WITHDRAWN

The Age of Extravagance

an Edwardian Reader

an *Edwardian Reader*

◆―◈―◆

The Age
of Extravagance

◆―◈―◆

edited by

MARY ELISABETH EDES

and

DUDLEY FRASIER

Rinehart & Company, Inc.   New York · Toronto

Published simultaneously in Canada by
    Clarke, Irwin & Company, Ltd., Toronto
Copyright, 1954, by Mary Elisabeth Edes and Dudley Frasier
Printed in the United States of America
Library of Congress Catalog Card Number: 54-9864

Foreword

---◆◆◇◆◆---

The editors confess to having made a highly personal selection from the literature of the Edwardian era—possibly to reinforce their private notions about the period—for inclusion in this volume. Neither of us was around when Edward VII and Theodore Roosevelt were. But the warm memories of those who were, and our own reading in the period, have convinced us that the dominant note was extravagance, an extravagance reflected in the writing of the time, the dress, food, theater, sports, everything. It was a time when social and "society" arts were valued as never before (or since). Pleasure was pursued with almost fanatic desperation. The charge of vulgarity has been leveled at the age; it has been characterized as the apotheosis of the stockbroker. But it was undoubtedly the last age of elegance, unclouded by world wars and the atom, that we shall know.

The reader will find, therefore, that most of the stories, essays, and memoirs in this sampler recall the era with charmed delight. Others show the shadows as well as the light. The reader will also note that the age of extravagance was very definitely the age of London and New York. For this reason, most of the selections are metropolitan in

v

feeling. The Edwardian era (roughly 1900 to 1914) was a time of great advances in science and of growing political awareness, but for the most part, such things didn't occupy those who set the pace. In fact, they hardly "showed" at all before the First World War. Security, real or imagined, was the keynote.

Just as Victorian, Early American, Regency and other periods have had their "revivals" and often secured permanent spots in contemporary decoration and design, so the Edwardian era seems on the verge of a similar comeback. It is our hope that interest will not stop with the donning of a velvet weskit or a bit of soutache. We hope that at least some of the readers of this volume will want to delve further into the literature of the period. We think they will find it delightful.

The editors are happy to have this chance to thank those who have aided and encouraged them in putting this reader together, especially Seth M. Agnew, Wendell T. Palmer, and Jean Crawford.

M. E. E. *and* D. P. F.

Acknowledgments

—◄◄◄●►►—

Grateful acknowledgment is made to the following authors, publishers, agents and copyright owners who have so generously granted permission for the use of excerpts from their publications:

Appleton-Century Crofts, Inc., New York, N. Y., for permission to reprint "Disaster" from *San Francisco: A Pageant*, by Charles Caldwell Dobie, copyright, 1933, 1939, by D. Appleton-Century-Co., Inc.

Curtis Brown, Ltd., New York, N. Y., for permission to reprint "Teresa" from *The Edwardians*, by V. Sackville-West, copyright, 1930, by Mrs. Harold Nicolson; and for permission to reprint "Before the Sunset Fades" by The Marchioness of Bath.

Cambridge University Press, New York, N. Y., for permission to reprint "Christmas Day" from *The Small Years* by Frank Kendon.

Henry Seidel Canby, New York, N. Y., for permission to reprint "College Town" from *American Memoir*, copyright, 1947, by Henry Seidel Canby.

Doubleday & Company, Inc., New York, N. Y., and A. P. Watt & Son, London, England, for permission to reprint "Mrs. Elinor Glyn" from *Books and Persons*, by Arnold Bennett, copyright, 1917, by Doubleday & Company, Inc.

Doubleday & Company, Inc., New York, N. Y., and George Weidenfeld & Nicolson Limited, London, England, for permission to reprint "Take One Hundred Larks" from *The Glass of Fashion*, by Cecil Beaton, copyright, 1954, by Cecil Beaton.

E. P. Dutton & Co., Inc., New York, N. Y., for permission to reprint "The Christening" from *The Ideal Home* by Matilda Lees-Dods.

E. P. Dutton & Co., Inc., New York, N. Y., and James Bone, Surrey, England, for permission to reprint "The Twilight of the Horse" from *London Echoing* by James Bone.

Harcourt, Brace and Company, Inc., New York, N. Y., for permission to reprint "A Second Start in Life" from *Life and Gabriella*, by Ellen Glasgow.

Harcourt, Brace and Company, Inc., New York, N. Y., and Harold Nicolson, London, England, for permission to reprint "The Edwardian

Weekend" from *Small Talk*, by Harold Nicolson, copyright, 1937, by Harcourt, Brace and Company, Inc.

Harcourt, Brace and Company, Inc., New York, N. Y., and Leonard Woolf, Sussex, England, for permission to reprint "1907" from *The Years*, by Virginia Woolf, copyright, 1937, by Harcourt, Brace and Company.

Houghton Mifflin Company, Boston, Mass., for permission to reprint "Newport" from *Good Old Summer Days*, by Richmond Barrett, copyright, 1941, by Richmond Barrett, copyright, 1952, by Houghton Mifflin Company.

Houghton Mifflin Company, Boston, Mass., and John Murray (Publishers) Ltd., London, England, for permission to reprint "Take Me Back to Dear Old Shepherd's Bush" from *All Done From Memory*, by Osbert Lancaster, copyright, 1951, 1953, by Osbert Lancaster.

Little, Brown & Company and the Atlantic Monthly Press, Boston, Mass., Macmillan & Company, London, England, and Pearn, Pollinger & Higham, Ltd., London, England, for permission to reprint "Between Season" from *The Scarlet Tree*, by Sir Osbert Sitwell, copyright, 1946, by Sir Osbert Sitwell.

W. Somerset Maugham, A. P. Watt & Son, and Messrs. William Heinemann, Ltd., London, England, for permission to reprint "Some Novelists I Have Known," Henry James, from *The Vagrant Mood*, by W. Somerset Maugham, copyright, 1952, by W. Somerset Maugham.

John Murray (Publishers) Ltd., London, England, for permission to reprint "The Edwardian" from *Homes, Sweet Homes*, by Osbert Lancaster.

The New Yorker, New York, N. Y., for permission to reprint "The King Is Crowned," by Dorothy Brett, copyright, 1953, by The New Yorker Magazine, Inc.

Random House, New York, N. Y., for permission to reprint "The Wicked Hansom" from *More Studies in Murder*, by Edmund Pearson, copyright, 1936, by Edmund Pearson.

Rinehart & Company, Inc., New York, N. Y. for permission to reprint "The Annual Exodus" from *Tempestuous Petticoat*, by Clare Leighton, copyright, 1947, by Clare Leighton; and a selection from *The Southern Part of Heaven*, by William Meade Prince, copyright, 1950, by William Meade Prince.

Charles Scribner's Sons, New York, N. Y., for permission to reprint "Expiation" from *The Descent of Man*, by Edith Wharton, copyright, 1904, by Charles Scribner's Sons, 1932, by Edith Wharton.

The Viking Press, Inc., New York, N. Y., and John Lane, The Bodley Head Limited, London, England, for a selection from "The Unbearable Bassington" by Saki, from *The Novels and Plays of Saki* by H. H. Munro, copyright, 1933, by The Viking Press, Inc.

Willis Kingsley Wing, New York, N. Y., for permission to reprint "The Unsinkable Mrs. Brown" from *Timber Line*, by Gene Fowler, copyright, 1933, by Gene Fowler.

Contents

Osbert Lancaster

"EDWARDIAN"

from *Homes, Sweet Homes*

To-day the epithet Edwardian has perhaps acquired, thanks to Miss Sackville-West's charmingly expressed nostalgia, and the prodigious memoir-writing feats of the surviving Edwardians, a rather too exclusively aristocratic application. Its syllables summon up for most of us a confused vision of electric broughams, the portraits of Laszlo and Sargent, Patti in Manon, Homburg and Miss Cornwallis West. In fact this glorious vision, in so far as it corresponds in any degree with reality, is illumined by the after-glow of the Victorian era while the cheerful rays of the new dawn (subsequently discovered to be false) with which the majority of Edwardians considered the reign to have been ushered in, fall on a totally different collection of symbols.

Large areas of shiny white paint, masking the mahogany dear to the previous generation; sticky-looking but cheerful chintzes patterned with large cabbage roses on a white background; the beautiful and moving pictures of Herr Böcklin, made available to a large public through the commercial acumen of the Berlin Photographic Company; these, together with the early plays of Mr. Shaw and the novels of Mr. Meredith, were some of the more characteristic signs of the times. But in addition there was one trait, which found ample expression in the contemporary interior, that particularly distinguishes the Edwardians from their immediate forbears—their pathetic faith in the benefits of science.

3

Soon the home was invaded by an entirely new collection of furniture and fittings in the design of most of which the supporters of *Art Nouveau*, by no means yet moribund, had secured an unfortunate monopoly. From the heart of a tinted glass flower at the end of a terrifyingly sinuous brass stalk there now peeped the electric light bulb, while in the fireplace a strange collection of stalactites, in a black lead sarcophagus embossed with a design of water lilies, glowed with gas-produced heat. Pendent from the wall a complicated contraption of vulcanite, mahogany and polished brass carried the householder's voice, at the mere turning of a handle, to such of his neighbours as were similarly equipped, while the hanging book-case, itself a striking testimony to little Willy's skill with that popular scientific toy the fret-saw, groaned beneath its load of Mr. Wells's marvellous romances. Everything in the garden, to use a contemporary phrase, was lovely.

And then one day the largest and most impressive miracle of modern science hit an iceberg in mid-Atlantic, and the prevailing optimism received a shock which two years later was repeated on a scale and at a length sufficient to banish it for ever.

Dorothy Brett

"THE KING IS CROWNED"

$\mathcal{W}$ith the Coronation of Queen Elizabeth drawing near, I often find myself thinking back to the spring of 1902, when I was a young lady, and my father, Reggie Brett, was deeply immersed in the problem of the Coronation of Edward VII. As Permanent Secretary of the Office of Works, Father was responsible for much of the planning for that great event. His job wasn't easy. One big difficulty was that Queen Victoria, who had died the year before, had ruled for sixty-four years, and nobody in the government had ever seen a Coronation.

We were living at our country place near Windsor at the time, and I can remember that Father would disappear for hours into a small farmhouse at the edge of a forest that was full of nightingales. There he pored over the Rolls Books—historical records that he had inherited from his father, along with the title Viscount Esher. Even as he examined the Books for accounts of previous Coronations, he kept scouting about for anybody who had seen one. "The old Duke of Cambridge!" he said with elation one day as he came in for lunch. "He's seen two of them." Gradually, from the memories of old men and from all sorts of records, including letters and private memoirs, a pattern began to emerge. Father took his discoveries to the Duke of Norfolk, who, as the hereditary Earl Marshal of England, was in charge of the Coronation ceremony, and

6

it was through their joint effort, and with the help of countless heraldic authorities, that the Coronation of Edward VII was made possible.

Naturally, I was almost breathlessly eager to see the crowning of the King, which was to take place in June, and as the daughter of a peer, I was entitled to a seat in the Abbey. Then, one morning in March, I was stricken with appendicitis. The disease was a mysterious one in those days. There was no general agreement on the proper method of treatment, and many doctors even thought appendicitis was contagious. As I lay writhing on my bed, our old country doctor appeared baffled. My parents, thoroughly alarmed, insisted that our London doctor be called in. He came, took one look at me, and requested another opinion. Our footman was then sent up to London to find the distinguished surgeon Sir Frederick Treves, and managed to intercept him on his doorstep just as he was starting off for a weekend. Sir Frederick immediately caught the train down to Windsor. After examining me, he announced that he must operate the next day, although he feared that it was too late. The next day, accordingly, I was operated on, at home.

My recovery was so slow that Father told me I would probably have to miss the Coronation. In the days that followed, he did his best to comfort me by sitting beside my bed in the evening and discussing some of the details of the event that were worrying him and that he knew would fascinate me. He also told me some things about other Coronations. I remember he described the spectacular procession through London of the first Queen Elizabeth. Thousands of pounds had been spent on street decorations, he said, and along the royal route beautiful children stood and made speeches of welcome as the Queen rode by in her carriage. Later in the day, at Westminster Abbey, the Queen objected to the anointing oil.

"The oil was grease and smelt ill," she remarked to her maids. One evening as I lay in bed feeling particularly unhappy, Father diverted me with some facts about the Coronation of Queen Victoria. He said she had walked up the nave with a bishop on either side of her, looking tiny in her massive robes but lively as a cricket. When the Archbishop of Canterbury, old and feeble, asked her the questions of the oath, he could not be heard by most of the audience, but the Queen's voice rang out clear as a bell. Further on in the ceremony, when she complained aloud of the weight of the orb, the symbol of spiritual power, which she carried in one hand, and asked what to do with it, a courtier standing nearby told her politely, "Hold it, Ma'am." There was a bad moment, later on, when the Archbishop of Canterbury awkwardly forced the Coronation ring on the wrong finger of the Queen's hand; she afterwards had a painful time getting it off.

The work Father did was most exacting, and he soon was looking worn and haggard. There was no end to the questions that must be settled. One, for example, had to do with trumpets and drums. As Their Majesties entered the Abbey, there would be a devilish fanfare of trumpets and a rolling of drums. The sound was shattering even in the open air; what effect would the vibrations have on the old Abbey? After long and heated discussions, involving not only Father and the Duke of Norfolk, but various architects, builders, and musicians, it was decided to risk a demonstration. The trumpet-and-drum corps from the band of the Horse Guards was marched into the Abbey, the instruments flared and rattled—and the old walls stood firm.

Along the streets of London, enormous white poles were erected, on which to hang shields and garlands. Velvet flags were suspended from balconies and windows.

Wooden stands were set up along the route the procession would follow, and as each section was completed, a detachment of guardsmen was marched onto it to test it. At a word of command, the men flumped down hard on the seats. If the stands didn't collapse, they were considered safe.

Crowds began pouring into London. Colonial troops and royalty arrived from abroad. Rehearsals went on constantly in the Abbey, sometimes with Their Majesties but more often with stand-ins. The Prince of Wales' little children, who were mischievous and high-spirited, had been taken to see the decorations in the Abbey. They had scrambled over pews, climbed onto tombs and monuments, and returned home covered with dust. The younger of my two brothers was not happy when he heard this report, since he had been assigned to guard the children during the Coronation and see that they didn't disrupt the ceremony.

My family started getting their costumes ready. Mother and Father would both wear crimson velvet robes. Underneath his, Father would wear a black velvet coat, a white silk shirt, and white satin knee breeches; the dress Mother would wear was a beautiful combination of velvet, satin, and lace, with a train that fell in long, sweeping folds. My brothers, as Gold Staff officers, would wear court dress, including coat, waistcoat, and knee breeches of black velvet. My sister would have a white evening frock, with long white gloves, and with three white ostrich feathers pinned in her hair at the back. I would be dressed the same way, if only I were going. The thought of not being there almost broke my heart.

The King was to be crowned on June 26th. On June 24th, Father went to London for the final rehearsal in the Abbey. For some time, he had been unusually quiet, and he seemed depressed. We children knew that he was fatigued from an almost endless round of state dinners and court receptions, and that he was still working hard on the last details of the Coronation. When he returned home that evening at dinnertime, he looked utterly spent and dispirited. He sat down by my bed, where I was still recuperating—and lamenting my ill fortune at having to miss the Coronation—and said to me quietly, "The Coronation is off. His Majesty has suffered an attack of appendicitis. He may need an operation."

I gasped. Father went on to say that he felt personally involved in the calamity. As I've said, little was known about appendicitis in those days. Father was faced with the appalling possibility that he had carried a germ from me to the King!

Sitting there, he told me of the scene in the Abbey. Among those present for the rehearsal were the Bishop of London, the canons, and the orchestra and choir, with their director, Sir Frederick Bridge. It was about noon. At three o'clock, the King and Queen were expected. Suddenly a messenger appeared and asked nervously for the Duke of Norfolk. He was not there. So the messenger whispered to my father, and my father whispered to the Bishop of London. The Bishop turned white. Standing by the empty throne, he announced simply that the King was seriously, perhaps dangerously ill, and that the Coronation was cancelled. There was a moment of awful silence. Then the Bishop knelt by the throne, and everybody else sank to his knees, as Sir Frederick Bridge asked the choir to sing a portion of the Litany. While they sang, the Bishop intoned, "In all time of our tribulation; in all time of our wealth; in the hour of death, and in the day of judgment . . ." And the choir answered, "Good Lord, deliver us." When the choir finished, the Bishop blessed the assemblage, and one by one the people departed, leaving behind the splendid trappings in the dim Abbey.

London, of course, was shocked. Throngs stood around Buckingham Palace, watching for bulletins, Father reported to me. A friend of his wrote him, "What next, *miserere, Domine?* The festive look of London jars horribly." That look was not to last long. The gay hangings along the streets were taken down. The colonial troops sailed away. The visiting royalty returned to their homes.

In the next few days, my feeling of depression almost equalled Father's, I think, not only because I realized I might have been the source of the King's illness but also because I knew, from what Father said, that the King himself was aware of where the appendicitis "bug" might have come from. But my gloom, as well as Father's, was almost dispelled when the surgeon who had operated on me, Sir Frederick Treves, successfully operated on the King. His Majesty's recovery was rapid, and a new date, August 9th, was set for the Coronation. I felt grateful to the King. I told my parents that if His Majesty would be well enough to attend the Coronation, I would, too. They agreed.

At last it was four o'clock on the morning of the great day. We had moved up the day before to our house in London, and it was ablaze with light. As my sister and I were struggling into our white dresses, we heard the slam of the front door that meant my brothers had gone off to the breakfast given for the Gold Staff officers and other officials in the Statesmen's Court of the Palace of Westminster.

We grabbed our gloves and joined our parents, who were already in a carriage outside. How gorgeous they looked in their crimson robes! The horses were fidgety, made nervous by the booming of the minute guns in Hyde Park. As we rode slowly along the streets jammed with carriages, my father said that Stanley Quick, his private secretary, had managed the day before to smuggle a steel box marked O.H.M.S. (On His Majesty's Service) into one of the crypts of the Abbey. The box contained sandwiches and champagne for our lunch. It would be well into the afternoon before we could get our carriage and leave the Abbey, and, of course, with the heavy traffic, we would be slow reaching home. Lunch at the Abbey was desirable, especially as I had been sick. A crypt was the only place that could be decently used, we all knew, for one would hardly resort to the indignity of eating on a tombstone or in a pew. Father did not explain how Stanley got the steel box past the sentries, police, soldiers, and plainclothesmen swarming about the Abbey; he said he simply didn't know and Stanley had sworn he would never tell. The story of Guy Fawkes and the Gunpowder Plot was still strong in the minds of all good Englishmen. Stanley's feat was not only ingenious but dangerous. My sister and I shuddered with delight.

Our horses plodded along. Soldiers and sailors were lined up at the curbs. Mounted police were clattering up and down. In the crowds that had waited along the royal route all night long, women fainted and children got stepped on or lost.

Once inside the Abbey, my sister and I were led by an usher to a balcony near the roof, where we had a magnificent view of the nave. Directly below us, slanting rays of sunlight were flickering on gold epaulets, bright scabbards, and waving plumes and feathers.

The ceremony went off without any real hitch. When the King entered the Abbey, the huge congregation watched anxiously to see if he would falter because of his recent illness—*my* illness, perhaps. But the King—I

learned later that he had been laced into a metal girdle—
walked confidently to the throne. When the Archbishop
of Canterbury, who, like the earlier one attending Queen
Victoria, was old and feeble, advanced to place the crown
on the King's head, *he* stumbled, but he managed to get
it there. At once, the congregation shouted, "God save the
King!" England had a new monarch.

After my sister and I climbed down from our perch, we
were lost in a swirling mass of people until Stanley Quick
suddenly stepped from behind a tomb. Presently, my
brothers appeared, grinning happily and with time only to
give us a friendly nudge before hastening off to attend the
luncheon at Statesmen's Court for the Officers of the College of Arms and the Gold Staff Officers. Father was supposed to lunch there, but he preferred to stay with us.
Stanley waved at us, and we followed him through the vast
crowd, estimated at seven thousand people, and down
what seemed like endless stone passages and stairs, into
the crypt where he had hidden the steel box. The crypt, a
square room with gray stone walls and a single electric-
light bulb, was cold and gloomy, and I began to think it
wasn't such a good idea, either for me or for anyone in
sturdier health. Then Father and Mother opened the door
and came in looking gay and full of fun, Father particularly. He seemed immeasurably relieved that the ceremony
had gone off successfully.

We sat on the floor in a circle, with the steel box in the
center. My parents spread their red robes about them. Father opened the box, and all of us, by now famished,
devoured sandwiches of chicken, ham, tongue, or jam. Father cautioned us to speak softly, as we were, of course,
not supposed to be in the crypt, and the guards on the
Abbey floor above might hear us. Stanley was about to
open a bottle of champagne when Father spoke of the

loud pop the cork would make. Stanley took care of this by wrapping a napkin around the top of the bottle.

As we ate, Father told us about some peers whose ancestral coronets had slipped down on their faces, because the coronets had originally been made to fit over wigs. He had been amused, too, at some peeresses he had overheard expressing their indignation at the lack of comforts in the Abbey. And he also told us, much to our pleasure, that my younger brother had managed to control the Prince of Wales' little children.

With all our precautions over the popping of corks, we had forgotten to keep our voices lowered. Abruptly there was a loud rapping at the door. My father called out, "Come in," as if this were his own living room. The door was flung open and there stood the Duke of Norfolk, several policemen, and a group of armed guardsmen. The policemen, who recognized my father, turned crimson, and the guardsmen grinned. The Duke, a kind, homely-looking man with a shaggy beard, stared in amazement.

Father rose politely and, with a charming smile, said, "My dear Duke, won't you join us?"

The Duke, who seemed tired, looked longingly at our lunch. "I can't," he said reluctantly. "I have to go to the Statesmen's Court. But I don't mind a glass of champagne." As Father handed him one, the Duke glanced around him and asked, "How did you do it?"

My father shook his head. "That's a secret," he said, "but someday I may be able to tell you."

The Duke drank his wine, looked longingly at our feast again, and started to leave.

"And how did you find us?" Father asked.

The Duke nodded toward an embarrassed policeman. "He heard strange noises and was sure it was another Guy Fawkes," he explained. "He insisted we come down to investigate. I borrowed the soldiers and came." He laughed.

"You don't know how I envy you," he said, and with a genial wave of the hand he marched off with the guardsmen and policemen.

Father sat down again, and we all munched away. After we had finished up everything, Father sent Stanley out to see if the coast was clear. Stanley returned in a few minutes to report that most of the crowd had gone. We went out of the crypt, walked back up the stairs and through the passages, and finally emerged into the sunlight outside. Then we got into our carriage and started for home.

"Look," said my father as we were leaving the Abbey yard. A pretty young peeress was sitting on a pile of old planks, with her crimson robe folded around her and her long train spread out behind. Something had evidently gone wrong about her carriage and she had to wait. As she sat there, the sunlight was reflected from the tiara in her blonde hair and the jewels in her ears. She was, I have since thought, a lovely emblem of old feudal England.

V. Sackville-West

◆◄◆►◆

"TERESA"

from *The Edwardians*

"Teresa" is a section from Miss Sackville-West's novel, THE EDWARDIANS, which is set in London and at Chevron, a large English country house which is, perhaps, not unlike Knole, the home of the Sackville family at Sevenoaks, Kent. Earlier in the story Sebastian, the young duke who has inherited Chevron, has had an unhappy love affair with an older woman. He has met Teresa, wife of a London doctor, John Spedding, when, alighting from a hansom cab, he suffered a sprained ankle almost on her doorstep. To the concern of his mother, Lucy, and his sister, Viola, he has invited the middle-class Speddings to a Christmas house party at Chevron.

*C*hevron was even more beautiful in winter than in summer; so Sebastian thought. (But then, whatever the season, Sebastian always decided that it suited Chevron better than any other season.) He had now been there for two days alone with his mother and Viola, and, as usual, had forgotten all about London and was deep in his Chevron mood. He had a full day left, before the Christmas party arrived by the six o'clock train. He had looked forward to this party, having arranged in his own mind that matters should come to a head between himself and Teresa, but now it merely irritated him to think that by the evening the house would be full of people, even though Teresa should be of their number. He had long since discovered why he resented parties at Chevron, although in his sardonic way he could enjoy them elsewhere; it was because they forced him to mingle the two sides of himself, for Sebastian was honest enough to dislike mixing his manners. He could come to terms with himself only if he kept his two selves sharply separate. Then he could manage to sustain himself by thinking that the one self redeemed the other. In this way, since we first met him rebelliously sitting astride the roof, had he tidied himself into compartments; but still parties at Chevron had the same distressing effect, of confusing him by pitting reality against unreality—one mood against the other. The presence of Teresa would complicate matters. He was clear-sighted enough to know well that he would play up to Teresa; would consent to the rôle that she expected of him; would hate himself for doing it; and would exaggerate out of sheer exasperation. He wished by all his gods that he had not invited Teresa.

Meanwhile, Teresa and the party were distant by twenty-five miles of space and eight hours of time, and Sebastian, with Sarah and Henry at his heels, was out in the park on a frosty morning. For the moment he could afford to be happy. Chevron was going about its business as usual, as though no discordant strangers were expected; the internal agitation of the house was not here apparent; Sebastian could forget that within doors his mother was interviewing the *chef*, Mrs. Wickenden sorting out the sheets, Wacey struggling with the dinner-table, Vigeon descending into the cellar, the groom of the chambers going round the writing-tables with ink, pencils, and paper, the still-room-maid making scones in the still-room. All that housekeeping business concerned Sebastian not at all. He roamed round the outer walls, meeting first a waggon charged with a fallen tree, and appreciated the rounded rumps, like Spanish chestnuts, of the straining horses; then he looked into the slaughter-house, where Hodder the keeper was skinning a deer slung by all four feet from a rafter; then he met two gardeners pushing a hand-cart laden with beetroot and potatoes; then he looked into the pimping-shed, where old Turnour was chopping faggots. Old Turnour, a frill of white beard edging his face, looked up, grinned cheerfully, and touched his hat, then went on with his chopping.

"Well, how are you keeping, Turnour? Nice weather, isn't it?"

"Nice enough, your Grace, but not seasonable, not seasonable."

"Well, it's cold enough, Turnour; but I suppose you expect snow at Christmas?"

"Ah, the climate isn't what it was, your Grace; a Christmas without snow is onnatural."

"I daresay we'll get it before we're done, Turnour."

"Maybe, your Grace, but still the climate isn't what it was. Anyhow we're getting a touch of frost to set the sprouts. I had a nice lot of sprouts this year, your Grace, and it would have been a pity to lose them for lack of a touch of frost."

"So it would, Turnour, a great pity. And how's the rheumatism?"

"Not onreasonably bad, your Grace, considering. But I'm getting on, and it tells."

"Seventy-eight is it, Turnour?"

"Ah, your Grace has his late Grace's memory. Seventy-eight it is—seventy-nine come Easter."

"Well, Turnour, there's a Christmas surprise for you and everybody on the estate—five shillings a week rise from the first of January."

"No, your Grace, you don't say so?" said Turnour, desisting from his chopping to push back his hat and to stare; "not that it won't be welcome to all, with prices going up as they do. Well, now!" said Turnour, still marvelling at this piece of fortune, "if I haven't always said: a gentleman is a gentleman, but his Grace is a real gentleman. And here I get my words proven out of my mouth."

"It isn't that, Turnour," said Sebastian, compelled to honesty; "only I can afford it, where others can't."

"Ah, your Grace makes light of it. But it isn't all who would think of it, even them as can afford it. And your Grace pays a decent wage already, next to some. Thank you kindly, your Grace. My old woman will dance when she hears it; stiff joints or no."

Sebastian smiled and nodded and walked away, with no

very great satisfaction at his heart. He felt that he had
received more gratitude, and had acquired more merit,
than was his due. Five shillings a week meant thirteen
pounds a year, and—say that he employed a hundred men
—that meant thirteen hundred pounds a year; very little
more than his mother would spend on a single ball; a neg-
ligible sum in his yearly budget. He felt ashamed. His
conversation with Viola had shamed him. Money apart,
he felt that his relationship with old Turnour was false.
What did he really care for old Turnour's rheumatism? or
for his age? or for the fact that he walked three miles at
five o'clock every morning to his work, winter and summer, and three miles back every evening? Sebastian could
stroll into the pimping-shed every now and then, and gossip with old Turnour in a friendly way for ten minutes,
and he knew that old Turnour liked it, and retailed every
word of the conversation to his old woman in the evening; but supposing that on a cold winter's night Sebastian had found his fire unlit, and, on ringing the bell, had
been told by Vigeon that old Turnour had omitted to
cut any faggots that day—would not he, Sebastian, have
damned with rage, and demanded what old Turnour
thought he was there for, if not to cut faggots? And would
have thought himself a lenient master in that he did not
sack Turnour without further enquiry. He walked on, un-
happily shaking his head. Viola had upset him. Turnour's
gratitude embarrassed him. He felt, rather, that it was he
who should thank the old man for rising at five o'clock
every morning and for walking three miles, that the bath
should be hot by eight and the fires fed throughout the
day.

But the morning was too lovely, and Sebastian too
young, for his depression to last for long. He took his way
across the park, throwing sticks for Henry to retrieve—
Sarah did not care for sticks—and every now and then he

turned round to look at the house which lay beneath him, spread out like a mediaeval village with its square turrets and its grey walls, its hundred chimneys sending blue threads up into the air. It was his; and he remembered Teresa's question, 'Tell me what it feels like to be you.' At that moment he knew exactly what if felt like to be himself.

The turf was white with frost, and each separate blade of grass stuck up, as brittle as an icicle. The grass crunched beneath his feet, and looking back across the plain he could see the track of his footsteps, making a dark line across the rime. Sarah stepped delicately, and from time to time she lay down to lick the balls of ice which gathered between her pads; Henry, who was made of coarser stuff, careered madly round and round in circles, galloping like a little horse, bounding over the tussocks, his ears flying, his feathers streaming. Sebastian cheered him on. He wished he could tear about like Henry. They came to the edge of the plain; Sebastian broke into a run down the slope; now they were in the valley; still they ran, startling the deer that nosed about among some armfuls of hay thrown down for them. They bounded away, the spaniels after them; they bounded up the slope, over the dead bracken, bouncing as though they had springs in their feet, their white scuts flashing between the trees. Sebastian stood still to watch; he felt so happy that he thought his heart would burst. Henry and Sarah, returning, dragging themselves on their bellies up to him, were astonished when they were not beaten.

By the morning of Christmas Eve, snow had fallen. Sebastian was amused by this, when he first looked out of his bedroom window and saw the white garden. He was amused, because Teresa would now see Chevron as she had expected to see it. "Quite an old-fashioned Christmas," she would say. He was in such a good temper that he could anticipate Teresa's careful platitudes with affection. He looked out at the familiar scene. Two gardeners were already sweeping the snow from the path. Swish, swish, went their black brooms, and the men moved after them, waddling from foot to foot, in a caricature of the scytheman's beautiful rhythm. The snow was powdery, and flew readily under the twiggy swish of the broom, heaping itself on either side in a low wedge-shaped rampart, clean and glittering; the yellow gravel of the path came through, streaked with thin semi-circles of snow between the brushings. Blackbirds walked over the lawn, printing the snow with their neat marks. Sebastian could not bear to remain indoors on such a morning; he pulled on a pair of trousers and a sweater; called to Sarah and Henry, who were still at the stage of stretching and yawning in their respective baskets—Sarah especially was always a slow waker, and liked to jump on to Sebastian's bed for five minutes' sentimentality before she was officially awake—and going downstairs he tried to get out into the garden, but was checked everywhere by fastened shutters and locked doors, for the indoor servants were not allowed in this part of the house so early, and had neither undone the fastenings nor pulled up the blinds. Sebastian tugged impatiently, unreasonably irritated with his servants for the efficiency with which they performed their duties. He was as irritated as when he sometimes arrived at Chevron without warning during the London season and found all the furniture piled into the middle of the rooms under dust-sheets. Then he grumbled at Mrs. Wickenden for the thoroughness that he really respected. At last he got out, having triumphed over the library shutters; Henry rushed in advance into the snow, tossing it up with his nose; Sarah followed more circumspectly, snuffing, looking back at Sebastian to know what this unfamiliar white grass might portend; they both ran, little brown shapes, snuffing, hither and thither, and Sebastian came after, at first reluctant to break the thick white carpet, then kicking it up with pleasure, seeing the powdery snow fluff up before his toe-caps as he kicked; and so he crossed the space to the path and the brushing gardeners, and taking a broom from one of the men he sent him off on other business.

A red ball of sun was coming up behind the trees; there was now a long stretch of path swept clear; Sebastian swept with such vigour that he constantly found himself outdistancing his companion. The cold air and the exercise made him tingle; his spirits rose; he chaffed the other man on his slow, steady progress. "See if I don't clear my share in half the time, Godden." "All very well, your Grace; but your Grace hasn't got to work for all the rest of the day. Slow and steady—that's what keeps you going from breakfast to dinner." Yet he knew that Godden was good-humoured and amused; amused, as any professional is amused, at the precipitate enthusiasm of the amateur. He looked up at the grey house; all the blinds were down, and he instantly despised his guests for being still asleep, in a rush of that superiority which afflicts all those who are astir earlier than other people. Then he remembered that his own windows alone, of all the bedrooms, looked onto the garden; and another rush of satisfaction took him, that he slept isolated in his fat tower, where no one could spy on him, and where for neighbours he had none but the portraits hanging on the walls of the unused state-rooms, or a Pontius Pilate who could no longer judge, on the tapestry in the chapel. How often, going to his room at night and leaning out to breathe the air from his window, had he felt himself in silent communion with Chevron, a communion which others were denied!

He liked the feel of the broom-handle in his hands, the wood polished by usage until it was as sleek and glossy as vellum. Even the knots in the wood were smooth. Sebastian had paused to straighten his back, and was running his fingers up and down the handle, enjoying the pleasant texture. Godden also paused, and watched him with a smile. "Blisters coming, your Grace?" "It takes more than that to give me blisters," said Sebastian, injured by the assumption that his hands were soft, and he fell to his sweeping again, though he would have liked to stand still for a moment, gazing round at the glistening snow, sprinkled with diamonds, and at the low red sun just topping the trees, and at Henry and Sarah, who, mad with delight, were rushing round and round after one another.

TERESA decided that it would be suitable for her to make her first appearance at twelve o'clock that morning. Thus she would display no undue eagerness. She had arrived at Chevron determined to behave with the utmost caution; by no impetuous word would she betray her agitation, by no imprudent question would she expose her ignorance. She would be very quiet and self-contained, and, by carefully copying what other people did, she would manage to get through the three days of this thrilling, agonising, exquisite ordeal without shame or ridicule. Her manner should be reserved and dignified; she would allow nothing visibly to impress her; she would conduct herself as though staying at Chevron were quite the ordinary thing for her to do. Inwardly, of course, she was more flustered than she had ever been in her life. The size of Chevron, the luxury, the number of servants, the powdered footmen and their red velvet breeches, the great fires, the gold plate, the conversation, the fashionable company, their air of taking everything for granted—all this had far surpassed Teresa's expectations. Cinderella going to the ball was not more overwhelmed than she. "Keep your head, keep your head," she kept repeating to herself; "don't give yourself away."

It was only when she had been shown to her bedroom before dinner, and was presently joined there by John, that she had let herself go. She had flown round the room, examining everything, clasping her hands in an ecstasy of delight. The familiar "Oh, look, John! look!" came tumbling from her lips. The dressing-table, the washstand, the writing-table with its appointments, the vast four-poster on which some unseen hand had already laid out her clothes, the drawn curtains, the brightly burning fire, the muslin cushions, the couch with a chinchilla rug lying folded across it—all these things led Teresa from transport to transport. She lingered for a long time over the writing-table, fingering all its details. There was a printed card, gilt-edged, which said: "Post arrives 8 a.m., 4 p.m.; Post leaves 6 p.m. Sundays: Post arrives 8 a.m.; leaves 5 p.m. Luncheon 1.30. Dinner 8.30." Nothing about breakfast; thank goodness, then, ladies were not expected to go down to breakfast. Then there were three different sizes of notepaper—"Look, John! MacMichael's best vellum-laid," said Teresa, showing it to him, "and I know that costs a pound a ream"—but what fascinated Teresa above all, so that she could scarcely take her eyes from it, was the address, Chevron, under a ducal coronet. "Just Chevron, John!" said Teresa; "nothing else! no town, no county! You see, it's so well known. Just Chevron, England. If you addressed a letter like that, from any part of the world, it would get here," and she sat staring at the sheet in her hand, remembering that she had once had a note from Sebastian on that paper, but had imagined that it was some special paper of his own, and now here it was, in quantities, in her own bedroom, all fair and unused; "I must write to Maud and Mother," said Teresa, privately resolving that she would send belated Christmas greetings to everybody she could think of; but she refrained from

saying this to John—for she did observe a few little reti-
cences towards him.

Nor was the writing-table the end of her delights, for
everything in the room seemed to be marked with the
sign of its ownership. Even the beribboned cosy which
went over the hot-water can had the crossed C's, and the
coronet embroidered upon it; likewise the sheets, when
Teresa turned down the counterpane to see; and they, fur-
thermore, had a wide pink satin ribbon threaded through
them. Teresa kept on exclaiming what all this must cost,
"and fancy, John," she said, "it isn't only one bedroom,
but twenty bedrooms, thirty bedrooms! so all this has to
be provided twenty, thirty times over. But I don't like the
Duchess; do you, John? I'm sure she's very snappy in private life. Such a funny crumpled face, and I bet she dyes
her hair. I wish Lady Roehampton was here. I don't like
that Mrs. Levison either, though I know she's terribly
smart—really the cream of the cream. I bet she has a
tongue. And Lady Viola—she looks as cold as ice. Isn't it
funny, John, that a nobody like Mrs. Levison should be
so smart? You never can tell with these people, can you?
They say that she is trying to set the fashion for women
to dine alone with men in restaurants. I don't like that
sort of thing; do you, John? Fast, I call it. Oh, dear, I do
wish I had some jewels to put on for dinner. Do you think
the ladies will wear their tiaras? No, perhaps not in a private house. Who do you think will take me in to dinner?
I wish it could be the duke, but I suppose that's impossible, with all these ladies of title about. I must say, I
think he was very nice when we arrived, and what dear
little dogs he has; I daresay he thought we might be a bit
shy. I wasn't; were you, John? One is all right so long as
one doesn't put oneself forward, don't you think? What a
lovely big room that was, and, oh! did you notice the flow-

ers? Lilac, and roses! At Christmas! Do you think the duke would show us the hot-houses? Could I ask him, do you think? Or would it look silly?" So Teresa had run on, until it was time to dress for dinner, when a maid scared her by coming to ask if there was anything she wanted.

At home, when doing her packing, she had looked with some satisfaction upon her clothes. Nothing there that might not meet the critical eye of the Chevron housemaids! Except, perhaps, her bedroom slippers. She had scrutinised them, then had decided in their favour; they were a little worn on one side, certainly, but that might be overlooked, and really she could not ask John for any more money; he had given her a generous cheque already. But here, at Chevron, in this luxurious bedroom, her poor little chemises and her nightgown looked paltry; and as for the slippers, they had turned unaccountably shabby. She wondered if she should hide them away; but it was too late; the housemaid had unpacked and had seen them. Teresa felt vexed. She regretted that she had given up her keys before dinner, when a footman came to ask her for them. But how could she have said that she would unpack her trunk herself? That would have revealed a woeful lack of *savoir faire*; and *savoir faire* for the moment was Teresa's god. She had given up her keys as though all her life she had been accustomed to have a maid; indeed, she had hoped that everybody within hearing would assume that she had brought her own maid, and that her retention of the keys was accidental. The Chevron housemaid was the only blot on Teresa's paradise.

Then she made a fresh discovery, which again scattered her regrets in the wind of her excitement. She discovered a nosegay upon her dressing-table: two orchids and a spray of maiden-hair fern. She flew into John's dressing-room next door, and there discovered the masculine counterpart: a buttonhole consisting of one exquisitely furled yellow rosebud. John by then was in his bath. She stood, cupping the rosebud within her hands as though it represented the total and final expression of everything refined and luxurious.

That had been last night. At dinner, the butler had thrown Teresa into a fresh fluster by saying to her, "Champagne, m'lady?" After dinner they had sat upstairs, in the great drawing-room, surrounded by more lilac and more roses, and the family portraits had looked down on them from the walls, filling Teresa with curiosity and admiration; but as nobody else made any comment, she judged it prudent to make none either. She had felt acutely uncomfortable during the half-hour she sat up there alone with the ladies, for Teresa did not care for women at the best of times, and these ladies who addressed a few remarks to her out of good manners, but who could certainly not fail to wish her out of the way, were especially not calculated to put her at her ease. Click, clack, click, clack, went their conversation, like so many knitting-needles, purl, plain, purl, plain, achieving a complex pattern of references, cross-references, Christian names, nicknames, and fleeting allusions; until Teresa, unable to do anything but observe, came to the conclusion that they thought their topics not merely the most absorbing in the world, but, rather, the only possible topics. She watched them wonderingly, much as Anquetil, also an outsider, had once watched them, but her reflections were very different from his. She envied, instead of scorning, their prodigious self-sufficiency, their tacit exclusion of all the world outside their own circle. She marvelled at the uniformity of their appearance: tall or short, stout or thin, young or old, there was an indefinable resemblance, something in the metallic glance of the eye, the hard line of the mouth, the movement of the hands with their many rings and bangles. This glance of the eye was peculiar; although penetrating, if had something of the deadness of a fish's eye; glassy, as though a slight film obscured the vision; and the eyelids moreover were sharply cut, as though a narrowing tuck had been taken in them, still further robbing the eyes of any open generosity they might once have possessed. Altogether, Teresa thought that these ladies ought properly to be sitting under glass cases in a museum, so fixed did they appear, so far removed from any possible disorder; their coiffures elaborate and perfect, their gowns so manifestly expensive and yet so much a part of them, their manner so secure from any conceivable bewilderment or confusion. Surely no natural element would ever disturb that fine complacency; no gale would dishevel that architectural hair, no passion ravage those corseted busts. No passion, thought Teresa with an exquisite shiver, but a chill and calculated wickedness. She did not criticise; she admired. She thought that they were like all the portraits by Sargent that she had ever seen—and she went to the Academy every year with John, so she had seen a good many—divine inhabitants of a world apart, for whom nothing sordid, nothing petty, and nothing painful had any existence at all; served by innumerable domestics, prepared for the day or the evening by innumerable maids, hairdressers, manicurists, beauty specialists, chiropodists, tailors, and dressmakers; sallying forth, scented and equipped, from their dressing-rooms, to consort as familiarly with the Great as she herself with Mrs. Tolputt.

Yet she was forced to admit that they did not seem to be saying anything worth saying.

She had expected their conversation to rival their appearance. She had expected to be dazzled by their wit and thrilled by their revelations. Try as she might, she had not been able to imagine what form their conversation would take; but had resigned herself humbly in anticipation, telling herself that she was in the position of a London child

who had never seen the sea, or of a beggar suddenly promised a meal at Dieudonné's. She did not know what it
would be like, only that it would be wonderful. And now
she found that it differed very little from the conversation
of her own acquaintances, only the references were to people she did not know, and the general assumptions were
on a more extravagant scale. They even talked about their
servants. "Yes, my dear," Lady Edward was saying, "I have
really had to get rid of the *chef* at last. We found he was
using a hundred and forty-four dozen eggs a week." They
went into screams of laughter at phrases that Teresa (reluctantly) thought quite silly. In particular, there was one
lady whose name Teresa did not know, but who could not
open her mouth without pronouncing some quite unintel-
ligible words that instantly provoked hilarity. Nevertheless, Teresa was interested. She supposed it must be some
kind of jargon confined only to the most exclusive circles,
and the fact that it should be used in her presence gave
her a sense of flattering privity. She tried to dismiss the
idea that it was really rather tiresome and affected, and
that it reminded her of nothing so much as of a secret language used by herself and her fellows at school, which
consisted in adding the syllables 'jib' and 'job' to every
alternate word. 'Are-jib you-job going-jib to-job play-jib
hockey-job to-jib day-job?' The language had been known
as Jib-job, and only the élite of the school had been allowed to use it. This language of the élite of London was
apparently composed on much the same principle. It consisted in adding an Italian termination to English words;
but as that termination was most frequently the termination of Italian verbs of the first declension, and as it was
tacked on to English words irrespective of their being
verbs, nouns, or adjectives, it could not be said to be based
on any very creditable grammatical system. Smartness,
Teresa couldn't help thinking, was cheap at such a price.

"And after dinn-are, we might have a little dans-are," said this anonymous lady; a suggestion greeted by exclamations of "What a deevy idea, Florence! There's nobody like Florence, is there, for deevy ideas like that?" The critical faculty, raising its head for a second in Teresa, though immediately stamped upon, suggested that there was nothing very original or divine in the idea of dancing after dinner. But, "How lovel-are!" cried Lucy, and suddenly recollecting her obligations as a hostess, she added, "You must tell Sebastian to bring Mrs. Spedding as his partnerina." All those searchlight eyes were turned upon Teresa, modest in her corner. She was just shrewd enough to realise that the Duchess with a twinge of social conscience had remembered her, left out in the cold. Hitherto, nobody had addressed any word to her but some phrase such as, "Do you live in London or the country, Mrs. Spedding?" a phrase which clearly could have no sequel but the actual timid reply. Now, thanks to Lucy's effort, Teresa became the momentary focus of interest. All the ladies took up Lucy's cue. They examined Teresa with a stare that was meant to be flattering, but which, in effect, was so patronising as to arouse Teresa's defiance. "I'm afraid I don't dance," she said, knowing that she danced extremely well; far better, probably, than all these ladies getting on in years. No sooner had she said it, than she wished to bite her tongue out for thus obeying an unregistered instinct. Involuntarily she had been rude; and, though half of her was pleased at daring to be rude, the other half was frightened. But their good manners were, apparently, not to be shaken. "We don't believe that," said Lucy with her light laugh; "we just don't believe that—do we? I'm sure Mrs. Spedding dans-ares like a ballerina. And anyway, if you won't let Sebastian bring you as a partnerina, I shall ask you to bring Sebastian as a partnerino. I'm sure you would never be so unkind as to refuse an anxious mother."

After that, they had left Teresa in peace. She was at liberty to recover from the flutter into which they had thrown her. She could look round once more at the vast drawing-room, and, unobserved, could take in the details of the panelling with the frieze of mermaids and dolphins, tails coiled into tails, scales overlapping onto scales in Elizabethan extravagance; she could look at the portraits while the click-clack of the conversation crackled in the background of her consciousness; she could leap across the centuries from the painting of Edward the Sixth holding a rose between finger and thumb, to the silver-framed photograph on a table of Edward the Seventh in a Homburg hat, his foot lifted ready upon the step of his first Daimler. Teresa devoted a good deal of her attention to a furtive observation of the photographs. Thanks to her own private collection, she was able to identify most of them. There was Lady de T., very dark and lovely, sitting, in evening dress, on the ground in a wood, a scatter of faggots beside her. There was Lady A., seated on a Louis Quinze *bergère*, occupied with a spinning-wheel at which she was not looking—a favourite composition of Miss Alice Hughes. There were the three beautiful W. sisters leaning over a balcony with a poodle. "For darling Lucy," ran the inscription in a flowing feminine hand. There was Mrs. Langtry wrapped in furs, her profile turned to display her celebrated and lovely nose. There was Queen Alexandra wearing a crown, and Queen Alexandra wearing a bonnet, and Queen Alexandra surrounded by her grandchildren and dogs. There was the German Emperor in uniform, with an eagled helmet, his hands clasped on the hilt of his sword. These indications of intimacy sent associative shivers of delight down Teresa's susceptible backbone. She longed to prowl about the room alone, and savour the treasures that every table offered. But this, she told herself, was foolish. Was she not better employed in observing the flesh-and-blood that surrounded her? Photographs, after all, could be cut out of any illustrated paper. Teresa floated away on a dream. She considered the possibility of cutting out the next available photograph of the Duchess; buying a silver frame for it; faking an inscription—"For dear Teresa," it would run; or would "For dear Mrs. Spedding" be more probable and more convincing? "Chevron, Christmas 1906"—and standing it upon her own drawing-room table for the benefit of Mrs. Tolputt and her friends. But what would John say? And what would she do if Sebastian unexpectedly came to call? Reluctantly she discarded the idea. The champagne must have gone to her head.

She decided that she did not like women. She felt much happier when the men came upstairs, and Sebastian immediately made his way to her side. She said again to John, that night in her bedroom, that Sebastian had been "very nice."

Now she lay in her vast bed, having breakfast on a tray. She had already written a great many letters, and had boxed them into a pack, like cards, putting on the top of the pile a letter addressed to the only other titled person she knew—the wife of a surgeon who had recently been knighted. She looked very pretty, breakfasting in bed as to the manner born, and felt as luxurious as a cat in the sun. John teased her by saying that she would now never be willing to return with him to the wrong end of the Cromwell Road. Outside the window, the snowflakes were falling silently; the great courtyard was all white, every battlement was outlined in snow, and every now and then came a soft plop, as men shovelled the snow off the roofs. "Doesn't one feel," said Teresa dreamily, "that all this has been going on for hundreds and hundreds of years?— I mean, that the snow has fallen, and that men have gone up to shovel it off the roofs, and that it has fallen with that same soft sound, and that the flag has hung quite still, and that the clock has struck the hours. I wonder what Chevron is like in summer! I do hope the duke will ask us again."

Poor Teresa. She tried to be so artful, and was really so artless. She did not know in the least which particular attributes in herself appealed to Sebastian, and which did not. She had no idea of how to treat Sebastian. When she finally appeared, very neatly dressed in the new tweed coat and skirt she had had made for the occasion, he came forward to greet her with a smile, but within an hour she had contrived to exasperate him beyond endurance. "What do you think of this snow, Mrs. Spedding?" he had said; and going over to the window, Teresa had replied that it looked just like a Christmas card. It was precisely the response he had expected from her, but he caught a look of amusement on Lady Templecombe's face, and in an access of irritation had offered to show Teresa over the house. It was the readiest means of escape he could devise. She was his friend; he was responsible for her; he must get her away from these people who made her nervous and drove her into making a fool of herself. So he took her upstairs, away into safety. They wandered through the state-rooms together.

Hitherto she had been more or less her natural self with Sebastian; her attempts at affectation had been brief and unsuccessful; but for weeks now, in anticipation of the Christmas visit, she had been schooling herself to be on her guard. So it was not the Teresa he knew who went round the house with him. It was a sedate Teresa, determined at all costs to appear unimpressed. Secretly, she was overcome by this new revelation of the splendours of Sebastian's home; she imagined that she traced a family likeness to him in every one of the pictures; she gasped at the sumptuous velvets, at the extravagance of the silver sconces, the silver tables; she longed to ask whose were the coats-of-arms represented in the heraldic windows; she longed to ask a thousand questions, to pour forth her admiration, her bewilderment, her ignorance; but she allowed herself to do none of these things. Instead, she strolled nonchalant and lackadaisical by his side, making pert remarks; "Dear, dear!" she said, as they paused before a Titian of Diana and her nymphs surprised by Acteon, "aren't you glad that your ancestresses didn't carry on in that way?" Still more unfortunately, she tried to ape the fashionable jargon. "How you must love-are all these funny old rooms!" Sebastian clenched his fists in his pockets. He had not expected her to show any intelligent interest in the treasures of Chevron, but at least he had expected to enjoy the reaction of a naïf and unaccustomed mind; he had been prepared to laugh at her, fondly, affectionately, even though he knew that his motive in showing her his possessions was not a very estimable one. They were entirely at cross-purposes. Sebastian began to feel that this middle-class caution was the last thing he could tolerate. He wished that Romola Cheyne were his companion, or Lady Templecombe, or Julia Levison; or, rushing to the other extreme, old Turnour, or Godden. They would have been incapable of such airs and graces. What folly had possessed him, he wondered, to invite Teresa to Chevron? His world and hers could never meet. Old Turnour was a different matter; he liked old Turnour for talking about the frost and the sprouts; he appreciated the enormous, the vital importance of sprouts to old Turnour; he liked any reflection of a natural and practical nature, in character with the person who made it; thus he had liked Mrs. Tolputt for talking about the sales and the servants' sheets—but he remembered how Teresa had tried to interrupt her; he liked Lord Templecombe for saying at breakfast, "Damn this bloody snow, Sebastian,

can't you do something about it? Spoiling all my huntin'."
What he could not endure was the hypocrisy of Teresa's
gentility. He liked her when she was, frankly and crudely,
a snob. He could not bear people who pretended to be
something that they were not. He decided that Teresa
was nothing—neither practical, nor cultured, nor raw—
and he determined there and then to dismiss her from his
life for ever.

"Wacey," he said, bursting into the schoolroom after
this unfortunate expedition into the state-rooms was over,
"can I see the plan of the luncheon-table, please?"

The harassed Wacey produced it.

"Sorry," said Sebastian, "but this has got to be altered.
I can't sit next to Mrs. Spedding. Be ingenious, Wacey.
Shift everybody round."

"But her Grace said . . . ," Wacey began.

"Never mind what she said. Shift them round. Put me
next to Lady Templecombe. Or can I come and have my
luncheon with you in here?"

Wacey gasped at him. Was he mad? Was he simply in
high spirits, as he sometimes was, when he came and teased
her? or had something gone seriously wrong?

"I would much rather have my luncheon with you,
Wacey. And my dinner, too. Can't I? just you and me and
Viola? Then we could laugh together at everybody sitting
solemnly downstairs."

Miss Wace found the suitable formula. "That would be
very nice for me, but People in your Position have to Respect Appearances."

"I seem to have heard that before," said Sebastian,
thinking of Sylvia. "Do we really? But why? Why are people so careful of appearances? Mr. Anquetil, you know,
Wacey, wouldn't give a fig for appearances."

"There was a bit about Mr. Anquetil in the *Daily
Mail*," said Miss Wace.

"No?" said Sebastian, greedily. "Was there? When? Show me."

"I don't know that I've kept it," said Miss Wace with caution.

"Nonsense, Wacey; you know you keep everything, even old newspapers in case they should come in handy for lighting the fire. You were born to hoard. Produce it."

Wacey rose and unlocked an enormous cupboard, where indeed, as Sebastian had implied, lay a pile of newspapers neatly folded. From these she drew a two-days-old copy of the *Daily Mail*.

"Adventurous Englishmen Missing," he read. "It is now three months since news has been received of a party which left Manaos in September in an attempt to discover the sources of the Upper Amazon. Mr. Leonard Anquetil, who will be remembered as a member of . . ."

Sebastian put the paper down. He looked out at the snow falling past the window.

"Will this snow prevent the children from coming to the Christmas tree?" he asked irrelevantly.

"Only those who live far out," replied Miss Wace, immediately well informed and brisk.

"Poor little devils! What a disappointment for them."

"But Mrs. Wickenden sees to it that they get their toys and crackers just the same."

"That isn't the same at all, Wacey. They miss their tea and their games. Do you think they like coming?"

"Of course they like coming," said Miss Wace, shocked. "It's the great treat of the year for them. They look forward to it, all the year through. So would you, if it was the only treat you had."

"Yes," said Sebastian, "I expect I should. As it is, I find that treats always turn out to be disappointments. And now some of them won't be able to come at all." He stared out at the falling snow; for one reason or another, he had forgotten the plan of the luncheon-table lying before him.

MATTERS went better between Teresa and Sebastian after luncheon. The morning is always an unpropitious time for emotional relationships. Lovers, or potential lovers, ought never to meet before the afternoon. Morning is bleak and unerotic. During luncheon, Sebastian had sat between Lady Templecombe and Mrs. Levison, and had been bored by their conversation, which was the replica of a conversation he had heard a thousand times before. Once or twice he had caught Teresa's eye, and had again imagined that a certain understanding ran between them—a fallacy readily credited by any person temporarily deluded by physical desire. Those airs and graces, he decided, were not the true Teresa; they were but defences that she put up, as much against the male in him as against the duke in him. He saw them in a new light now, and was as leniently touched and diverted by them as he had originally been by Teresa's anguished efforts to control Mrs. Tolputt. In this mellower mood, he perceived that Teresa's pretences were as much a part of her as was Turnour's anxiety about his sprouts.

Still, he remained uneasily solicitous on Teresa's behalf; he was disinclined to trust her for the rest of the afternoon with his mother, Lady Templecombe, and the others. He proposed that they should make a snow-man in the garden. This suggestion was received with horror by all but Teresa herself, and, unexpectedly, John; Teresa forgot herself and clapped her hands; John took his pipe out of his mouth and said he hadn't made a snow-man since he was a boy, by Jove! he hadn't. Lucy was all too obviously relieved. She rapidly summed-up three bridge-tables, and

cast an approving look at Sebastian, who had thus solved
the problem of amusing his two incongruous friends for
the afternoon.

Snow had ceased to fall; it was freezing hard; the lying
snow was in admirable condition. Sebastian, John, and
Teresa went out in hearty spirits. Teresa, moreover, was
looking deliciously pretty, dressed in a tight bolero of
stamped velvet, a sealskin cap on her head, and her hands
buried in a little sealskin muff. She tripped gaily between
them, chattering, and turning her happy face from one to
the other. This was better than London, she said; snow
got so dreadfully dirty in London, and before you knew
where you were it had all turned to slush. She chattered
on, while John and Sebastian chose a site for their snow-
man. But before they engaged on their work they must
have implements; so ambitious a snow-man as they pro-
jected could not be built by the unaided human hand.
Sebastian and Teresa left John stamping among the snow
while they went off to find the necessary shovels. Wooden
shovels they must be—Sebastian knew from boyish experience that snow stuck to ordinary steel shovels—but he
must find the shovels for himself, for he knew that on
Christmas Eve the men would have knocked off work
early. The door of the gardeners' bothy, indeed, was
locked when they reached it. The discipline of childhood
was still strong in Sebastian; he hesitated for an instant
before the locked door; he went back to the days when
Chevron, although officially his, was not his to treat in
such high-handed manner; then, taking up a mallet with
sudden determination, he broke down the door, and
Teresa exclaimed in mixed dismay and admiration. Sebastian, while pleased with himself for showing off his
strength and his mastership before Teresa, could not escape a private sense of guilt, as though he were still a
little boy. Plunging into the dark bothy, stumbling over

benches and mowing-machines in his search for the shovels he wanted, he remembered analogous defiances of law in years gone by, when no one but his mother and his nurse dared to reprove him; he remembered getting out of the house at five on summer mornings, climbing over the garden wall because he was not then allowed the master-key that would unlock the wrought-iron gates (he put his hand into his pocket now, and fingered the key buried there); he remembered running across the park to the kitchen garden; he remembered creeping under the nets to eat the full, fresh strawberries with the dews of dawn still on them; he remembered the way his fingers had got entangled in the meshes, and how he had deliberately held up the nets for the frightened thrushes to escape, having meanwhile an unpatriotic feeling about Chevron as he did it, for it was surely wrong to let the thieving thrushes go. He remembered having once stolen two peaches out of the hot-house. It was not quite so criminal to eat fruit that grew in the open air—homely fruit: but not hot-house fruit. He remembered how he had once met Diggs the head-gardener carrying a basket of grapes, and how he had begged for some grapes, but Diggs had drawn the basket aside, saying, "No, your Grace lied to me," and how he had never understood, to this day, what Diggs had meant. He was sure that he had never lied—he hated lies; and even now, at the age of twenty-one, he cherished a resentment against Diggs, good servitor though Diggs undoubtedly was, all for that phrase spoken thirteen years ago. So he felt glad that he should have broken down the door of the bothy; it would annoy Diggs, but Diggs would not be in a position to complain. And Wickenden would have to mend it. His Grace could do what he liked with his own. Meanwhile, he had found the shovels.

It was not a snow-man that they made, but a snow-lady. She was all complete, even to the buttons down the front of her bodice, and the bun at the back of her head, and the hat tilted over her nose, and two pebbles for eyes. They laughed a great deal over the making of her, while the sun that Sebastian had seen climb up over the trees in the morning sank slowly down into the trees on the opposite side of the lawn, the same red ball that it had been all day. Absolute stillness reigned, the stillness which comes with a heavy fall of snow, and which to Sebastian, the country-bred, seemed expected and in the right order; but which Teresa, the little Cockney, thought unnatural, and which, she maintained, could only portend a storm. Sebastian scoffed at her, but amiably, very different from his sulky monosyllables of the morning. "A storm! This snow, unless we get a sudden thaw, will lie for days; to-morrow you will see the whole village out, tobogganing in the park. Our snow-lady will have an icicle dripping from the end of her nose." They worked on, putting the finishing touches in the fading daylight, all three of them in good humour, their shouts and their laughter ringing over the snow and echoing back from the walls of the house. Even the taciturn John expanded; he displayed himself as quite a competent sculptor, modelling the lady's bust and paring away the snow at her waist, till Sebastian cried out that if he made her any more like an hour-glass she would snap in half; while Teresa arranged the lady's train on the ground, and scolloped the snow into flounces. Kneeling on the ground, her face glowing beneath her sealskin cap, she laughed up at Sebastian as she beat her hands together to shake the snow from her gloves; he thought only how pretty she was, how charming, and had no longer the slightest desire for the company of Mrs. Levison or Lady Templecombe.

"IN A FEW moments we must go and give the children their presents," said Lucy, after tea. "You will have to make up the bridge-tables without me. I can cut in when I come back. What a nuisance these entertainments are, but I suppose one must put up with them."

"What children are they, Lucy, dear?"

"Only the estate children. We have a tree for them of course, every Christmas. It means that we can never dine in the Hall on Christmas Eve, and I used to be so terribly afraid that Sebastian and Viola would catch something. Really I don't know that it is a very good plan to spoil poor children like this; it only gives them a taste for things they can't have; but it is very difficult to stop something which has always been an institution."

"In my opinion," said Mrs. Levison, who had neither estates nor children on them, but had always maintained herself somewhat precariously by her wits, "we do a great deal too much for such people. We educate their children for them for nothing—and I don't believe they want to be educated, half the time—we keep the hospitals for them entirely out of charity, we give them warm old clothes and almshouses: what more do they want? Alfred Rothschild even gives the bus-drivers a pair of gloves and a brace of pheasants for Christmas."

"We always give our beaters a hare and a pheasant each, after every shoot," said Lady Templecombe, self-righteously.

"They've earned it, too," said Lord Templecombe, unexpectedly; "how would you like to go plunging through hedges and brambles from morning to night, tearing all your clothes?"

"Now, Eadred, you know they enjoy it," said Lucy, with her light laugh. "You're as bad as Sebastian: do you know what he has done now? Given every man on the estate a rise of five shillings a week this Christmas. Did you ever hear of such a thing?"

"My dear boy!" said Lord Templecombe, screwing in

his eyeglass to stare at Sebastian, "what made you do that? Not my business, of course, but it's a great mistake. A great mistake. Spoils the market for other people less fortunate than yourself. Besides, they won't appreciate it. They'll only expect more."

They all looked at Sebastian as though he had committed a crime.

Vigeon, followed by two footmen carrying trays, came in to clear away the tea.

"The children are quite ready, when your Grace is ready," he said in a low voice to Lucy.

"Oh, heavens! then we must go," said Lucy, getting up off the sofa. "Let's get it over quickly. I always believe in getting boring things over quickly. And I always believe in doing things well if you do them at all. I always change into my prettiest frock for the children; I'm sure they like it. Anyway, their mothers do. Come along, Viola. Come along, Sebastian. You must both support me."

Teresa took an enormous decision; she knew that none of the other ladies would want to go to the Christmas tree, but partly because she dreaded being left alone with them, and partly also because she so desperately wanted to see the ceremony of the tree, she resolved to abandon her policy of imitating what other people did. "May I come too, Duchess? You see, I don't play bridge. . . ."

The roar of voices and the stamping of feet in the hall ceased abruptly as the door opened to admit the Duchess and her party. The hall was full of children, and there, on the dais, in isolated splendour, stood the great tree, shining with a hundred candles and glittering with a hundred baubles of coloured glass. Silver tinsel ran in and out of its dark boughs; tufts of cotton-wool suggested snow-flakes; the pot was swathed in cotton-wool; and a spangled doll, a fairy queen with a crescent in her hair, gloriously crowned the topmost spike. Toys were heaped upon the table; a hamper of oranges and a hamper of rosy apples stood ready on either side, the lids thrown back. The children seethed excitedly in the body of the hall, even while the Chevron housemaids flitted about, trying to marshal them into order. The mothers sat grouped round the blazing fire, many of them with babies on their knees, but as Lucy entered they all rose, and some of them curtseyed, and a murmur ran round the hall, and some of the little boys, who had been carefully primed, saluted.

Now that Lucy was actually in the presence of her audience, standing above them on the step, all trace of boredom vanished from her manner. She believed, as she had said, in doing things well if you did them at all; moreover, she was not insensible to the favour she was conferring, or to the dramatic quality of her own appearance, backed by the shining tree that cast an aureole of light round her fair head and sparkled on the diamonds at her breast. She paused for a moment, surveying the mob of children, while the last murmurs and shufflings quieted down; then she spoke. Her clear voice rang out, in the formula she had used for the past five-and-twenty years: "Well, children, I hope you have all had a nice tea?"

More murmurs; here and there one could distinguish a "Yes, thank you, your Grace."

Lucy pursued, after rewarding them all with a bright smile, "And now I expect you all want your presents?"

Here Mrs. Wickenden came forward; she had been hovering in the background, waiting for Lucy to give this signal. The estate children's treat was always a great day in Mrs. Wickenden's calendar. She came forward now with a long list in her hand.

"Should I read out the names, your Grace?"

"Yes, please, Mrs. Wickenden, would you?"

For five-and-twenty years the list had been read out by the housekeeper, whether Mrs. Wickenden or her prede-

cessor, but that little ceremony was never omitted. Mrs.
Wickenden would not have believed her ears had she
heard Lucy say, "No, I'll read it myself." So now, clearing her throat and carefully settling her spectacles, she advanced to the edge of the step and began calling up the
children one by one. They were listed in families, from the
eldest to the youngest, and the families were arranged in
strict order, the butler's children coming first, then the
head-carpenter's, then the head-gardener's, and so down
to the children of the man who swept up the leaves in the
park. Each child detached itself from the rows and came
up to the step as its name was called out; the little boys
wore thick suits of dark tweed, the little girls wore frocks
of pink, mauve, blue, or green, voile. An elder sister sometimes had a younger brother by the hand. Lucy, stooping
very graciously to bestow the present into eager hands,
had a kind word for all. "Why, Doris, what a big girl you
are growing! . . . Now, Jacky, if I give you this lovely
knife, you must promise not to cut your mother's furniture. . . . And so this is the new baby, Mrs. Hodder?"—
Lucy was very quick at picking up the names—"let me see,
how old is he now? seven months? only *four* months! well,
he *is* a fine boy, you must be very proud of him, and here
is a lovely rattle for him. He must wait a few years before
he gets a knife, mustn't he?"—this was a joke that, however often repeated, never failed to arouse laughter. Mrs.
Wickenden stood by, beaming; yet she kept a sharp watch
on the children's manners: "Say thank you to her Grace,
Maggie; Bob, you've forgotten your salute; now touch your
forehead nicely to her Grace," and Lucy herself in the
midst of her benevolence could preserve discipline too,
saying, "Well, if you won't say thank you for your knife,
Jacky, I shall have to take it away from you." Sebastian, listening, was slightly embarrassed to hear the children re-
proved in this way; he tried to tell himself that his mother

and Mrs. Wickenden were probably quite right; his discomfort would have been lessened, however, had he been able to convince himself that his mother did not really enjoy doing it. He and Viola had their share in the ceremony; they presented an apple, an orange, and a cracker to each child after Lucy had given the toy. Here, again, Mrs. Wickenden supervised and intervened, taking the forgetful child by the shoulders and turning it round; "Look, Stanley, his Grace and Lady Viola have something for you, too."

But every now and then there was no response to the name called out, and after a suitable hesitation there would come a murmur from amongst the mothers round the fire, and Mrs. Wickenden would say, "Not here?" and would turn with the explanation to Lucy, "Mumps, your Grace," or else, "They live too far out, your Grace, to get here through the snow."

Teresa was spell-bound. She stood modestly to one side, fascinated by the lights, by the great hall, by the rows and rows of faces, by this list of names that never seemed to come to an end. She noticed, too, how many families there were of the same name, Hodders and Goddens and Bassetts and Reynolds. "Feudal!" she kept saying to herself; "really feudal!" It was a source of enormous satisfaction to her to be standing on the dais with Lucy, Sebastian and Viola; she felt privileged and elevated; though had she overheard the whispers round the fire her vainglory might have received a check. The mothers had been so anxious to know who the stranger was, for her Grace was not usually accompanied by a guest, and they had enquired of the Chevron housemaids, who stood amongst them in their quality of part-hostesses, dandling the babies in their arms. But the housemaids had sniffed. "A Mrs. Spedding," they said; "wife of a doctor," and poor Teresa had unwittingly provided a disappointment.

The last present had been given, the last apple, the last orange, and the last cracker: Lucy was preparing to make her little farewell speech. A threat of rowdiness had to be suppressed, for the impatient children had already begun to pull their crackers, hob-nailed boots clattered on the stone floor, and one or two of the little boys had loosed off a pistol with deafening caps; so "Hush, children!" cried Mrs. Wickenden, holding up her hand, and the noise subsided. "Well, children," Lucy began again, "I hope you all like your presents, and now I hope you will all have a good game, and so I'll say good-bye till next year. Good-bye, children, good-night, good-bye to you all."

Vigeon rose very stately in the body of the hall.

"Three cheers for her Grace, children!" he cried. "Now lift the roof! Hip, hip . . ."

"Hooray!" they shouted, lifting the roof.

"And again for his Grace. Hip, hip . . ."

"Hooray!"

"And for Lady Viola. Hip, hip . . ."

Teresa blinked the tears back from her eyes. How beautiful it was! How young, how handsome, how patrician were Viola and Sebastian! How the children must adore them!

"Hooray!"

Bang went a cracker. Lucy made her escape. Sebastian slipped round the tree to his sister. "Shall we stay and play games with them, Viola?"

"But what about Mrs. Spedding?"

"Oh, she can stay too."

They all stayed. Vigeon had already wound up the gramophone, and its enormous trumpet brayed forth, but the children were in no mood to listen even to Dan Leno. They wanted to make as much noise as possible themselves. If they were to be controlled at all, regular games must be organised. Sebastian and Viola knew all about

this, for they had always been allowed to stay behind with
the children, and Sebastian indeed had always been puzzled as a little boy by "Nuts in May," because, as he explained to his nurse, nuts grew in September, not in May.

The housemaids were admirable hostesses. They wore
their best black dresses; enjoyed their rôle thoroughly;
knew all the children by name; were inventive and competent; could produce enough chairs for "Musical Chairs,"
or a clean handkerchief for "I wrote-a-letter-to-my-love,"
or a thick honest scarf for "Blindman's Buff"; in fact, anything that was wanted. Mr. Vigeon was a terrible Blindman. He had to be saved a dozen times from falling into
the fire. He plunged about, his arms whirling, so that one
scarcely dared to creep up and poke him in the back or
tweak his coat-tails, he was so quick on his feet and could
nip round so fast. He caught his Grace, who was too daring—he had always been too daring, even as a little boy—
and everyone stood round breathlessly while he felt his
Grace's head and nose, and finally gave the pronounce-
ment right. There were shrieks of laughter when his Grace
blundered into the panelling and caught one of the heraldic leopards; felt its tail very carefully, right up to the
tip; and then said, "Mrs. Wickenden." Then they wanted
to play "Hunt the Slipper," but Mrs. Vigeon said it was
too cold for the children to sit on the stone floor. So they
played "Musical Chairs" instead, with Mr. Vigeon working the gramophone very ingeniously; his Grace and Mrs.
Spedding were left in last, and had an exciting scramble
over the last chair, which ended in their both sitting down
on it together and trying to crowd each other off. By now
everyone was in very high spirits, and even Mrs. Wickenden forgot to reprove the children for lacking in respect
to his Grace. They played "Nuts in May," swaying in two
long lines up and down the hall after the invidious business of picking sides had been completed; Mr. Vigeon had

picked one side and Mrs. Wickenden the other, as befitted
their dignity. Mr. Vigeon had very gallantly picked Mrs.
Spedding, and Mrs. Wickenden had retaliated by picking
his Grace. So Teresa and Sebastian were ranged opposite
to one another, each with their hands clasped by the hot
little hands of two excited children. Teresa was conscious
of a strange agitation, which in her innocence she ascribed
to the general ferment of the evening; Sebastian, just as
much troubled but less innocent, watched her closely; this
intimacy with her, in the midst of their apparent frivolity,
was of the very nature that whipped his taste. Ever since
they fetched the shovels out of the bothy, ever since they
made the snow-lady, he had been wooing Teresa, not very
openly as yet, but still more openly than he had hitherto
dared. Now he laughed at her gaily, as his enemy on the
opposite side; she saw his laughing face across the gap that
separated them. And, since such humours are contagious,
the line of children and servants rocked backwards and
forwards, taking Sebastian and Teresa as on a tide with
them, and as they rocked they sang:

"Who will you have for nuts in May? nuts in May? nuts
in May?"

"We'll have Mrs. Spedding for nuts in May, nuts in
May, nuts in May. We'll have Mrs. Spedding for nuts in
May, all on a frosty morning."

"And who will you send to fetch her away? fetch her
away? fetch her away?"

"We'll send his Grace to fetch her away, fetch her away,
fetch her away. We'll send his Grace to fetch her away, all
on a frosty morning."

A handkerchief was laid down in the middle, and Sebastian and Teresa advanced amidst much laughter to pit
their strength.

"It isn't fair!" cried Teresa, resisting the many hands
that pushed her forward.

"Nonsense," said Sebastian firmly; "all's fair . . ." and he looked at her, but did not complete the sentence.

They joined hands across the handkerchief; there was a brief struggle, and Sebastian pulled her easily over to his side. She came, panting, laughing, submissive; looking at her captor while everybody applauded. For the first time in their acquaintance she was frightened of him; for the first time in their acquaintance he was sure of her. Viola observed them; she sized up the situation; she felt sorry for Teresa, sorrier for John Spedding. But, of course, it was no good trying to interfere with Sebastian.

Sebastian himself was well aware of this. He had been circumspect, he had been forbearing, but now he was bent on hunting Teresa down, and nothing could stop him. He turned everything into a circumstance that drew her closer to him, and he did it with a certainty and a recklessness that swept her along with him on his crazy course. The control was entirely in his hands. All through the maze of children he seemed to be chasing her, so that she found him always behind her, or beside her, or facing her, where she least expected him, mocking her lightly, or alternating his gaiety with a smouldering look that disturbed her to some unexplored region of her soul. Everything piled up for Teresa: the new experience of Chevron, the lights of the Christmas tree, the shouting of the children, the fantasy, the improbability, the sense of this young man burning his way towards her, a remorseless young man who would spare her nothing—all this turned Sebastian from the most unhoped toy that she had ever had into an urgent but still undefinable terror. He saw the fright in her eyes, and, skilled in reading the signs, exulted. How ludicrously he was misled, he had yet to learn.

Meanwhile they played. They played the childish games, with the adult game lying behind them. They played "Oranges and Lemons," with Sebastian and Viola making the arch; they let a dozen children pass, but snatched Teresa, as she tried to slip past them, and for the first time Sebastian felt Teresa's small body imprisoned in his arms. He could feel her heart beating against his ribs. She, for her part, clipped between brother and sister, turned laughing and dizzy in her imprisonment from one to the other, seeing Viola's grave brows bent inquiringly towards her, and Sebastian's eyes dark with a question that exacted an answer. "Oranges?" said Sebastian. "Lemons?" said Viola, and Teresa knew that she must take her place in the string of children behind one or the other. "Lemons," she said, casting Viola a glance that was an appeal. It was as though she had said, "Save me from him!" divining that in this cold, secretive girl she might hope for some masonic, feminine support; but at the same time the oranges that Sebastian offered her seemed luscious and warm, opposed to the sour lemons of Viola's following. The very colour of the fruits, which in her sensitive state she visualised, seemed symbolic: the reddish fire of the orange, the unripe yellow of the lemon. Yet "Lemons!" she said, and took her place behind Viola, in a gesture that repudiated all that Sebastian had to offer.

Still he would not let her go, for her defiance had only served to stimulate him; he persecuted her, softly, stealthily, even when the Christmas tree caught fire and the hall was suddenly filled with the acrid scent of burning fir. One of the candles had burnt out, and the little candleclip had tipped over; the hall-boy, who had been left in charge with a damp sponge on the end of a pole, had been tempted by the games to desert his post, thinking that no one would notice—he was only fourteen, so there was some excuse for him—a flare resulted; everyone rushed to help; fire-buckets were brought and the water flung sizzling over the conflagration; this happened nearly every year, but still for some reason Vigeon's theory of discipline refused to accept the fact that a hall-boy aged fourteen was not a suitable person to be left in charge of a Christmas tree whilst other fun was in progress. No harm was done, only a little excitement added to the general excitement; and Sebastian's hand had caught Teresa's wrist and had pulled it away from a blazing patch of cotton-wool. No further harm. But somehow the incident broke up the games. The guilty hall-boy ran off to lay the table for the servants' hall supper; a baby by the fire woke up and began to squall; Mrs. Wickenden realised that she was tired; mothers remembered that they were faced with a long trudge home through the snow; a sudden weariness descended upon the children; the housemaids bethought themselves of the hot-water cans they must fill; it occurred to Sebastian that it was time to dress for dinner; and Vigeon finally put an end to the jollity by calling upon everybody to sing "For he's a jolly good fellow." Sebastian stood on the step between Viola and Teresa while they sang it. He did not enjoy it as his mother would have enjoyed it, but he endured it as inevitable. Teresa was again compelled to blink the tears back from her eyes.

"Mrs. Spedding, do come and talk to me. You don't play bridge, neither do I—at least, not when I can do anything better. Let's go and wander through the house. We'll take a candle. Look—they're all settled down. No one will notice. Let's creep away. Shall you be cold?" Impetuous, he caught up a cloak thrown down on the back of a sofa.

"But that is your mother's cloak."

"Never mind." He put it round her shoulders. It was of gold tissue lined with sable. Teresa's feminine eye had appraised it already, earlier in the evening. The soft fur caressed her bare shoulders. It seemed fitting that Sebastian should swathe her in such a garment; but still she cast a glance at John, conscientiously sorting the cards in his hand. John had let drop a hint to her that he was a little alarmed by the high stakes they played for. He hoped that he would not lose more than he could afford. Poor John, who had given her fifty pounds to spend on clothes, in anticipation of this party! Poor John. But the sable was warm and soft to her bare skin; she had never felt just such a caress before; Sebastian opened the door for her, and she passed through it into the dark galleries, hoping that the other women had seen them go, hoping that John had not looked up.

Sebastian carried a three-branched candlestick in his hand; it lit up his face, but left the rooms in shadow. He proved to be in a mellow mood, neither sarcastic, nor excited, nor scoffing; but dreamy, as though he had plenty of time before him, and were disposed to betray something of himself as he had never done to Teresa before. They sauntered down the long gallery, talking softly, and every now and then Sebastian would pause before a picture, and, holding up the candlestick, would make some comment or recount some anecdote, while the three little spears of light flickered over the stomacher of a lady or the beard of a king. Then the gilding of the frame came to life, and the face looked gravely down at them, until, moving on, they left the portrait to re-enter the darkness, and woke some other image out of its painted sleep. There was now no friction between them, as there had been in the morning, when Sebastian was irritable and Teresa cautious. They talked naturally but softly, lowering their voices almost to a murmur out of respect for the hushed and sleeping rooms, where the moonlight spread in chequered lakes across the boards and the muting hand of the centuries seemed to have laid itself gently over the clamour of life. They breathed the air of a world that was completely withdrawn from reality—a world of which Sebastian was a natural inhabitant and to which he had admitted Teresa as

by the unlocking of a door. She felt that with a princely
generosity he had now shown her all his jewels. He had
shown her his friends—and, though Sebastian might not
value his friends, Teresa valued them extremely—he had
shown her his boyishness and simplicity; now by leading
her into this enchantment he had revealed another aspect
of himself, the most secret, the most romantic of all. For
it goes without saying that Sebastian was the essence of
romance in Teresa's eyes. Whether he came to tea with
her in the Cromwell Road out of the mysterious background of his London life, or sat at the head of his table
half-hidden by the plate and the orchids, or laughed as he
tossed the snow, or murmured in the moonlit rooms, it appeared to her in turn that he could play no other part.
And now, seeing him in the crowning magic of the moon
and the ancient rooms, she thought that she at last saw
him in the round. She could put all the pieces together;
he was, triumphantly, a unity. Out of the jumble of her
impressions emerged a perfectly clear figure. She had her
moment of revelation; she experienced the ecstatic shock
of truly apprehending a work of art.

So, at least, thought Teresa; except that she did not put
it to herself in terms of apprehending works of art. Sebastian was wiser, and colder. He had estimated—and, up to
a certain point, with accuracy—the effect that the dark
galleries would have upon Teresa. When he chose, his
technique could be faultless; it was faultless now. (He
was not really to blame for his miscalculation of one essential particular.) He was very gentle with Teresa, warning
her not to stumble over a step, holding the tapestry aside
that she might pass beneath; he was protective, though impersonal: the stories he told her were just such as would
lead her deeper into this poetic world where reality ceased
to have any weight. He wanted her to feel that he and she
were its only inhabitants, and that it was their possession,

for them to re-enter at any moment which left them alone together. So gradually he began to speak of the people they had deserted in the drawing-room—"chattering magpies," said Sebastian—and of the difference between herself and them, speaking with eloquence because he had half-persuaded himself that he believed what he was saying. Teresa believed it too. With her final putting-together of Sebastian, she had come to the sustaining conviction that she "understood" him. He must know it, she thought; for otherwise he would not have led her away into this beautiful, secret house of his. Her reverent adoration of him became slightly maternal.

Despite their lingering, they had wandered through two galleries and found themselves now in Queen Elizabeth's Bedroom, where the great four-poster of silver and flamingo satin towered to the ceiling and the outlines of the famous silver furniture gleamed dimly in a ray of the moon. Sebastian went to the window and pulled back the curtains. He knew that this was the moment for which the whole day had been but a preparation, yet he almost forgot Teresa and his wary plotting in the first shock of the beauty that met his eyes. The white garden lay in the full flood of the moon. The dark room was suddenly irradiated; the figures on the tapestry seemed to stir, the bed was full of shadows, the bosses on the silver shone, the polished floor became a lake of silver light. Softly he blew out his candles, and as their three spears of gold vanished, the room was given up entirely to that argent radiance. Teresa's gold cloak turned silver too as she slipped into the embrasure of the window and leant there by his side. They were both silent, now gazing through the lattices into the white garden, now turning to let their eyes roam and search the recesses of the beautiful room. Teresa's arm, escaping from the cloak, lay along the window-sill. Sebastian recollected himself; he remembered the purpose

with which he had brought her there; his desire revived—
but he was a little shocked to discover that his delight in
Chevron, ever renewed, could eclipse even for a moment
his desire for a woman—it was, however, not too late to
repair the mistake; his hand stole out, and he laid it upon
hers.

Teresa also came to her senses as his touch recalled her.
She looked at him in some surprise. She had been weaving
a dream about him, in which she saw him straying end-
lessly as a wraith among this incredible beauty. That moment in which she fancied she saw him in the round had
been very valuable and illuminating to her. But it had
slightly accentuated his unreality. On the whole, in spite
of her maternal impulse when she told herself that she
"understood" him, it had helped to make him into something more of a peep-show, something more definitely
apart from herself. As his romance increased, so did his
reality diminish. So now, when his slim fingers closed upon
her hand, she was surprised, and baffled, and could not re-
late the physical contact with the image she had formed
of him.

They were once again at cross-purposes.

He leant towards her, and, to her intense perplexity, began to pour words of love into her ear. "Teresa," he said,
in a tone she had never heard him use, just as she had
never heard him use her Christian name; and she found
that he was speaking of the great shadowy bed, and of his
desire for her body, and of their solitude and safety, and
of the loveliness and suitability of the hour. "They will be
stuck at their bridge until at least midnight," he said, and
proceeded to paint a picture of the joys that might be
theirs for years to come. But the immediate moment was
the most urgent, he said. The snow outside, the moonlight, their isolation; he pleaded all this in fulfilment of his
desire. Her mind flew to John, sitting in the great drawing-

room, playing bridge for stakes which he knew were beyond his means; John, whom she had persuaded against his will to come to Chevron for Christmas; John, who had given her a cheque for fifty pounds; John, who had searchingly asked her once whether there was 'nothing wrong' between herself and this young duke, and had instantly, almost apologetically, accepted her indignant denial. She pushed Sebastian away. She almost hated him. "You must be mad," she said, "if you think I am that sort of woman." Sebastian, in his turn, was equally perplexed. Had he not spent all his life among women who made light of such infidelities? Besides, had he not seen the adoration in Teresa's eyes? "Teresa," he said, "don't waste our time. Don't pretend. You know I am in love with you, and I believe you are in love with me—why make any bones about it?" Teresa put her hands over her ears to shut out the sudden voicing of this crude and shocking creed. "John!" she cried in a low voice, as though she were crying for help. "John!" said Sebastian, taken aback; the very mention of her husband at such a moment struck him as an error of taste. "Why, John knows all about it, you may be sure; else, he would never have consented to bring you here." "What?" said Teresa, taking her hands away and staring at him in real amazement; "you think that? You think that John knew you were in love with me, and condoned it? You believe that? You think that John and I are that sort of person?" "Oh," said Sebastian, maddened into exasperation, "don't go on saying 'that sort of woman,' and 'that sort of person'; it means nothing at all." "But it does mean something," said Teresa, suddenly discovering a great many things about herself, and feeling firmer than she had ever felt before; "it means that John and I love each other, and that when we married we intended to go on loving each other, and to be faithful to one another, and that that is the way we understand marriage. I know that it is not the way you understand it—you and your friends. I am sorry if I gave you the impression that I was in love with you. I don't think I ever was, and if I had been I should have asked you to go away and never see me again. I was dazzled by you, I admired you, I used to watch you and think about you, in a way I almost worshipped you. I don't mind admitting it, but that is not the same as being in love."

She paused for breath after rapidly delivering this little speech. She clutched the cloak about her and fixed Sebastian with a distressed but courageous gaze. "I don't want to hurt you," she said more gently, "but I must tell you exactly how it is. I suppose it is as difficult for you to understand our ideas as it is for us to understand yours. I know what you are thinking—you are disgusted with me, and you are wondering why you ever wasted your time over a conventional little *bourgeoise* like me. To tell you the truth, I used to wonder too. To tell you even more of the truth, I knew I attracted you and I was pleased. But I never took it seriously. If I had taken it seriously I should have told John at once. But I didn't take it seriously, and anyway I was weak, because you represented everything I had always longed for. I am being so frank with you because I want you to understand. Perhaps I never really thought about it very much; I was so excited about you, and when you asked me to Chevron I nearly died of joy. There, now, you know all the depths of my silliness. You were offering me sweets, and I took them. But I love John, and he's my husband."

"And if you did not love him?" asked Sebastian curiously.

"It would still be the same," said Teresa; "marriage is marriage, isn't it?—not in your world, perhaps, but in mine—and I should hold on to that. Not one of my relations would ever speak to me again if I were unfaithful to John. Surely you must know that?"

Sebastian could not sympathise with these sentiments. He had acknowledged her dignity when she first spoke, but now she seemed to have switched over from something fundamental to something contemptible. Love was one thing; middle-class virtue was another. This was as bad as Sylvia Roehampton, who could sacrifice him and herself to her social position. Sebastian was angry, because he saw his caprice broken against a rock. Was he never to find moral courage anywhere in the world, he demanded? It now seemed to him that that was the only quality worth having. (Reference has already been made, perhaps too frequently, to the intemperate nature of his moods.) He had tried the most fashionable society, and he had tried the middle-class, and in both his plunging spirit had got stuck in the glue of convention and hypocrisy. The conventions differed—Sylvia had not hesitated to give herself to him—but the hypocrisy remained the same. He raved and stormed. He tried anger, only too unfeigned; and he tried persuasion, but neither could move Teresa. She was grieved, she was sorry, but she was softly stubborn; she even appeared incapable of understanding half he said. Indeed, he poured out such a torrent that no one but himself could have followed his arguments; no one, that is, who had not grown up as he had grown up, with the sense of being caught and condemned to a prearranged existence; who had not alternately struggled against his bonds and then drawn them tighter around him; who had not loved his good things and despised himself for loving them; who had not tried to solace himself with pleasures and with women who meant nothing to him; who had not wavered, in unhappy confusion, between an outward rôle that was almost forced upon him, and the inward passion

for Chevron that was the one stable and worthy thing in
his life. It was not surprising that Teresa should be puzzled by the abuse that he poured upon her or by the bitterness that he heaped upon himself.

The big clock, striking overhead, abruptly reminded her
of her absence. What would John think, what would they
all think? she cried. "We must go," she cried, tugging at
him; she was frightened now by this scene that had taken
place between them; she only wanted to get back to safety
and to John. "Do come," she implored. Sebastian would
not move; he leant against the window-sill, looking wild
and indifferent to earthly pleadings. "Please!" she cried
childishly; and desperately added, "I can't leave you here
alone, but I must get back." She made the only appeal that
meant anything to her; it was an unfortunate choice. "Do
think of me," she said; "think of John, think of my reputation." At that Sebastian laughed. The contrast between
her plea and his own feelings was—or seemed to him—too
ironically discrepant. "Your reputation?" he said; "what
does your reputation matter? You timid, virtuous wife!"
The inner knowledge that he was behaving not only badly
but histrionically increased his obstinacy. He was acutely
ashamed of himself, since, for the first time in his life, he
saw himself through other eyes; and saw his selfishness, his
self-indulgence, his arrogance, his futile philandering, for
what they were worth. Still he would not give way. He was
as childish as she; for he was in what Wacey would have
called a Regular State; and when people get into Regular
States all the problems of their life rise up and join forces
with their immediate sorrow. He had wanted Teresa; he
had been thwarted by Teresa; so he remembered that he
had wanted Sylvia and had been thwarted by Sylvia, and
so by a natural process he had remembered everything else
—Chevron, and his hatred of his friends, and the shackles
that had been tied round him like ribbons in his cradle,

and the sarcasm of Leonard Anquetil. "You shan't go," he said, making a movement towards Teresa.

She escaped him; she fled out of the beautiful room, leaving her cloak where it fell, lying in a pool of moonlight. Sebastian stared at it after she had gone. Its wrinkled gold was turned to silver. Its sable lining was as dark as the shadows within the great bed. It was as empty and as crumpled as everything that he had ever desired.

Henry Seidel Canby

"THE COLLEGE TOWN"
from *American Memoir*

$\mathcal{I}$ remember first the college town. Surely it is amazing that neither history, nor sociology, nor even fiction, has given more than passing attention to the American college town, for it has had a character and a personality unlike other towns. And quite as surely, its imprint of small-town respectability, convention, and common sense is deeper upon American education than has ever been guessed. With the rarest exceptions the home of the college has been a small town, even if that town was a suburb or a section, self-contained, of a city. There were hundreds of such towns in the period of which I write, and all with a family resemblance.

Cleaner, neater than other towns, with green spaces somewhere toward the center, and white spires or Gothic towers or windowed dormitories half hid by trees, they were the little capitals of the academic states. As trading or industrial centers their life might be indistinguishable from towns or cities of a like size, but in their social consciousness there was always some recognition of peculiarity. For the heart of the community was a college. Its subtle influences were as pervasive if less noticeable, than the quite unsubtle symbols of college life—playing fields, cafés, and collegiate clothing.

And in the early nineteen-hundreds the college town was no luncheon stop for automobiles. It was secluded,

even if it was a town within a city, like the Yale section of
New Haven; it knew its boundaries and kept them; it was
jealous of its distinctions; if it was uneasy, it was also
proud. The campus and the college buildings dominated
its architecture like the temple and citadel of a Greek city-
state, a difficult relationship since there was always some
doubt in the minds of the town folk whether the college
was an asset or a parasite. The town with its college was
like a woman's club committee with a celebrity in tow, a
credit to them but also an embarrassment and sometimes a
nuisance; it was like a French village built upon a Roman
camp to which tourists resort; it was like the mistress of an
actors' boarding house, pleased by the notoriety but worried by the manners, or the morals, of her boarders; it was
like almost anything but a town without a college. And
many a college town was like a resentful mother who, ex-
pecting a quiet and manageable infant, had given birth to
a Gargantua that swallowed whole streets and squares in
its gigantic growing. I do not wish to be fantastic, yet only
such similes will express how very unlike the rest of the
United States was the college town.

New Haven, as I first knew it in the late nineties, was a
decorous and beautiful town set in the midst of a sprawling industrial city of slums, factories, and long, undistinguished avenues. The college town was old New Haven,
with its Green, its bordering business streets, its campus
and blocks of residences north-stretching into park and
country beyond. The elm-shaded streets of this old town
were lined by sedate houses which in various modes still
kept the impress of the Greek revival of the early nineteenth century. Eight out of ten had a portico of wood
with two Doric columns painted brown or gray or white.
Down the length of shady streets these columns made a
pleasant arcade, broken here and there by high brick man-

sions of the eighties, or charming green-shuttered, white-walled reminder of the better proportions of a Colonial day.

It was a guarded town, very unlike the ample if ugly spaciousness of the mansarded avenues of my youth, where broad porches and open gates welcomed relatives and friends. There were no open doors in the New England college town. Behind the twin Doric columns, which might have been labeled Respectability and Reserve, two squint lights seemed always to be looking down their noses at the passer-by, fearful lest he should wish to enter. The college town, unlike the rest of America, was jealous of privacy, and doubtful of casual relationships.

Lights went out early in these bosky streets, often to be relit in upstairs studies. When the chapel bell rang ten, and the undergraduate navigating homeward across the Green filled the night with shouts and melody, the prim town pulled up its covers, shut its ears, or burrowed deeper in a book. Nights in the college town were consecrated to sleep or work.

Along these town streets, professors lived, students wandered, but also the social and professional leaders of the city sought residence, because, after all, it was the college that gave tone to the community. Academic society was therefore both town and gown, and had a double flavor which recalled in homely fashion the atmosphere of those small European courts where both prince and bishop had their following. It was not an exciting society, yet certainly it was not dull. New Haven had never forgotten that it was once a colony, all of itself, and might have been a state had it not sheltered republicans and regicides. There was a stiff, aristocratic quality in the old families, now entirely lost there as elsewhere in America. From their harsh stalks sprouted personalities of extraordinary independence, so that it was hard to tell sometimes whether decorum or eccentricity was the dominant note of the town's society. These families belonged to the college world, yet were not wholeheartedly of it. They arranged its finances, fought its lawsuits, supplied a president or a professor now and then, were mysteriously powerful sometimes in academic affairs, yet in general their attitude of respectful but slightly contemptuous toleration of learning, so characteristic of America, was tempered only by the belief that the college belonged to them and put them a cut above the aristocracies of Hartford or Springfield, and made them able to take rank even in New York. Hence the teacher, who in this money-making age lived on the edge or beyond of society, in the college town might have a definite place, though he was not society himself. Wealth and position did not so much stoop to him as restrain their privileges so that he could enter. By a self-denying ordinance tacitly understood, the rich in the college set (and no other society counted) spent only a part of their incomes at home, eschewed butlers, denied themselves broughams, and later, for a while, automobiles, kept dues low in the clubs, and, if they did spend, put their money into that good wine and costly food which the scholar has always enjoyed. And he responded with an unexpected geniality which was sometimes grateful and sometimes lumbering, and sometimes only a courteous irony.

Thus the college was privileged socially, not only in the hand-picked sons of the cultivated or the well-to-do that came as students, but in the close contacts between the faculty and the aristocracy of the college town. But it was conditioned also by the life of a small-town community, which, no matter how good its traditions, how admirable its character, how genuine its culture, was, by definition, a little provincial, a little priggish, and very much inbred. And yet there was a raciness in this mingling of town and gown that gave its own flavor to the college society, and was some compensation for the gustier airs which blew through capitals and metropolises.

I can see now a characteristic 'reception' in a great house behind the broad sweep of the elms of Hillhouse Avenue, which was to the college town of New Haven what Fifth Avenue once was to New York—a terminus of social pride. Tables were laden with heavy, mind-satisfying food, champagne bubbled on the sideboards, stiff-backed professors were trying to relax, while their wives with the curious pursed mouth of the academic woman, showed more concern for their dignity than for the entertainment. Among them moved the grand dames of our town society, soothing vanities by a kind word, snubbing with a vacant look the strange uncouth creatures that science was bringing into the university, but not too emphatically, since one never knew nowadays who might become famous. And with them were our town eccentrics, women usually of old families, too sure of themselves to bother about social distinctions. Worse dressed than the professors' wives, they had a confident distinction of ugliness which lifted them above our small-town limitations, and they spoke the language of the academic world with understanding and tolerance, like missionaries among an Indian tribe. Trailing behind them, yet always heading back toward the champagne, were our faculty 'characters'—the great hearty souls that scholarship which is not pedantry creates in its happier moods, men whose broadcloth might be shiny and spotted, their linen none too clean, yet with minds and faces of the great world, known in Europe and conscious of it, witty often, sarcastic usually, ill-mannered, inclined to lash out at this pompous bourgeois society, which nevertheless gave them their only chance to eat, drink, and be merry with their own kind. There was our famous Chaucerian scholar, Lounsbury, his sparse white beard wagging under his rapid tongue, his eyes a little bleary, an epigram worth quoting with every glass of champagne. 'Why do they want to inscribe old Whitney's name on the Court House wall? All he knew was Sanskrit. What did he ever do for New Haven?' says a banker. 'Do!' Lounsbury shoots back, 'By Gorry! It's enough that he lived here!'

There were subtle jealousies between town and gown which could not be assigned to differences in income. The town had inherited a Yankee distrust of ministers who talked about God but made no money, and now that ministers were less and professors more it transferred this distrust with increments. It was irritated by its own deference to an institution that did not make for profits. Energy that in other communities was organizing machine tools or life insurance, here in this college community leaked away in a trickle that sometimes carried sons and heirs with it into the academic world where it was transformed into the teaching of adolescents or into books that nobody but professors read. The town derived a goodly share of its income from the rapidly increasing expenditures of the college and its students, and this, too, it resented, feeling that it was committed to an approval of what the college was doing. It endured the noisy night life of the students, the untidy boarding houses that crowded its streets, the frequent arrogance of the academic mind, but it disliked the haunting sense of inferiority which came from knowing that it was celebrated because of the college. It listened to the endless shoptalk of the faculty and pretended to take the 'big men' of the undergraduate world at their face value, but it could not entirely respect, still less understand, the creature upon which it lived and which it believed it had created. Not until the expansive twenties when alumni, enriched by the war and prosperity, upset their applecarts of gold into the college coffers, and made education, or at least the side-shows of education, a big business, was the town convinced that the college, its own college, was worthy of its birthplace. No Commencement orator was ever so persuasive as gifts in the millions and a building program that was a major industry.

And yet, as with Christians and Infidels living together in old Spain, there was more interpenetration than appeared on the surface. The college taught the town to discuss ideas; it taught also friendship and a delight in the companionship of like-minded men. The two blended in the adult life of the community, for the habit of the undergraduate fraternity persisted in dozens of little clubs of talkers which flourished throughout the town because their members had learned clubability. It was a rash hostess who gave a dinner party on Wednesday or Friday nights, their favorite meeting times. In these clubs scholar, lawyer, and business man ate, drank, and read papers explaining their jobs or their social philosophy. Ideas spread through the college town, freed from that taboo on abstractions which was the curse of the small town elsewhere in America, and many a scholar was saved from pedantry, or a paralysis of the emotions in the arid wastes of specialist theory, by his contacts with men whose daily task was the handling of men. Even the women became clubable; and indeed it was in New Haven that by happy inspiration Our Society was born, whose inestimable privilege after the meeting was to inspect every closet in their hostess's house. But it was a man's town.

Still another institution the college gave to the society of the town, the college widow. I knew two of them in their old age and profited greatly from my friendships. For the college widow had a depth and richness of emotional experience never developed in American life of that day outside of the few metropolises, and seldom there. She began at sixteen or eighteen as a ravishing beauty, the

darling of freshmen; she passed on in the years of her first
blooming from class to class of ardent youngsters, until,
as her experience ripened, she acquired a taste, never to
be satisfied by matrimony, for male admiration abstracted
from its consequences; and more subtly for the heady stim-
ulant of intimacy with men in their fresh and vigorous
youth. By her thirties she had learned the art of eternal
spring, and had become a connoisseur in the dangerous
excitement of passion controlled at the breaking point, a
mistress of every emotion, and an adept in the difficult
task of sublimating love into friendship. The students
lived out their brief college life and went on; she endured,
and tradition with her, an enchantress in illusion, and a
specialist in the heart. Twenty, even thirty years, might be
her tether; and when suddenly on a midnight, a shock of
reality, or perhaps only boredom, ended it all, she was old
—but still charming and infinitely wise. To smoke a cigarette with her when cigarettes were still taboo for women,
and drink her coffee and liqueur, was a lesson in civiliza-
tion.

Yet in fostering in its midst the sprawling infant, gray-
headed but still growing, which was the college, the town
sacrificed its own youth. There was childhood and maturity in a college town, but no youth in between. Youth
male was absorbed into the undergraduate community and
came home only on Sundays, youth female was usually
sent off perforce to school or woman's colleges, away from
the dangerous glamour of college streets. Hence the young
folk in the college town settled back into their home environment only in their mid or late twenties, and then
only did social life in a community begin for them.
There were no calf loves in the society of the college
town, no gawkish immaturity, no giggling, no rebellious
escapes. And since the young had reached the earning and
marrying stage in a society where the scale of living was

based upon an instructor's salary, their pleasures were necessarily simple. Relative poverty was regarded as a virtue, doing without was a pride. One walked, not rode; went to concerts rather than to the theater; danced to a piano and a cornet; gave books not jewelry; sat down four at a table, not eight; kept married instead of toying with expensive ideas about lovers and divorce.

The results for the college town were by no means ill. The tittle-tattle of a small town had little fuel here. It was an educated society, and since it could not afford to be frivolous, and both puritan custom and economy held the passions in check, every opportunity was given to vivacity and ideas in conversation. Talk was cheap, which did not prevent it from being good. It was often stiff with convention and sometimes pedantical, yet the fun was more civilized than country-club horseplay, the wit, when any, aware of the nature of wit.

And yet it was all a little arid. The young people had come together too late. They had no sentimental memories to share, and thanks to the restrictions of what was, after all, a small town, and to the official nature of their college society, and to relative poverty, the sex in relationships was weak. Every emotion had its inhibition. Like the columns of the houses, the twin shrines in every heart were Reserve and Respectability.

The college town was thus the imperfect resultant of two worlds in a physical merger where souls and minds remained desperate. Even this understates the difficulty. The undergraduates belonged to the faction of the gown, but had themselves come in a vast majority from uncollegiate small towns, and so in ideas and attitudes toward learning were far closer to the Philistines of the streets than to the Israelites of the campus faculty. Their relations with the faculty could too often be described as passive resistance, usually with the sneaking sympathy of both parents and town. Hence, there was a split in the college itself, so that in my days not a duality but a trinity —town, gown, and sweater—would have best described our community.

I have written of the college town with pleasure because I was happy there, and excited, and amused, and also cabin'd, cribb'd, confined; yet also with a very definite purpose. For it is impossible to think of the college of that day without its encircling town. This was the air the professor breathed, and which the student absorbed from his freshman year onward. For him the town often provided his first experience in adult social life. Nor in discussing the internal conflicts of the college itself which have been so decisive in shaping the type known as the college graduate, is it right to forget for a moment the influence of these nests of puritan respectability, given tone by the American aristocracy that clung to them for shelter from the make-money world outside. Here is a factor in education and in the faiths and prejudices of the educated and educator which has escaped the theorist and the statistician alike. We have forgotten that the types we analyze so readily—professors, alumni, humanists, scientists, scholars —were in their conditioning period American boys in a small college town.

W. Somerset Maugham

$\blacktriangleleft\!\diamond\!\blacktriangleright$

"SOME NOVELISTS I HAVE KNOWN"

Henry James, from *The Vagrant Mood*

$\mathcal{I}$ saw Henry James long before I knew him. Somehow or other I was allotted two seats in the dress circle for the first night of *Guy Domville*. I can't think why, because I was still a medical student and one of George Alexander's first nights was a fashionable affair and seats in the better parts of the house were distributed among critics, regular first-nighters, friends of the management and persons of consequence. The play was a dreadful failure. The dialogue was graceful, but perhaps not quite direct enough to be taken in by an audience and there was a certain monotony in its rhythm. Henry James was fifty when he wrote the play and it is hard to understand how such a practised writer could have invented such a tissue of absurdities as was that night presented to the public. There was in the second act a distressing scene of pretended drunkenness which gave one goose-flesh. One blushed for the author. The play reached its tedious end and Henry James was very unwisely brought on the stage to take a bow, as was the undignified custom of the time. He was greeted with such an outburst of boos and catcalls as only then have I heard in the theatre. From my seat in the dress circle he seemed oddly foreshortened. A stout man on stumpy legs, and owing to his baldness, notwithstanding his beard, a vast expanse of naked face. He confronted the hostile audience, his jaw fallen so that his mouth was slightly open and on his countenance a look

76

of complete bewilderment. He was paralysed. I don't know why the curtain wasn't immediately brought down. He seemed to stand there interminably while the gallery and the pit continued to bawl. There was clapping in the stalls and dress circle, and he said afterwards that it was enthusiastic, but there he was mistaken. It was half-hearted. People clapped in protest at the rudeness of pit and gallery, and out of pity because they could not bear to see the wretched man's humiliation. At last George Alexander came out and led him, crushed and cowed, away.

In a letter he wrote to his brother William after that disastrous evening Henry James, like many another dramatist who has had a failure, said that his play was "over the heads of the usual vulgar theatre-going London public." That was not the fact. It was a bad play. It is possible that the outcry would have been less violent if the audience had not been exasperated by the incredible conduct of the characters. Their motives were, as in so much of Henry James's work, not the motives of normal human beings, and though in his fiction he was persuasive enough very often to conceal the fact from the reader, presented on the stage they glaringly lacked plausibility. The audience felt instinctively that people did not behave with the lack of common sense with which he made them behave and, so feeling, felt that they had been made fools of. In their boos there was more than irritation because they had been bored, there was resentment.

One can see the play Henry James wanted to write and perhaps thought he had written, but it is wretchedly evident that he fell very far short of his intention. He despised the English theatre and was convinced that he could write much better plays himself. Years before in Paris he wrote that he had "mastered Dumas, Augier and Sardou," and claimed that he knew "all they knew and a great deal more besides." Why he failed as a dramatist is obvious enough. He was like a man who, because he can ride a bicycle, thinks he can ride a horse. If under that impression he goes out for a day with the Pytchley he will come a cropper at the first fence. One unfortunate result of Henry James's misadventure was that it confirmed managers in the belief that no novelist could write a play.

It was not till many years later, when I had myself written successful plays, that I met Henry James. It was at a luncheon party given by Lady Russell, the author of *Elizabeth and Her German Garden*, in a flat she then had, if I remember rightly, near Buckingham Gate. It was by way of being a literary party and Henry James was of course the lion of the occasion. He said a few polite words to me, but I received the impression that they meant very little. I forget how long it was after this that I happened to go to an afternoon performance of *The Cherry Orchard* given by the Stage Society and found myself sitting next to Henry James and Mrs. W. K. Clifford, the widow of the mathematician, and herself the author of two good novels, *Mrs. Keith's Crime* and *Aunt Anne*. The intervals were long and we had ample time to talk. Henry James was perplexed by *The Cherry Orchard*, as well he might be when his dramatic values were founded on the plays of Alexandre Dumas and Sardou, and in the second interval he set out to explain to us how antagonistic to his French sympathies was this Russian incoherence. Lumbering through his tortuous phrases, he hesitated now and again in search of the exact word to express his dismay; but Mrs. Clifford had a quick and agile mind; she knew the word he was looking for and every time he paused immediately supplied it. This was the last thing he wanted. He was too well-mannered to protest, but an almost imperceptible expression on his face betrayed his irritation and, obstinately refusing the word she offered, he laboriously sought another, and again Mrs. Clifford suggested it, only to have it again turned down. It was a scene of high comedy.

Ethel Irving was playing the part of Chekov's feckless heroine. She was herself moody, neurotic and emotional, which suited the character, and her performance was excellent. She had made a great success in a play of mine and Henry James was curious to know about her. I told him what I could. Then he put me a very simple question, but he felt it would be crude and perhaps a trifle snobbish to put it simply. Both Mrs. Clifford and I knew exactly what he wanted to say. He led up to his enquiry like a big-game hunter stalking an antelope. He approached stealthily and drew back when he suspected that the shy creature winded him. He wrapped up his meaning in an increasingly embarrassed maze of circumlocution till at last Mrs. Clifford could stand it no longer and blurted out: "Do you mean, is she a lady?" A look of real suffering crossed his face. Put so, the question had a vulgarity that outraged him. He pretended not to hear. He made a little gesture of desperation and said: "Is she, *enfin*, what you'd call if you were asked point-blank, if so to speak you were put with your back to the wall, is she a *femme du monde*?"

In 1910 I went to America for the first time and in due course paid a visit to Boston. Henry James, his brother having recently died, was staying at Cambridge, Massachusetts, with his sister-in-law, and Mrs. James asked me to dinner. There were but the three of us. I can remember nothing of the conversation, but I could not help noticing that Henry James was troubled in spirit, and after dinner, when the widow had left us alone in the dining-room, he told me that he had promised his brother to remain at Cambridge for, I think, six months after his death, so that if he found himself able to make a communication from

beyond the grave there would be two sympathetic wit-
nesses on the spot ready to receive it. I could not but reflect that Henry James was in so nervous a state that it
would be difficult to place implicit confidence in any report he might make. His sensibility was so exacerbated
that he was capable of imagining anything. But hitherto
no message had come and the six months were drawing to
their end.

When it was time for me to go Henry James insisted on
accompanying me to the corner where I could take the
street-car back to Boston. I protested that I was perfectly
capable of getting there by myself, but he would not hear
of it, not only on account of the kindness and the great
courtesy which were natural to him, but also because
America seemed to him a strange and terrifying labyrinth
in which without his guidance I was bound to get hopelessly lost.

As we walked along, he told me what his good manners
had prevented him from saying before Mrs. James, that he
was counting the days that must elapse before, having ful-
filled his promise, he could sail for the blessed shores of
England. He yearned for it. There, in Cambridge, he felt
himself forlorn. He was determined never to set foot again
on that bewildering and unknown country that America
was to him. It was then that he uttered the phrase which
seemed to me so fantastic that I have never forgotten it.
"I wander about these great empty streets of Boston," he
said, "and I never see a soul. I could not be more alone in
the Sahara." The street-car hove in sight and Henry James
was seized with agitation. He began waving frantically
when it was still a quarter of a mile away. He was afraid
it wouldn't stop, and he besought me to jump on with the
greatest agility of which I was capable, for it would not
pause more than an instant, and if I were not very careful I might be dragged along and, if not killed, at least

mangled and dismembered. I assured him I was quite accustomed to getting on street-cars. Not American street-
cars, he told me, they were of a savagery, an inhumanity, a
ruthlessness beyond any conception. I was so infected by
his anxiety that when the car pulled up and I leapt on I
had almost the sensation that I had had a miraculous
escape from certain death. I saw him standing on his short
legs in the middle of the road, looking after the car, and I
felt that he was trembling still at my narrow shave.

But homesick as he was for England, I don't believe
that he ever felt himself quite at home there. He remained a friendly but critical alien. He did not know the
English as an Englishman instinctively knows them and
so his English characters never to my mind ring quite true.
His American characters, at least to an Englishman, on
the whole do. He had certain remarkable gifts, but he
lacked the quality of empathy which enables a novelist to
feel himself into his characters, think their thoughts and
suffer their emotions. Flaubert vomited as though he too
had swallowed arsenic when he was describing the suicide
of Emma Bovary. It is impossible to imagine Henry James
being similarly affected if he had had to narrate a similar
episode. Take *The Author of Beltraffio*. In that a mother
lets her only child, a little boy, die of diphtheria so that
he should not be corrupted by his father's books, of which
she profoundly disapproves. No one could have conceived
such a monstrous episode who could imagine a mother's
love for her son and in his nerves feel the anguish of the
child tossing restlessly on his bed and the pitiful, agonizing struggle for breath. That is what the French call *littérature*. There is no precise English equivalent. On the
pattern of writer's cramp you might call it writer's hokum.
It signifies the sort of writing produced purely for literary
effect without a relation to truth or probability. A novelist may ask himself what it feels like to commit a murder

and then may invent a character who commits one to know what it feels like. That is *littérature*. People commit murders for reasons that seem good to them, not in order to enjoy a curious experience. The great novelists, even in seclusion, have lived life passionately. Henry James was content to observe it from a window. But you cannot describe life convincingly unless you have partaken of it; nor, should your object be different, can you fantasticate upon it (as Balzac and Dickens did) unless you know it first. Something escapes you unless you have been an actor in the tragi-comedy. However realistic he tries to be, the novelist cannot hope to give a representation of life as exactly as a lithograph can give a representation of a drawing. With his characters and the experiences he causes them to undergo he draws a pattern, but he is more likely to convince his readers that the pattern is acceptable if the people he depicts have the same sort of motives, foibles and passions as they know they have themselves and if the experiences of the persons in question are such as their characters render plausible.

Henry James regarded his relations and friends with deep affection, but this is no indication that he was capable of love. Indeed he showed a singular obtuseness in his stories and novels when he came to deal with the most deeply seated of human emotions; so that interested and amused as you are (often amused at him rather than with him), you are constantly jolted back to reality by your feeling that human beings simply do not behave as he makes them do. You cannot take Henry James's fiction quite seriously as, for instance, you take *Anna Karenina* or *Madame Bovary*; you read it with a smile, and with the suspension of disbelief with which you read the Restoration dramatists. (This notion is not so far-fetched as it may seem at first sight: if Congreve had been a novelist he might well have written the bawdy narrative of promiscuous fornication which Henry James entitled *What Maisie Knew*.) There is all the difference between his novels and those of Flaubert and Tolstoi as there is between the paintings of Daumier and the drawings of Constantin Guys. The draughtsman's pretty women drive in the Bois in their smart carriages, luxurious and fashionable, but they have no bodies in their elegant clothes. They amuse, they charm; but they are as unsubstantial as the stuff that dreams are made of. Henry James's fictions are like the cobwebs which a spider may spin in the attic of some old house, intricate, delicate and even beautiful, but which at any moment the housemaid's broom with brutal common sense may sweep away.

It is not my purpose to criticise Henry James's work, yet it is impossible in his case to write of the man rather than of the author. They are in fact inseparable. The author absorbed the man. To him it was art that made life significant, but he cared little for any of the arts except the one he practised. He was little interested in music or painting. When Gosse was going to Venice he conjured him without fail to see Tintoretto's *Crucifixion* at San Cassiano. It is odd that he should have picked out this fine but stagey picture to commend rather than Titian's grand *Presentation of the Virgin* or Veronese's *Jesus in the House of Levi*. No one who knew Henry James in the flesh can read his stories dispassionately. He got the sound of his voice into every line he wrote, and you accept (not willingly, but with indulgence) the abominable style of his later work, with its ugly Gallicisms, its abuse of adverbs, its too elaborate metaphors, the tortuosity of its long sentences, because they are part and parcel of the charm, benignity and amusing pomposity of the man you remember.

I am not sure that Henry James was fortunate in his friends. They were disposed to be possessive, and they

regarded one another's claim to be in the inner circle of
his confidence with no conspicuous amiability. Like a dog
with a bone, each was inclined to growl when another
showed an inclination to dispute his exclusive right to the
precious object of his devotion. The reverence with which
they treated him was of no great service to him. They
seemed to me, indeed, sometimes a trifle silly: they whispered to one another with delighted giggles that Henry
James privately stated that the article in *The Ambassa-
dors* on the manufacture of which the fortune of the
widow Newsome was founded, and the nature of which
he had left in polite obscurity, was in fact a chamber pot.
I did not find this so amusing as they did. I think it
would be unfair to say that Henry James demanded the
admiration of his friends, but he certainly enjoyed it. English authors, unlike their fellows in France and Germany,
are chary of assuming an attitude. The pose of *Cher
Maître* makes them feel faintly ridiculous. Perhaps because
Henry James had first come to know distinguished writers
in France he took the pedestal on which his admirers
placed him as a natural prerogative. He was touchy and
could be cross when he was not treated with what he
thought proper respect. On one occasion a young Irish
friend of mine was staying at Hill for the week-end in
company with Henry James. Mrs. Hunter, their hostess,
told him that he was a talented young man and Henry
James on the Saturday afternoon engaged him in conversation. My friend was petulant and impatient, and at
length, driven to desperation by James's interminable
struggle to find the one word that would express exactly
what he wanted to say, blurted out: "Oh, Mr. James,
I'm not of any importance. Don't bother about rooting
around for the right word. Any old word is good enough
for me." Henry James was deeply affronted and complained to Mrs. Hunter that the young man had been very

rude to him, whereupon Mrs. Hunter gave him a severe scolding and insisted that he should apologise to her distinguished guest. This he accordingly did. Once Jane Wells inveigled Henry James and me to go with her to a subscription dance in aid of some worthy object in which H. G. was interested. Mrs. Wells, Henry James and I were chatting in a kind of anteroom adjoining the ballroom when a brash young man bounced in, interrupting Henry James in his discourse, and, seizing Jane Wells's hands, said: "Come on and dance, Mrs. Wells, you don't want to sit there listening to that old man talking his head off." It wasn't very polite. Jane Wells gave Henry James an anxious glance and then with a strained smile went off with the brash young man. Henry James was too little accustomed to be treated like that to take it, as he might sensibly have done, with a good-natured laugh, and he was much offended. When Mrs. Wells came back he got up and a little too formally bade her good night.

When someone transplants himself from one country to another he is more likely to assimilate the defects of its inhabitants than their virtues. The England in which Henry James lived was excessively class-conscious, and I think it is to this that must be ascribed the somewhat disconcerting attitude he adopted in his fiction to those who were so unfortunate as to be of humble origin. Unless he were an artist, by choice a writer, it seemed to him more than a little ridiculous that anyone should be under the necessity of earning a living. The death of a member of the lower orders could be trusted to give him a mild chuckle. I think this attitude was emphasized by the fact that, himself of good family, he could not have dwelt long in England without becoming aware that to the English one American was very like another. He saw compatriots on the strength of a fortune acquired in Michigan or Ohio received with as great cordiality as though they belonged to the eminent families of Boston and New York, and in self-defence somewhat exaggerated his native fastidiousness in social relations. Sometimes he made rather ludicrous mistakes and would attribute to some young man who had taken his fancy a distinction which he obviously did not possess.

If in these pages I have made Henry James, I hope not unkindly, a trifle absurd it is because that is what I found him. I think he took himself a good deal too seriously. We look askance at a man who keeps on telling you he is a gentleman; I think it would have been more becoming in Henry James if he had not insisted so often on his being an artist. It is better to leave others to say that. But he was gracious, hospitable and, when in the mood, uncommonly amusing. He had uncommon gifts and if I think they were too often ill-directed that is only what I think and I ask no one to agree with me. The fact remains that those last novels of his, notwithstanding their unreality, make all other novels, except the very best, unreadable.

Matilda Lees-Dods

"THE CHRISTENING"

from *The Ideal Home*

"The Christening" is one of the shorter chapters from Miss Lees-Dods's 958-page, eight-pound tome, THE IDEAL HOME. Subtitled "How to Find It, How to Furnish It, How to Keep It," this encyclopedic work was published in New York in 1916 and in London many years earlier. In her foreword, the author states that, in the course of long lecture tours through the British Isles, Canada and the United States, "no fact has impressed me so much as this, that the world is full of good housewives, but that the bookshops are singularly destitute of good domestic guides."

$\mathcal{T}$he first baby has arrived in the house. Forever the old order has passed away and the house is under a new reign. As Napoleon said, "My baby rules me, I rule the world, therefore my baby is universal King." We must at least agree with Napoleon on this point, for a birth in the house brings a great self-abnegation, though at the same time there is a spring of pure joy flowing into our hearts. If the family is a rich one, a boy is always most welcome. But as a lady once said to me when the heir to a dukedom gave place to his younger sister, "Baby Margaret is just a week old, but we have all long ago forgotten that babies could ever be boys."

It is a time of general rejoicing amongst the grandfathers and grandmothers, "the uncles, the cousins, and the aunts," and both sides of the family generally vie with each other in the quality and nature of the presents the first baby receives. However, when the eighth or ninth child arrives there is no flourish of trumpets, but rather a sort of suppressed sigh of pity for the father and the mother. Luckily, as a rule the older sisters and brothers make up in affection and adulation for the outside relatives' indifference.

When the home is not a palace or something akin to it, the arrival of the first baby changes much of the general arrangement. New rules have to be made. Fresh servants have to be engaged, and one or more rooms have to be set

aside for the new-comer and his caretakers. At this stage
in the Ideal Home the young wife has to be very careful
of her treatment of her baby. Man is a jealous being. He
may rub shoulders with his equals in the House of Lords,
or he may have a seat in the House of Commons, or he
may be a City man wringing six or eight hundreds a year
out of the Stock Exchange or the law or the great mercan-
tile interests; and he may be, above all, the proudest and
most affectionate of fathers. At the same time, he watches
his wife's attention to "our baby" with a jealous eye.

Far be it from me to incite a young wife or any other
woman to artifice, but surely a little—shall we call it
finesse?—at this stage would not be unforgivable. The
young wife must therefore make an effort to induce her
husband to see that the baby has only drawn them closer
together, and that he is even dearer to her than ever. This,
of course, is the case in many hundreds of homes; but
there are as many where the coming of the baby is not altogether an unqualified blessing. It has always occurred to
me that when in the girl-mother's nature lies a little of
selfishness, the baby has first place. The baby is given to
her as her very own, and she treats the little life as a possession which is outside and between her and everything
else. A very wise young mother, the happy possessor of
two little children, told me some time ago that she was
more particular over the home comforts and arrangements
than ever, since the children had come, adding, "I see
how much harder my husband works now for me and
mine, so I put him first in everything."

I am not wandering away from the christening, but
leading up to it. The name of the baby must be settled
upon before the christening, and it goes without saying
that all the near relations expect their names to be carried down to the new generation. And when there is a
question of expectations, the young parents are apt to give

way and take a selection from both sides. I knew a boy who had so many names that his school companions called him "Alphabet Barrie," and thus he lived and died. I have never been able to see, when grandmother's name is perhaps Sarah Ann, that the baby should be burdened with it. A good plan is to ask the grandmother the name of her favorite flower and to adopt that. Again there may be difficulties, for the grandmother, with the perversity of old age might say, "Hollyhocks," instead of what one had hoped might be Violet or Rosemary, or perhaps Pansy. But the best plan of all is to boldly choose a name you prefer. Let the name be what it may, it is always best to state it on a tiny card affixed to the larger card announcing the baby's birth. Then the relations know the truth irrevocably once and for all. All near relations expect to be invited to a christening, and the best way is to invite them to the church and afterwards to the house. The baby should be prepared specially for the ordeal, for ordeal it must be, if one is to judge from the way I saw a baby lord behave in his grandfather's private chapel. His screams almost shook the rafters, and his pretty blushing mother tried to hide his little open-mouthed red face in the folds of lace on her bodice. But he only screamed the more, for a diamond grazed his nose. In this case the nurse had planned badly; his waking hour was coincident with his christening.

The nurse can always arrange the baby's sleeping hour for the same time as his christening. The mother must be certain she has engaged a woman as nurse who would be above bringing a drug to ensure the baby's good behavior. There are two cases which have come under my observation where the baby had a little gin given him by the nurse, and the result was highly injurious. But surely in these days of expert training a mother need not fear this. Still, "precaution is worth ten armed men."

Lily of the valley is a favorite flower at christenings, and a tiny spray should be fastened in some bow or piece of lace of the baby's dress. The most popular and most sensible entertainment for a christening is afternoon tea. A luncheon is more or less harassing to the mother and hostess, and in these days, unless in exceptional cases, a dinner is absurd. At afternoon tea the nurse can bring in the baby in his pretty dress—be it ever so simple, a christening dress is always pretty—and he can be passed round for admiration, enough to satisfy the proud mother. The arrival of the baby brings a large amount of necessary expenditure, and very few young people in these days have much more money than they require, so even the question of entertainment at a christening has to be thought out.

Afternoon teas do not run into much money; but one little inevitable expense is the "christening cake," and that, after all, is not a serious monetary affair.

Frank Kendon

"CHRISTMAS DAY"

from *The Small Years*

In 1950 the Cambridge University Press issued a third edition of Frank Kendon's enchanting memoir of childhood, THE SMALL YEARS, containing a new chapter, "Christmas Day." The book originally appeared in England in 1930, and in 1937 it was reissued in a pocket edition. Mr. Kendon was born in England in 1893 and grew up at a boarding school for boys conducted by his father.

$\mathcal{A}$utumn, I suppose, had taken us by usual surprise; we had been busy chattering with the Summer, and had not dreamt that she was leave-taking, when unexpectedly she dropped our hand, and turned, and here was her freckled follower, that changeful season.

On a day in any autumn someone—(probably Stella)— was sure to exclaim, "Only six weeks, and then it will be Christmas!" And the year itself suffered a shock at such words, sheared into unequal parts: a vast, crowded past; but how tense and brief a future.

Christmas was the natural climax of any year. For John and me, for Stella and Carrie and those of the small fry who had any power at all over time, there were two such days and no more in every year—birthday, and Christmas Day. These had the closest association in our minds, though the only factor common to both was this receiving of presents. Nobody under fourteen had any doubt about the matter. It was not greed. We depended for our possessions entirely upon gifts, and chiefly upon what fell to our lot on these two generous days.

The penny that came on Saturday was improvidently spent on Saturday; and even so simple a necessity as a pocket-knife was beyond hope of purchase. Thus, also, with pencils and rubbers, rich crayons and paints, drums, whips, hoops, printing outfits, pistols, autograph albums, telescopes, compasses, snakes-and-ladders, balls, carpentry sets (to speak only in a masculine way) and suchlike necessities. We were bound to be dependent upon presents; an unfortunate Christmas meant an ill-equipped life; it meant borrowed paints, hunting for someone to sharpen a pencil, handicaps.

Christmas being so all-important, Stella's discovery (if it was Stella's) at once gave Time a strange double reality: the ominously brief days still dawned and dawdled, died and succeeded one another, and Christmas drew nearer and yet no nearer, and yet again drew nearer. We were, for instance, continually forgetting it—in the prolific and useless harvest of elm leaves along the road and in the playground, in bonfires on Saturdays, in the startling strangeness which solid white morning fogs bestowed on a well-known world, in frost on spider-webs, in the first aching nip of winter that brought fires into school—and then, suddenly, examinations, leading through a day's disorder, to Last Day at school. We lived at school; the others went home. One stood, that morning, in an echoing, fireless schoolroom, all lessons over; but one almost heard Christmas galloping down at last, no more than six or seven days ahead.

And the six or seven seemed so short precisely because there was so much to be done; for it need not be said, that, as distinct from birthdays, Christmas was, in the matter of gifts, everybody's birthday. Aunts one merely noticed in May both generously gave and rightly received presents at Christmas time; and no one wished to shirk responsibilities. Christmas was always a joint effort, and a joint enthusiasm. Even at six a child could, and would, fold pointed paper "hair-tidies" or spills, or blanket-stitch a kettleholder. At the least everyone could, and many did, paint easy plum puddings and holly for cards for the last remembered. There was fever of work and secrecy in those last days, until the afternoon before Christmas, when blessed with permissive weather, we got together the pence we had come by, and an extra sixpence or so from relenting parents, and we set out to walk the two miles through the winter lanes over the hills to shop at Gowdhurst.

I cannot go into the arithmetic, which was simply the problem of suiting as many relatives as remained unsuited (a variable) out of a small and definite, and hampering total. But rare country shops had an atmosphere above arithmetic in those days—an intimacy and a clustering bounty, cheerful and anything but reticent—which depended largely upon the acceptable combined ignorances of architecture, electricity, salesmanship, or good taste. I am not sure whether Miss Button's shop was built for a shop or merely "thrown out" or just converted. To us it was unquestionable and right. It was a small triangular room, with the door (automatically ringing a shaker bell as you entered) at the pointed end.

If it had been purposely built for a shop, the architect had not thought to consider what kind of a shop, indeed Miss Button herself clearly felt no limits of that sort, except food—she never stocked food. Thus her place, helped by the hot air of a Gothick lamp-stove, had a dry and drapery smell. Ribbons, I should say—ribbons and lace— hairpins, hatpins, collar-supports—were characteristic of the all-the-year-round Miss Button; but all such gear as this was swept out of her mind by the Christmas excess. Do you know those limp, canvas-bodied dolls, with shiny china-ware heads and necks, no clothes, but pointed black glossy heavy cold clicking french boots on the leg-ends? Miss Button had boxes of them. She had packs of parlour games, Snap, Happy Families, Ludo, crisp Dominoes, rattling Halmas, and of course such things as marbles (in tape-tied bags), lead soldiers (not much in our line), popguns, and wooden symbols of engines and horses so hardened in convention by an ancient ritual of toymaking that they bore no more resemblance to real trains and horses than the pegged knees and hips and flat bellies of wooden dutch dolls bore to our own well-known anatomies. But the smell, and then the touch, of newness was everywhere, and though drums and musical boxes were, as Miss Button knew, for ever out of reach of our purses, we might linger over them, see how they worked, enjoy them in all but the having. When at last we set out on the long walk home, easily carrying our parcels, we knew that the last turnstile had been passed. No more presents could be bought, no more now could even be finished off. It was supper and bed as soon as we had labelled the last of our packets and told our mother all, over the cocoa. Bed of course by candlelight, eagerly sought tonight; for we were to hang up our stockings. Carol singers faltered in the dark below us while we undressed and said our prayers.

Santa Claus was a game with us; we knew and respected the rules quite as well as the grown ups. They smilingly admonished; we knowingly responded. And when we were in bed, John and I, newly determined this time to see the thing through to the exact truth, did all we knew to keep awake. There was always, in spite of our democratic large-family rationalism, just a chance. Though we knew it was not Father Christmas; who it was we did not know. But we graduated into sleep. (How did they know when we were asleep?)

We woke in black morning, long before day. We stretched out a groping hand to the stocking, and felt that weighty and angular sausage and brought it rustling in itself to bed. There was always an apple, an orange, a twist of sweets—tom-tit jellies sanded with sugar, and crescents and stars and circles of chalky peppermints. There was always a penny; also, perhaps a rolled sheet of transfers, a magnifying glass, or a little raffia basket. For Santa Claus

—it was well devised—brought only delicate tokens, little foretastes to begin the day well. In a cold that we would not feel and in a darkness that added to our fingers' mystification, we went through the wrapped contents of our stockings, and knew everything, and had eaten most by the time that dawn arrived.

It was characteristic of Christmas Day that, sharing a touch of both Sunday and weekday, it belonged to neither class. We put on clean linen and best suits without resentment; we found that we were not late for breakfast, because breakfast (for once) was smilingly waiting for *us*, in sustenance a normal breakfast, porridge and eggs, but eaten under the influence of the holly and ivy behind picture-frames, and towards the end transmuted by the loaded arrival of the postman with millions of cards and not a few pretentiously shaped parcels. Cards were distributed; parcels, by customary agreement, were put on the pile unopened.

Could it be true? We scattered from breakfast, and somehow filled in the long morning with Sunday School (where the collection gave us a penny instead of taking one from us), and a few suspiciously ordinary occupations. But when we got back—still too early for the fabulous Christmas dinner—someone had transformed the great school dining-room. A long wide board, covered with many white cloths, ran down the room. It was decorated with holly sprays, coloured papers, vases of chrysanthemums, towers of Blenheims and Cox's, boxes of candied figs with fragile leaf-metal servers, pyramids of mince pies, and enough cutlery and drink to serve nearly thirty people. For what is the use of living at a school in the holidays if you may not, on a Christmas Day, sit thirty down to dinner? It was of such a feast as this that I thought (and still think) whenever I read the parable of the marriage feast and the man without a wedding garment who was cast out—terrible thought—"and there shall be weeping and gnashing of teeth."

The bell sounded now, and from all quarters the people mustered immediately, threaded by children whose coiled-up excitement was beginning to have its way with them at last. We were seated, grace was sung, the menfolk were busy at the carving table, plates began to pass from hand to hand. Must I go on?

Singly, and at odd times during the significant forenoon, Stella and John and I had, casually if we could, passed down that narrow, windowless passage outside the Front Dining-room (this was its name; I never knew us to dine there). The table had been taken away; more than twice its company of chairs now sat there unoccupied, vacant with expectation. The grate was prepared already with a hissing log fire. It was a dark, one-windowed room, low-browed but cosy. In a corner of its deepest twilight, piled up on the floor and half burying two great baskets, lay a quite uncountable heap of wrapped presents. In this room, at the classical right time, the middle movement of the great Christmas symphony would unfold; but before that moment, with all our will, but much against our heart, we had to accept the discipline of a walk. No doubt it began as a device to get the company away while the wreck of dinner was washed up and the table subtly altered for tea. But in my days the walk was official in its own right; Father came with us, a holiday-father, easy-humoured and primed with riddles. So we met the wind and saw the village empty by December daylight, for none of the cottagers had the ritual reason that we had to face the uncosy elements. There were no demurs; the day allowed for the discipline. By half-past three we crowded into the Front Dining-room, lit now by mixed firelight and soft lamplight.

The Mother (as Aunt Mary called her) was in her

chair, her two or three babies (for safety against the strain of excitement) on footstools close to her; the rest of us anywhere. And, waiting his cue from the fall of silence among us, Father was in office by the pyramid and baskets.

His was the great part; he was the superb soloist, king in this movement, and he needed no help from red mantle or white whiskers. Father Christmas was a well-enough legend: Father himself was a reality. Through his lips every label on every parcel was given a voice. One at a time he picked them up and dwelt on them. He would be puzzled, or would make mistakes and correct them, or would talk tantalizingly and wrongheadedly about the largest packet—what it felt like or looked like, keeping the company in a tickle of tolerant excitement. He knew when to spin it out, and when to hurry it up, which packets must be handled with frightening care, and which neatly flung to the addressee's knees.

We loved it, as under his endless performance his hair grew disordered, his pretence more extravagant, and our spirits more varied and nearer riot. For now discipline properly began to give way. Strings were cut and papers publicly torn off, and still the fantastically unexpected parcels accumulated, and still were unwrapped, till the floor below became a sea, with billows of brown paper, and the cosy room, so Sundayish and dim on most days of the year, rang with exclamations of joy surprised.

At length, however, the pyramid had gone and the baskets were empty; Father's work was done. He had few parcels of his own, but he didn't seem to mind. Mother, of course, had her parcels; she had been the first on every list, even as far back as November, and she best liked the things we ourselves had made. I think it seemed redundant, if not presumptuous, to give presents to Father; and indeed the presents to Mother truly included him, and he accepted the intention even though Mother got the pincushion or the fretwork. And now, while we were yet caressing our treasures and demonstrating them, here he was collecting the string and the paper, tidying up.

By and by the girls began to whisper together, and then to go out; tea was in half-an-hour, and they had frocks to try—and, suddenly, the great third movement had ended, the rooms grew in half-way towards its own size again, the fire was mended, the lamp-wick was lowered, the afternoon's gains were piled and taken to quarters.

Daylight had gone long ago. Now, at last we and Christmas together were safely walled in by conspiring night. John and I, boys, and untroubled by the need for re-dressing, lightly enjoyed the brief hiatus alone, thought over again our presents one by one, waited watching the great logs oozing their spittle, said little, but found in each heart a great safety and content. We wandered out into the passage. Christmas was here indeed and at last; it was now, it was beginning.

Steal a glimpse, with us, at the long schoolroom. Though as yet the lamps are unlit, there will be firelight enough from the two high fires in it. See all the chairs in order against the wainscot, see the soft feminine colours of paper chains looping down into the flamelight out of the high wooden ceiling. Notice the great boughs of holly and tots of berried ivy nailed above the mantels and above the doors and between the windows, dark and rich masses of luxuriant shape transforming the shadows. Look at the long trestle table laughing with dimpled oranges and apples, with dim bowls of nuts, and shut boxes of sweets.

Take this one look into the dancing dark and light, and shut the door quickly, for there is a noise like teatime; we hear girls' voices. Strangers, cousins and relations of the more distant sort, and Christmas partners from other houses, have come in out of the night—they say it is sprinkling with snow—and have hung up their wraps, and have kissed, and are moving down the steps to the big dining-room again.

The just perceptible grossness (shall I say) of the Christmas dinner-table is not a character of the tea-table. There is just as much to eat, but the food has art and charm and delicacy now, not merely alimentary goodness. Cakes are iced, biscuits are fancy, teacups and tea-urn have a twinkling, jewelled quality under coloured and shaded lamplight, and the crackers are there, things made with a charming excess, tufted, tinselled, lying (one over each plate) demurely yet. And there is chatter at tea. Surely, the afternoon's plunder has given everyone topics enough. Moreover, this time our visitors are guests, and deserve our smiling small-talk, and give as good as they get. There is no more hurry; this is time to spend: Christmas is here.

We move without haste from the tea-table at last, leaving the shaded lamps burning. Someone—some uncle—had preceded us, and the schoolroom, when we drift there, now seems blazing with extra lamps; the fires are twice themselves, well guarded against coming boisterousness within wire cages. With our Father as King again, and with Uncle Day and Uncle Ernest as his first ministers, we begin to sing games, we run games, we dance games, we shout games, we sit down to games, while the old folk, who have seen so many Christmases, sit by and gossip absently, or, watching us, hold out a kind hand to catch the glow of the fires, and smile, thinking, approving.

In order of age and tiredness as the evening advances, one after one the children will be persuaded and withdrawn to bed. Soon it will be my fate, and John's, and we know it. We must now cheerfully climb the four steps out of the schoolroom and look back at the party that shows no dimming of light and mirth because of our leaving. The bedroom is cold; the heart is satisfied; and while we take to the sheets and understand that we really are tired, the noise and laughter comes faintly up the stairway still.

No Christmas is quite perfect, for each waits to be proved—and at the height of the tune they end.

What is there now to look forward to? Why is John creeping out of bed again? He calls me; he has looked out to the stars and the roof. "It's snowing," he whispers.

Snowing!

Charles Caldwell Dobie

—◄◆►—

"DISASTER"

from *San Francisco: A Pageant*

*A*n enormous canvas is often filled with so much detail that one gets little but confused impressions from it. To attempt to contract the canvas does not help matters, for, then, the detail becomes microscopic. In war, in pestilence, in disaster, authentic fragments frequently etch the event more sharply than a complete history.

Moreover, the broad outline of what follows any cosmic upheaval in these United States has long since been without variety. Disaster, momentary confusion, organization, relief, rehabilitation. It matters not whether a community is visited by flood, tornado, or earthquake, the distant view is much the same. It is the intimate glimpses that provide variety. Which is the author's apology for suddenly abandoning the detached point of view and becoming personal.

Premonitions of disaster seemed singularly lacking in San Francisco on the evening of April 17, 1906. Spring was in the full flush of its enchantment and the only audible rumblings came from nothing more portentous than carriage wheels bumping over the cobbled streets toward the Grand Opera House. San Francisco was in a gala mood, as she always was when keyed to the excitement of an opera season. This year, Caruso was the star, and for days long queues of music lovers had stood in line before the box-office eagerly snapping up seats left over from the regular subscription.

I, myself, had succumbed to the blandishments of the advance notices. Thirty-six of my monotonously earned dollars—I was at that time a fire-insurance clerk—had been exchanged for bits of pasteboard entitling me to a perch on a level with the huge crystal chandelier glittering down upon expansive bosoms, jeweled dog-collars, diamond tiaras. On Monday night I had gone to see the season open. An incredibly homely Queen of Sheba had vamped the susceptible Solomon before an audience that was holding itself in check for the next evening when Caruso was billed to sing Don José to Olive Fremstad's Carmen. This second night was not on my list. So I retired early, setting my alarm-clock with the prudence of a man young enough to sleep past the hour of rising. This proved to be an unnecessary precaution. Something much more effective than an alarm-clock was scheduled to waken me.

I came out of a thick slumber with the confused notion that I was on a bucking horse. The plunging continued, followed by a deafening roar. I jumped out of bed to run down the hall to my mother's room. But the swaying of the house flung me from one wall to the other, very much as a passenger aboard an ocean liner would be flung about by a heavy sea. Then, quite suddenly, the vibrations ceased.

Fortunately it was daylight—in the neighborhood of five o'clock. The family ran to the front windows and looked out. A fine dust from crumbling chimneys filled the air. But the frame houses of the quarter in which we lived were standing valiantly. We had all felt earthquakes before, and ordinarily after the shock was over we were disposed to joke about it. But this time we knew that we had passed through an earthquake that was no joking matter. Although, even at this point, we did not realize just how serious matters were. Particularly, as an inspection of our apartment disclosed no damage beyond cracked plaster and one shattered vase.

We were not a family disposed to alarm after danger had passed, and so we dressed, lit a fire in the kitchen stove, and sat down to a cup of coffee. It never occurred to us that the chimney might be cracked and that we could set fire to the house in consequence. We noticed that the water trickled out of the faucet very slowly, but we were not disposed to be captious about a reluctant water spout on such a morning. By this time it was six o'clock. My brother and I discussed the matter of going down to our respective offices. We were not due to work until nine. We decided to take a turn about town in the meantime.

The streets were filled with excited people making ominous predictions. But we declined to share their pessimism. We felt that the worst was over, although disturbing plumes of black smoke began to appear upon the horizon. But what was a fire or two? San Francisco had one of the most efficient fire departments in the country. The fires would be under control in a half-hour. At this point, neither one of us remembered the trickle of water that had so slowly filled the coffee-pot a half-hour before.

By this time, we had reached the top of Nob Hill. It was here that we received our first shock. A few years before, a huge dome had been tacked on to the City Hall to provide the faithful with jobs. This dome stood up in the morning sunlight divested of every brick that had covered its steel nakedness. More than that, the black plumes of smoke were increasing. At a dozen different points they were smudging the sky-line. A man said: "The water supply has been cut off!" Another told us that Chief Sullivan of the Fire Department had been killed.

Catton, Bell, and Company, the firm I worked for, had offices in the Merchants Exchange Building on California Street at the foot of Nob Hill. Thither we went, somewhat sobered by the news that had come to our ears. The streets were littered with bricks from falling chimneys, fragments of shattered cornices, with here and there the front wall of a cheaply constructed building piled up on the sidewalk. But, on the whole, the city was still standing gallantly.

The earthquake had thrown the entire elevator system of the Merchants Exchange out of commission. I started to climb the stairs. Another sharp earthquake shock routed my intentions. Like most fools I wanted to be out on the street when the earth trembled, when, as a matter of fact, the interior of a steel-frame building was perhaps the safest place a man could find on such an occasion.

My brother was employed by the Mutual Savings Bank on Market Street. We decided to move in that direction. Our way led us through the shopping district. Here we found every plate glass front completely shattered. But it was not until we reached Union Square that we began to get a sense of portentous disaster. The square was swarming with refugees from the "South of Market" districts. This was the cheap, poor quarter of the town and many of the wretches who had fled from the flames looked as if they had not faced the morning sunlight for years. They were like rats startled out of their holes, this beer-sodden, frowsy crew of dreadful men and still more dreadful women. A breed that has passed out of American life completely—red-faced, bloated, blowsy.

It was eight o'clock when we reached the Mutual Bank. This building was on the north side of Market Street. Op-

posite, an inferno was raging. The cheap lodging-houses
of Third Street were shooting up flames, walls were crumbling, explosions were throwing débris into the air. On the
corner of Third and Market Streets stood the Call Building. It was one of San Francisco's first skyscrapers—a "fire-
proof" building. We watched the intense heat smash
window after window. In the wake of each shattered pane
would follow a burst of flame, a cloud of smoke. In ten
minutes the building was doomed. Now, for the first time,
we began to be truly apprehensive. If stone and steel and
concrete could burn like a cigar-box, what hope was left?
More than this, we knew by this time that the pessimists
were right: There was no water. The earthquake had dis-
located and smashed the main pipe-line.

We walked a block east to the Palace Hotel. Here everything was calm to a point of absurdity. In the lobby, the
Chinese servants in their immaculate white duck uniforms
were dusting off the furniture. Most of the tourists had
undoubtedly turned over and gone to sleep again, secure
in conviction that the cosmic prank of the morning was a
weekly occurrence. Only the native San Franciscans and
the great Enrico Caruso were unduly alarmed. And, even
then, it was only Mr. Caruso who was in tears. He swore
on that fateful morning that wild horses would never drag
him back to San Francisco. And they never did. Apparently, he preferred the volcanic earthquakes of his native
Italy to the fault-line earthquakes of California. But, I
suppose, one can be just as fussy about a brand of seismic
disturbance as about the brand of Scotch one drinks—it
is all a matter of habit.

By this time, there was no end to the wild rumors that
began to fly about. Thousands killed, tens of thousands
wounded, a half-hundred fires raging in as many parts of
town. Happily, all save the extent of the fire hazard was
exaggerated. Dead and wounded there undoubtedly were

but in insignificant numbers. The earthquake had occurred at the best possible hour. Most people were in bed and, unless one is in the path of a falling chimney, bed is as safe a place as any when the earth begins to cavort like a dragon in a Chinese parade. Personally, no one of my acquaintances was killed and only one prominent man, the fire chief, was listed among the casualties.

My movements during that first day have become blurred. I think I wandered more or less aimlessly from point to point. One thing I do remember, I saw no tears, no despair, no wailing. The public squares, the cemeteries, any open space, were crowded with refugees who had already been burnt out. The things that they had saved were pathetic, divine, laughable. Pets seem to have had first consideration—dogs, cats, parrots, canaries, rabbits, white mice. Bits of treasured finery came next. And the usual absurdities. I saw one woman dragging a clothes basket full of stove lids. And to Jefferson Square a man came running with two huge confectionery jars filled with peppermint candy.

Most people, even those whose roofs the fire had not yet burned away, slept out of doors that night. But not our family. My mother's sense of personal privacy made her willing to chance the hazard of four walls.

What followed had all the elements of delirium. We dozed, fully clothed, to a solemn undercurrent of marching feet. The fire had reached Chinatown and our house was on Jackson Street, in the path of the steady stream of Orientals fleeing to points of safety. At dawn, the exodus was at its height. They came, silently, with the fatalistic calm of the Far East—dragging trunks, chests, go-carts, baby buggies, wicker baskets, piled high with household goods. The woman who lodged beneath us was from the South. That morning I met her peering out at the disheveled stream. "It's like Sherman's March through Georgia!"

she said, and her lips quivered with the memory of that horror.

We made a fire in the garden. We had learned the hazard of cracked chimneys. But when we came to draw enough water for coffee, not a drop fell from the spigot. My brother, whose calmness was always equal to any emergency, remembered the hot-water boiler. He got a monkey wrench and unscrewed the waterback. Then, turning on the faucet, he blew into the disconnected pipe. A thin trickle slowly filled the coffee-pot.

After breakfast, we decided to seek out a vantage point where we could watch the progress of the flames. From indications the fire was creeping toward us from every side but the west. My mother insisted on going with us. She had bought, only a few days before, a street gown in the latest mode. It had sleeves, elbow length, and a pair of long black kid gloves added to its distinction. When she came downstairs to join us she was flaunting this new costume. She even had a veil drawn trimly across her face. Her cheeks were smudged and unwashed, her hair a bit snarled. But otherwise her toilette was irreproachable. In spite of the desperate situation, the three of us laughed, and, thus refreshed, we went forth to learn the worst.

The worst was very bad indeed. The fire was creeping up the slopes of Nob Hill, within a dozen blocks of our home. We sat in the shadow of the bonanza mansions of the incredible seventies and watched the blue-black menace snake up the heights. The lawns, the sidewalks, the roadways, were crowded with as silent a throng, I think, as I shall ever witness.

The entire downtown section, built of stone, brick and concrete, had been devoured as completely as if some insatiable monster had crept over it. It was a frame city that was being attacked, now. One hope for the doomed city was for the usual brisk afternoon wind to spring up from the west. A scant hour of April rain would have beaten out the flames. Even a thick blanket of fog might have smothered them. But the sky smiled down in blue, sardonic calm, as if to pay us back for every idle protest that we had ever lodged against wind and weather.

At one o'clock my brother suggested that it was time to go back to our flat and think of getting some necessary equipment together for flight. We had planned before to move on to a friend's garden, hedged in by cypress-trees, at the foot of Larkin Street. This half-block of ground owned by the de Bretteville family had the safety of comparative detachment and its trees were a great factor in warding off intense heat and by the same token combustion.

We arrived at our house to find a soldier ringing at our door to warn us out of the district. Martial law had been proclaimed by the mayor and the military was in command, closing up saloons, shooting down looters, clearing threatened quarters of their inhabitants. On every side, our neighbors were making ready to flee. Many of them were at that moment digging holes in their back yards in which they were burying their silver and treasure.

We tied all our clothes and bedding into bundles, with rope filched from a clothes line. These we slung over our shoulders. A huge basket my brother and I carried between us—piled with personal effects. My brother commented many times upon the heaviness of the basket. He did not know, until we had reached our destination, that I had hidden a collection of rare German beer mugs that had been my boyish delight between the layers of blankets. Nor did he suspect the volume on "Italian Gardens" by Edith Wharton and illustrated by Maxfield Parrish, which I had tucked under my arm. It had been given me the week before and I was loath to leave the history of so much loveliness behind.

My mother went on ahead, in her smart gown with the long black gloves, carrying the family canary and a large cream-colored pitcher made by Wedgwood that my grandmother had brought across the Isthmus of Panama in the fifties. For some reason, we were not unduly cast down. At least we had the courage, the hope, the absurdity, if you will, to save some of the unessentials. And, I have always treasured the picture of my mother on that fateful morning in her new dress, with a dotted veil drawn tautly across her shapely nose, carrying a canary and a Wedgwood pitcher to safety. The dauntlessness of San Francisco shone through the unconscious gallantry of her gesture.

Once in our flight we halted. Passing a wretched corner grocery we remembered that it might be well to stock up with some provisions. The old woman who waited on us had nothing on her shelves but canned spaghetti. This we bought, promptly. But it appeared, before we left, that she had one other commodity for sale—beer that the military authorities had not yet seized. She shuffled back behind a swinging door and brought us out three foaming mugs. I shall never forget that drink of cool beer to my dying day. It gave us such renewed courage that we felt like going back and attempting to save the town.

We set up a camp in the de Bretteville garden and hung the canary in a rose-bush. As we entered the gate we met Madame Emma Eames and a trio of other opera stars leaving. A continuous stream of people looking for an oasis in a desert of flames came and went all afternoon. It was as if our friends were holding a reception. That evening we dined off cold canned spaghetti washed down with hot coffee which we shared with other refugees who had crept into the inclosure. In the matter of serving coffee, my beer mugs, even at this early hour, justified themselves.

All night, the writhing flames danced their dance of destruction. The boom of dynamite began to shake the earth, now. It was rumored that the navy was blowing up blocks at a time so as to leave nothing in the path of the red monster. Our shelter stood upon sloping ground and we could see the bay alive with glittering ferry-boats carrying thousands away from the doomed city. The docks through some miracle had been spared and this made flight an easy matter.

About three o'clock in the morning, the block containing our home burned up. The suspense was over—for us, at least. We threw ourselves down upon our blankets and fell into fitful slumber, while all about us sparks and embers rained in a continuous downpour. We woke to stifling heat. A pall of smoke obscured the sun. The fire was moving relentlessly toward our safety zone. But all this did not prevent our silly canary from singing out his pleasure at his new home in the rose-bush.

We held a family council. The decision was that I should take my mother over on the Tiburon ferry to Belvedere where my brother maintained a house-boat. My brother was to stay behind to help our friends save their home. Sparks and falling embers were the chief dangers and vigilance might bring victory. We stored our belongings in the basement and walked along sizzling pavements to the Ferry Building. My mother still wore her long black gloves but her fingers were poking through them and her dotted veil had a rent in it. She carried her irrepressible canary in one hand and her Wedgwood pitcher in the other.

It was now Friday. The earthquake had occurred on Wednesday morning, but forty-eight hours of red terror had almost wiped out the memory of that cosmic insolence. Which may explain to the scornful why the average San Franciscan still talks fire instead of earthquake. The one sprang from the other, undoubtedly. Tidal waves spring from earthquakes, also. But one drowns in the tidal wave and not the earthquake, just as one is burnt out by a fire, instead of by the fire's contributing cause. However, there is really no harm in letting the cyclone belt and the electric-storm sectors have their little sarcasms.

That night was the most horrid of all, in spite of the fact that my mother and I were far removed from the flames. The city glowed in the distance like an angry dragon belching out fire and brimstone. And the heavy thunders from the relentless war upon conflagration which the navy was waging with guncotton kept up until dawn. At noon, the next day, my brother showed up. The de Bretteville house had been saved and with it our bedding and the book on "Italian Gardens." The fire had been halted at Van Ness Avenue. Which filled my mother with such elation that she trudged straightway to the village store in Tiburon and bought the last dozen clothespins remaining in stock, to the great envy and amazement of our refugee neighbors who began at once to quarrel over who should be the first to borrow them. Showing what a relative thing wealth is.

If you are a lover of statistics you will find a rich yield of interesting figures in the story of the San Francisco earthquake and fire. You will learn among other things that the "shake" lasted one minute and five seconds and that it was caused by a subterranean landslide or slip of faulty ground along 400 miles of coast-line. You will likewise discover that the flames destroyed over 2,500 acres of improvements or about 500 city blocks. The value of property destroyed is confusing and the estimates run all the way from its assessed value at some $50,000,000 to a more generous estimate which reached ten times that amount. But one set of figures is incontrovertible—the amount of insurance paid out, $163,713,330 to be exact.

Perhaps the most interesting of all is the degree of heat

thrown off by the flames which made so vast and altogether satisfactory a bonfire possible. This has been fixed
at 2,700 degrees Fahrenheit, and explains why bulwarks
of stone and steel crumbled like dust before its blast. However open to controversy any other of San Francisco's
claims to superiority are, there is no doubt about her pre-
eminence in the matter of fires. With six previous disasters
by flames to her credit she finally put on a show that
crowded out the heroic attempts of Mrs. O'Leary's cow to
give Chicago first place in conflagration finals.

It would be unfair not to mention the generosity which
San Francisco met at the hands of the world. Within
twenty-four hours after word went out that San Francisco
was burning, relief trains by the hundreds were started on
their way with food supplies. Not a soul went hungry,
even for a day. More than this, the Red Cross received
nearly $10,000,000 for San Francisco relief. It was a heart-
ening testimonial to the place which San Francisco held
in the affections of all who knew its own generous impulses.

This start toward rehabilitation did much to put spirit
into the people. Before the ashes had cooled they were
rolling up their sleeves for the greatest feat of the city's
career—or the career of any city in the world's history, for
that matter. But there was nothing grim about the performance. San Francisco met this last arrow of outrageous
fortune with her usual "heroic good humor." She donned
overalls and flannel shirts with a gusto that recalled the
old days of the gold rush. And she played as vigorously.
Not all of the $163,000,000 recovered from the insurance
companies went into necessities. The shopkeepers in their
temporary quarters on Van Ness Avenue found very soon
that silk gowns sold, but wash dresses languished on their
shelves. Cafés ran full blast, theaters turned crowds away
from their doors, the string of gay saloons, known as the

cocktail route, functioned just as blithely as of yore in their temporary locations. A hundred and sixty million dollars flowing in, brought back all the joy of living that had flourished in the Comstock days. But, with a difference—San Francisco was not spending her time, now, in the enervating bucket-shops of Pauper Alley. She was rebuilding a city by the sweat of her brow, she was working hard and playing hard, she was earning her gay moments.

She worked so hard that she fell into her old habit of letting civic matters take care of themselves. The result was a set of thieves and rascals in power that put any of her former rotten politicians in the shade. Abe Ruef, the boss who led this last band of highwaymen to power, said quite frankly that his gang were so greedy for plunder that they "would eat the paint off a house."

When things got too noisome San Francisco made a characteristic gesture. It organized another Law-and-Order committee called, this time, the Citizens' League of Justice and went mildly vigilante. Like every such committee it ignored law, even if it preserved order. But the rascals were thrown out and Abe Ruef was sent to the penitentiary. San Francisco then went all through the usual cycle of hatreds, persecutions, recriminations. But the air cleared to a more permanent tranquillity and graft on a big scale went out of fashion. The spectacle of a political boss wearing prison stripes was not reassuring to potential civic plunderers.

In this post-disaster period, San Francisco relived every former experience, made every mistake, save one. It refused to listen to the siren of inflation. It was through with speculation. Its boom days were over.

Ten years or more later when it threw wide the gates of the Panama-Pacific Exposition to commemorate the opening of the Panama Canal this hard-won conservatism was confirmed. Not a sand hill was subdivided, not a building was erected, not a lot changed hands in anticipation of the millions of visitors that San Francisco was to entertain. When the Fair started there was no inflation and, when it closed, the proverbial reaction was happily missing.

On the day the exposition opened, the wolves of war were devouring Europe and throwing their uneasy shadows over America. There were many who said that for this reason San Francisco's exotic venture would fail lamentably. It was pointed out that it was too far away from the centers of population to be anything but a financial disaster. Fairs depended for their success on visitors, never upon a local population for attendance and support. But, those who made this prediction left out the capacity for play which always had been one of San Francisco's chief characteristics. Visitors came in reassuring numbers, but it was not the visitors who put over the Panama-Pacific Exposition.

It was San Francisco, herself, without Federal aid, who built it. It was San Francisco, herself, who supported it to such an extent that it returned dividends to its subscribers. And it was San Francisco, herself, who made the entrance gates click merrily, who danced and sang and drowsed in its incomparable gardens.

It closed just as the war wolves were snapping at America's threshold. A year later, when San Francisco girded herself for the fray she carried the memory of these enchanted days with her to recruiting camp and battle-field. It was the last completely care-free era in San Francisco's age of innocence.

Cecil Beaton

"TAKE ONE HUNDRED LARKS"

from *The Glass of Fashion*

$\mathcal{D}$uring the early years of this century, about the time of my birth, France was producing an ornate fashion magazine called *La Mode*. In its pages, whose paper was of such good quality that it felt like kidskin to the touch, one might have run across an Helleu engraving, a Boldini drawing, an oil portrait by De la Gandara, or a snapshot taken at Auteuil or Chantilly of some lady whose identity would barely be suggested by her initials —Madame la Comtesse A. de N., or La Princesse B. Apart from the lady's initiates, who were certain to recognize her, this anonymity added a romantic quality and an air of ambiguity to the game of fashion; for personal values and fashion still retained a mystery and discretion.

That swift tenor of change inaugurated by the First World War has carried us a long way from the Edwardian age of my birth. The distance seems, in memory, to be curiously greater than my proper lifetime. My advent into this world had coincided with first horseless carriages and electric lights. Queen Victoria had died only three years previously, and Oscar Wilde was but recently buried in the cemetery at Père Lachaise. Their deaths signalled the end of Victorianism, though I think Wilde would have been quite happy in an England where affairs were being genially conducted to the aroma of good King Edward's cigars. After the monotony which had blanketed London in the latter years of Victoria's reign, there was to be a brief decade of dazzling seasons, which in their splendour were to recall if not recapture the days of Louis Philippe and of the Second Empire. Balls and entertainments became ever more lavish. At the court drawing rooms, ladies with tall Prince of Wales feathers in their hair wore trains that swept for many yards on the floor.

The Edwardian age was a period of gaiety, when life was so inexpensive that a dandy with four hundred pounds a year could go out dancing most nights of the week, wearing lavender gloves and a wired button-hole in the lapel of his tail coat. Theatre stalls cost half a guinea, operetta was in its heyday, and chorus girls, following the example of pretty Connie Gilchrist of "skipping-rope-gaiety" fame, began to marry into the peerage.

The women who leaned over my crib had not yet foregone the lines of the hourglass and were laced into corsets that gave them pouter-pigeon bosoms and protruding posteriors. Perched on their heads, and elevated by a little roll just inside the crown, were hats which had grown as frivolous as the milliner's trade could make them—enormous galleons of grey velvet with vast grey plumes of ostrich feathers sweeping upwards and outwards, or they would be trimmed with artificial flowers and fruit. One of the most flamboyant and generous exponents of the prevailing styles and modes was my godmother, Aunt Jessie, who was the first woman of fashion that I ever knew.

These ladies of the upper middle classes rolled along in hansom carriages as they paid afternoon calls. Their white kid gloves were of an immaculate quality. Over one wrist they carried a small, square gold mesh bag containing a gold pencil, a handkerchief, and a flat gold wallet which held their calling cards. If the lady of the house was "not at home," the visitor handed the servant two of her cards with the corner turned down to indicate that she had "left cards" in person. The shining wheels of her carriage revolved on the freshly gravelled surface of the road to the next place of call, their sound muted if they were passing a door where the sick or dying lay, for it was customary to spread a thick carpet of straw in the streets before houses of invalids.

Since the Edwardian period was a link between Victorian bourgeois security and the febrile modernity that was to follow it, the age of my birth was not unlike some rich, heavy cake with, fortunately, the magic leavening to make it digestible. The manners and morals of the time, though still strict, were beginning to yield, and a taste for spice could be detected: the opulence had a note of the frivolous; the sense of luxury was, in general, more sparkling than suffocating.

These changes showed themselves in the freer fashions of the day, though many in the upper middle classes still lived strictly by Victorian rules when it came to the exclusiveness of individual modes of dress. Exchanges of fashion confidence were unthinkable, for between the woman and her confidante, the dressmaker, there existed a relationship as private as a love affair. At times this reticence would be carried to such lengths that a lady of fashion might send her motorcar away from the establishment where she bought clothes, simply in order to maintain the mystery of their origin. Exclusiveness of style reached the point where it caused incalculable embarrassment to both parties if an identical dress was worn on the same occasion by two different women. With all the fervour of a mid-Victorian melodrama, a scene, or possibly even a scandal, might be precipitated if it was discovered that one lady had crept into the bedroom of another at a country house party to find out from which establishment the dresses had been bought, a matter easily ascertained from the silk labels sewn into the lining.

Set in such an atmosphere, it was only natural that the

spangled chiffon, filigree-embroidered tulle, veils, billowing ostrich-feather boas, and, trimmed with clover, honeysuckle, or paradise feathers, the ubiquitous cartwheel hats, which had superseded the stiff satins, brocades with rigid iris or bulrush patterns, starched linen skirts, and prim boater straw hats of a decade earlier, took on an enigma comparable to that which shrouded the alchemist in his search for the philosopher's stone.

Perhaps modern chemistry, for all its amazing laboratories, has nevertheless lost something valuable that the medieval wizard, with an almost primitive belief in the symbols of his trade, possessed. Without mystery, magic disappears. Even our unprofessional ladies of fashion have, today, through overpublicizing, been reduced to journalistic commonplaces. If some discreet individual becomes "news," then willingly or unwillingly she must go into the public domain and be exploited as a "celebrity." If distance lends enchantment, then there is little distance in our contemporary world.

The conformist way of life, whatever its virtues, infringes on one of the fundamentals of taste and fashion—exclusiveness. Formerly it was only in an overwhelming desire for difference and distinction that fashion found its incentive. Today that incentive seems to be reversed: there is a desire to seek safety in standardization.

I was too young, perhaps, to know that the *pêche Melba* had just been created in honour of a great singer; or that Escoffier, the master chef himself, was still preparing chicken in champagne at the Carlton Hotel in London and stuffing capons with one hundred larks as a dish to set before the King. . . . But I do remember that pet Pomeranians were called Ponto, while terriers were named Egbert. Anyone who dropped the ball was "a silly duffer." Grown-up games included the Diabolo, which was played with an hourglass spool balancing on a string between two sticks. My aunt Jessie's gramophone had a horn of crimson enamel, like some huge, exotic tropical flower, on which she played arias sung by Tetrazzini, Albani, or Caruso.

At Madame Sherwood's dancing school we children wore our patent-leather shoes with their silver buckles and learnt the polka and the hornpipe. The young girls were wrapped in Shetland shawls at children's parties and carried their dancing shoes in a bag, bronze leather pumps with an elastic round them and a little bead on top. Inevitably they were accompanied by their nannies, who would roll the sausage curls of their wards around their fat fingers. These curls were like rolled-up slices of bread and butter, or the ginger brittle rolls known as "elephants' tongues" that were served together with tea and ices. Fire stations had scarlet doors and white horses that were trained to rush out at the sound of a big brass bell, rearing and flaring their nostrils like the stallions in the chariot races of the *Decline and Fall*, at which the nursemaids screamed or fainted, for women were more hysterical then than they are today.

My inward child's eye, even as my adult vision, always sought out the detail rather than the conception as a whole. A particular trimming on a dress seen in childhood could make a profound impression on me, and certain details have remained in my memory to this day, with acute combinations of colour that have influenced my own creative work.

Thus it was always a thrill when my mother, who was a fair reflector of the feminine fashions of the day, would come to say good night to me, perhaps going out to a dinner party, dressed in miraculously soft materials. On one occasion she wore a large special bunch of imitation lilies of the valley on her bosom, pinned to a pale green chiffon scarf. This sunburst of artificial flowers was a revelation, because I had not thought lilies of the valley could be simulated.

I soon discovered that my mother had an entire drawerful of artificial flowers. She would fasten a clump of slightly crumpled "old-rose" coloured roses to her waist if she was going off to an "at home," where the baritone (one singer, I remember, was named Hubert Eisdale) might sing "Down in the Forest Something Stirred." Sometimes, when she decided to spend the afternoon "calling," my mother would perhaps choose a huge rosette of Parma violets. When she went to Ascot, she wore real flowers—three Malmaison carnations, fully five inches in diameter. To keep each of these flowers in place, a pale pink cardboard disc had been fitted behind them, with a center hole for the carnation stem to pass through.

Like any other hostess of the period, my mother gave luncheons or dinner parties. The day of these events she would be too busy to give any but the most cursory attention to her personal appearance, though the flowers were always tastefully arranged on all the occasional tables. The masterpiece of decoration, most usually sweet peas, was saved for the centre of the dining table, which would be dotted with olives, salted almonds, sugared green peppermints, and chocolates in cut-glass bowls or silver dishes. These were the signs of a gala, as they were never on the table in the ordinary course of events. At Christmas time preserved fruit made its appearance—splintery wooden boxes of *glacé* pears and greengages, which I seem to remember came from elsewhere than France, possibly Sweden or Denmark. There were also tins of caviar sent from Riga, and huge blue-and-white vases of preserved ginger from India, via Whiteley's or Harrod's.

The period of elaborate coiffures had not yet passed. Since she had no personal maid, my mother was usually obliged to dress her own hair. It was worn wide at the sides, stuffed out with pads and garnished with amber, tortoise shell, or imitation diamond combs. On black Mondays, after a long solitary session with her arms upraised, putting the waves and curls into place, the effect might still not please her.

Then she would take out the rats, glancing with alarm into the looking glass as the whole business started over again. Her face became flushed, her arms would be aching, and by the time she had finished she was more than late for dinner.

On special occasions a man with a moustache and sepia wavy hair parted in the centre would come to the house with a brown leather bag. He was shown to my mother's bedroom, where, armed with the spirit lamp or stove, he heated his tongs over a blue flame. I can still, in memory, conjure up the exciting scent of methylated spirit and singed hair, an accompaniment of the transmutation in this wonderful adult world which I watched with such spellbound admiration. There were almost regular intervals of alarms and a last-minute rush for a dinner party or a visit to the theatre. My mother's room, by the time she vacated it, looked as if a tornado had passed; powder was spilled onto the dressing table and floor, while the bed and chairs overflowed with discarded garments, trimmings, and feathers.

Another great thrill for me was provided whenever my mother indulged her interior-decorating fancies. Sometimes this coincided with spring cleaning, for spring cleaning caused a great upheaval in those days: the whole house was taken to pieces and put back together again. Invisible gnomelike creatures appeared early in the mornings to clean out the chimneys and were gone before you had rubbed the sand out of your eyes; carpets, pictures, looking glasses, and furniture were covered with dust sheets, while for days on end most of the house was "out of bounds." It was not unlike fumigating a ward where patients with contagious diseases had been segregated.

At this time of year my mother might well decide to alter the colours of her rooms, choosing curtain materials or chair covers for the drawing room or the "library" (a room in which, strangely enough, never a book was to be seen). One springtime the schoolroom was redecorated in grey and mauve, somewhat halfheartedly after the fashion of the *art nouveau* movement. There were pale mauve curtains of muslin with frills on them and what must have been daring touches of simplicity in grey papered walls edged with a geometrical mauve border. The pale grained furniture included a set of tall-backed chairs of grey wood, having stylized roses carved out of their centre panels. Later, when it became my privilege to accompany my mother on shopping expeditions to Hanover Square, new vistas and wonders were opened as I watched her choose flowered cretonnes, shot taffetas, and purple brocatelles.

With the passing of time I was not only conscious of colour and detail, but became aware of line and pattern and crystallized more developed aesthetic experiences. It was then that Bessie Ascough's fashion plates, which appeared each day in the *Evening Standard*, began to excite my curiosity. Soon I was in virtual paroxysms of impatience while awaiting my father to bring home the paper in which this lady's latest pen drawing would be ready to be smeared with my water colours or oddly smelling silver and gold paints. Sometimes, on red-letter days, Bessie Ascough sketched a picture of a lady in court dress, replete with feathers, bouquet, and train; or she might draw a *robe de bal*, giving a wonderful facsimile of all the embroidery on the dress. Her particular skill was manifest in the roses that she drew, roses like balloons or billiard balls, with great round centres. Often a whole cluster of them would be held by a worldly bride. At first my father may have attributed my excitement to his return from the city, though he could not have been long in remarking that the *Evening Standard* was the focal point of my attention. One evening he said he had forgotten to bring his newspaper home with him, and I was deeply hurt by his callousness in the face of such an important event. The next day I was told that Miss Ascough was on holiday and that her fashion plates would not be appearing for a while. Later I discovered this was not the case at all. The truth was that my family deemed it unwise to allow these apoplectic expectancies for Bessie Ascough's artistry to continue: the child was becoming peculiar.

Philosophers tell us that as we grow older we come closer to childhood. I was still a child when King Edward's death closed the covers of the book of opulence, if not forever, at any rate for my lifetime. I am glad that my early roots were Edwardian, for that period gave me a sense of solidity and discipline and helped to crystallize a number of homely virtues and tastes by which, consciously or unconsciously, I have been influenced in my life.

Richmond Barrett

---◄●►---

"NEWPORT"

from *Good Old Summer Days*

The following accounts of Tennis Week and the Annual
Horse Show in the "Cottage Colony" at Newport, Rhode
Island, are taken from "Newport," a section of Mr. Barrett's book, GOOD OLD SUMMER DAYS, first published in
1941, which contains his first-hand accounts of life in five
of America's most fashionable summer resorts: Newport,
Narragansett Pier, Saratoga, Long Branch and Bar Harbor. The American National Lawn Tennis Championship
Matches were held at the Newport Casino from the 1880's
until 1915 when they were transferred to the West Side
Tennis Club in Forest Hills, New York.

$\mathcal{T}$ennis week at the Casino, in the old days, marked the high point of the season. The very air seemed to have in it an electric tingle of excitement. The weather, unfortunately, was sometimes fickle, a less subservient handmaiden than she showed herself on the days Ward McAllister chose for his picnics. There was one melancholy August when it rained for a solid week; even after the skies had cleared, play could not be resumed for forty-eight hours. The championship court had been converted into a pretty little lake that placidly reflected the sky above it; and the Newport Fire Department had to be called in to pump it dry. Luckily, tennis week then was the United States National Lawn Tennis Tournament; if play had dragged on for as long as a month, the contestants could not have escaped from the clutches of the National Committee. The players were in Newport "for the duration" and that was all there was to it; but they were a highstrung crew, and stormy weather got on their nerves. Their antics up in the Club above the Bellevue Avenue shops were often a sad trial to their dignified hosts, the Board of Governors of the Casino. Some of the best players were also formidable drinkers, and there were some roaring orgies staged up in the Club. Why no bones were ever fractured on rainy days during tennis week has remained an insoluble puzzle in the history of Newport. Men had a curious tendency to plunge headlong down the staircase

132

into the entrance corridor. One day a National Doubles champion leaped from the center window overlooking the upper court; he landed astride the bracket of an iron lantern beneath.

When the skies cleared and play was resumed, the harassed barman in the club was given a blessed opportunity to rub Sloan's Liniment on his sore muscles while the masseurs took over down at the Locker Room. Like so many wine-presses, the more convivial of the players had the superfluous alcohol kneaded out of their systems; but even the deftest Swede couldn't seem to cure them of their thunderous headaches. Pails of cracked ice and portable medicine chests of digitalis and strychnine were carried out to the courts by the ball-boys. The spectators were blandly indulgent of the wide-open holes that began to show in their favorites' games; a Casino gallery was sure to be in possession of all the sorry facts. A standard joke for years was the newspaper report, "So-and-So was not up to his usual form yesterday. He was suffering from a recurrence of an old elbow complication."

The National Tournament had been inaugurated the year the Casino opened. At first, the gallery had been a very modest one—a scattering of a hundred people or so sitting in chairs around the Championship Court. Nobody bothered to watch the matches on the other courts. During its infancy, the National Tournament was pretty much of a family affair. Tennis was still considered "the gentleman's game"; most of the contestants were drawn from the summer colony. There were William Glyn and R. Livingston Beekman, for example, and the great Dick Sears of Boston; Sears won the championship eight times in succession. The brand of tennis they played, however, would not carry a man much beyond the second round at Forest Hills these days; even in the closing years of the eighteen-eighties, they had begun to drop behind in the quickening race for national honors. It is curious, this inability of theirs to keep the gentleman's game in their own hands. The men of the Newport summer colony have always been sturdy athletes, a superb fox-hunting breed, magnificent polo players and famous yachtsmen; but since the day of Dick Sears they have contributed very little to the extraordinary development of tennis.

Boys "from away," most of them college students, began to invade Newport in increasing numbers; and by 1890, the tournament had become a brilliant event, with a nation-wide fame and an international flavor. Eventually a few rows of chairs around the Championship Court could no longer accommodate the spectators, so the Casino Governors bought a grand-stand from Barnum and Bailey. It was a typical circus grand-stand, the reserved-seat section familiar to every American who has ever been under a big top. Set up along the south side of the court, with its round hinged seats of solid wood painted a bright vermilion, it looked rather like a great gaudy typewriter, with people scrambling about over it and finally perching on the keys. Underneath those hard little seats, the structure was a mere skeleton framework. People hung precariously suspended over a yawning emptiness. Women were forever dropping their parasols and their long white kid gloves into the wide-open spaces beneath them. The trips up the narrow aisles—and down again—were hazardous adventures. One morning Mrs. John Jacob Astor caught her heel at the very top of the grand-stand, lost her balance and fell the whole length to the ground. The moment is still remembered vividly by the few people alive to-day who were at the Casino that morning. Mrs. Astor happened to be the most beautiful woman of that period of beautiful women, a figure of almost legendary renown. In the eyes of her worshipers, she was by no means merely the reigning belle; before she was thirty, she had been unofficially deified. The goddess in her was never more apparent, or so it struck her contemporaries, than in the few seconds of her historic plunge down the tennis grandstand; apparently the whole episode was more in the nature of a gracious and unhurried descent from Olympus than an awkward human tumble. She reached the ground not only unhurt but unshaken; she was on her feet again in a moment and drifting nonchalantly toward the exit as if nothing untoward had occurred.

The first time the Casino Governors inspected the grand-stand, after the carpenters had hammered it together for its initial season, they had been aghast. It would never never do, they protested. For days, the manager of the Casino listened patiently to their complaints. Then he came forward with an offer: he would buy the thing from the Casino, accept all responsibility for it and reap for himself either the modest profits or the whirlwinds of damage suits that might accrue. The Governors, however, were just and generous men at heart; they considered themselves solely responsible for the wretched mistake. "Let it go for this year," they finally decided, "and we will assume the obligation in the name of the Casino." So, thanks to their fair-mindedness, the manager lost the one great chance that would ever come his way to make a comfortable fortune.

Within two years, that flimsy little grand-stand tucked away in the shady southeast corner of the Casino grounds was crowded with the highest and mightiest personages on the American scene. Into the erstwhile reserved seats of Barnum and Bailey had moved the Vanderbilts, the Astors, the Belmonts, the Goelets; and there they were to remain for many years, always occupying the same seats, regarding them at last as their own private property. Indeed, the seats on the Casino grand-stand had soon become as much a part of the family tradition as the red plush parterre box at the Metropolitan, the pew at Trinity and the shaving mug at Merker's barber shop. Not that a block of seats for tennis cost an outrageous sum of money; as a matter of fact, the tickets were absurdly cheap, six dollars apiece for the whole tournament. There were no scalpers on the Bellevue Avenue sidewalk shouting "Two good seats—fifty dollars for the pair!" The question was, not how much a man must pay but how under the sun he could get hold of one of those rare collector's items.

With such a background, it was inevitable that the National Tournament should continue to possess a good deal of its original atmosphere of a jolly family reunion. The players nowadays were for the most part "carpet-baggers," to be sure; but there was still a certain intimacy, a genuine give and take between them and the audience. The grand-stand crowd was sincerely interested both in the large outlines and the minutiae of a contestant's life. If a man was engaged to be married, his girl received a good deal of attention; the Newport lorgnettes swept over her, from head to foot, raking her with a sort of friendly machine-gun fire. When Bundy ate a bad lobster at Berger's, the bulletins about his ptomaine were followed with breathless interest. Once, at a critical moment of one of Bill Clothier's matches, an usher carried a glass of water up the grand-stand to the Clothier party; watching him, the audience held its collective breath in sympathy. Which member of the Clothier family could it be who was feeling faint—Bill's father or Bill's fiancée? People didn't ask a man for his autograph in those days; but in their well-bred way they were ardent fans just the same.

How pathetically antiquated the old Newport tennis week would seem to the sportsman who has watched National Tournaments only from the concrete stadium of Forest Hills! To the old-timer, however, that vanished scene will always be a precious and almost tearfully romantic memory. That it had some foolish opéra bouffe trimmings is undeniable. It must have been bad for a player's concentration, in the middle of a grueling fifth set, to hear Mullaly and his men strumming away at Offenbach's "La Belle Hélène" on the Horse-Shoe Piazza. Nor was it fair to hold the champion back till the very last day; if ever there was a theatrical trick, staged for the benefit of the audience and to the disadvantage of the aspiring tennis player, it was the "Challenge Round" at Newport. In those days, the more ancient followers of tennis may recall, the National Champion took no part in the tournament; he watched from the sidelines, shrewdly studying the good and bad points of the other men, one of whom was destined to win the tournament and thus become the challenger. Only then did the champion sally forth; coming out on the turf in the very pink of condition, he usually smothered the fagged and faded challenger.

Tennis in the Newport manner was a bit too much like command performances at court, some of the more hardboiled of the players began to think. The youngsters from California in particular, that historic band led by the brilliant flaming-haired comet McLaughlin, never for a moment felt at home under the benignant but faintly patronizing gaze of the Casino subscribers. So the grumblings began; but for a long time they went unheeded in the noisy bustle of a National Tournament that, year by year, was growing so fast that it was actually threatening to outgrow Newport.

The people sitting on their round red perches were delighted at the prodigious popularity their tennis week had attained; they were thrilled that their tiny inaccessible island should play host to thousands of visitors every day during the tournament. They did not realize what it cost these valiant strangers, in physical and mental wear and tear, to get aboard the inaccessible island. Sometimes, on the day of a big match, scores of tennis enthusiasts who had tumbled out of their beds before sunrise got no nearer to the Casino than the hill overlooking the Saunderstown ferry-slip. It is not to be wondered at that the Casino should have been roundly cursed by men and women who had watched the nine o'clock ferry, then the ten o'clock and the eleven o'clock, go chugging off without them toward Newport. The prospects of those who managed to get into the overloaded boat could not be considered enviable, either. By the time they reached the sacred enclosure of the Championship Court, they were confronted by a crowd packed at least ten deep around three sides of the famous rectangle; the fourth side—the shady side—was, of course, taken up by the grand-stand. To obtain even a distant view of the match, it was necessary to climb a tree or bake in the hot sun on the locker-room roof of the Court Tennis Building. There *was* a third horn to this dilemma, however: to throw one's self on the mercy of the ball-boys. For large bribes, those little blood-suckers would produce from some mysterious store-house battered old bureaus and chiffoniers and ramshackle pruning-ladders fifteen feet high. From these insecure roosting-places on the fringes of the crowd, the more adventurous visitors could obtain a pretty good slant on the match.

The author of this book once invited a girl cousin to tennis, hiring a pruning-ladder from the ball-boys for the festive occasion. It was a rickety old giant, that ladder, about the height of a giraffe. During the second set of the match, it suddenly buckled, folded up its four tired legs, tipped over backwards in a dead faint, and flung off the frightened youngsters to right and left. Again, by some miracle, no bones were broken; but a New York paper stated flatly the next day that things had reached a pretty pass when innocent children had to risk their necks to see a tennis game at the Casino.

Hotel accommodations at Newport remained notoriously inadequate during those years, and the summer colony was still very proud of the fact. They had a perfect right, of course, to cherish their inaccessibility and exclusiveness; but it did show a certain lack of foresight, after extending a bright welcome to the whole wide world for one brief period in the season, to let the guests go hungry and shelterless. After the match at the Casino was over, famished hordes ranged the streets, trying vainly to wedge their way into the overcrowded dining-rooms of Gunther's and Berger's and Hill Top Inn; and the guileless souls who had planned to stay overnight were summarily turned away from one "family" hotel after another.

The worst trial of all—far more exasperating than the attempt to reach the island or to get within sight of the court—was the interminable ordeal of getting *out* of the Casino after a championship match. The narrow entrance-hall was also the only exit; and it was perhaps the worst bottle-neck with which the United States has ever had to cope. The tennis grounds of the Casino were spacious enough to give the biggest crowd elbow-room; but when thousands of people jammed in the small upper court attempted to force themselves out into the corridor, the congestion was suffocating. The slow endless leakage, the agonizing dribble of humanity through that bottle-neck, went on literally for hours.

Naturally, the pushing new West Side Tennis Club at Forest Hills was turning out a great deal of insidious propaganda during these years of the Casino's dizzy prosperity. Players and spectators alike, not to mention certain influential papers in New York, took up the cause of Forest Hills. The grumbles were making themselves heard at last, were swelling into a loud martial chorus, a sort of frightening Marseillaise: "Down with Newport! On to West Side!" The well-behaved tennis-week guests of yesterday had turned into a vengeful mob; the charming Casino had become a monument of tyranny no less sinister than the Bastille itself.

The very ball-boys at the Casino began to catch the fever of sedition. Infernal nuisances they had always been; but they had never in the past come out in open and organized defiance of authority. When they finally did stage a mass demonstration, the Casino failed to recognize the significance of the affair, its connection with all the other alarming portents of a people on the march. Those ragamuffins, marching two by two up the grounds on the very morning of a championship match and delivering their ultimatum to the manager through a duly elected spokesman, were dealt with swiftly and ruthlessly. "An immediate increase in wages or we strike," the manager was informed. "Get the Hell out of here this minute or we'll have the cops in to *put* you out," was the immediate answer. In 1941, such a strike might appear to the world at large as a sort of Children's Crusade, very brave and very touching; people thought otherwise in the unenlightened old days at Newport. The boys were simply chased out into Bellevue Avenue, and telephone calls were put through to the parish priests. A whole new band of shackers was hired and was on the job in time for the match. On the stone wall of the old Jim Bennett estate across the street, the strikers sat in a row and shrieked "Scab! Scab!" as their successors scurried on the dead run into the corridor. The Casino had won out that time; the story of the great strike of the shackers highly amused the Governors.

Like all the despotic régimes of history, the summer colony of Newport awoke too late to its peril; and, when it did awake, it sought to ward off the inevitable doom by a series of weak, half-grudging concessions. The Championship Court was hastily moved from its modest pocket in the southeast corner of the grounds to the spacious Horse-Show ring with its big permanent box-enclosure.

The Barnum and Bailey grand-stand was overhauled and set up across the court; moreover, it was announced that henceforth the rule would be "first come, first served." Assuredly a gesture of real hospitality; but the carpers had soon taken due note of the fact that the former subscribers on the old grand-stand had already snapped up for themselves every box in the Horse-Show enclosure. The rule of first come, first served did not apply there.

It was too late, anyhow, for compromises; even the most drastic reforms could no longer have stemmed the tide of red revolt. The chant was still "On to West Side"; and on to West Side it was in the end. The angry crowds that had been cramming the proud inaccessible island to the gunwales had succeeded at last in scuttling it. As the capital of the tennis world, Newport sank beneath the waves.

Unlike the lost Atlantis, Newport proved to be incorrigibly buoyant; she bobbed up again the very next season with an Invitation Tournament. Strangely enough, a sizable proportion of the erstwhile saboteurs returned like dutiful sons to help make that annual invitation event a brilliant success in the years to come. To be sure, it was a smaller and much tidier affair than the unwieldy old "National"; but it was soon being spoken of everywhere as "*the* tournament, next to Forest Hills."

The annual Horse Show at the Casino ran a more sedate and seemly course than the National Tennis Tournament; and it died at last, quietly and unobtrusively, of sheer inanition. In its prime, the Horse Show was a charming and popular event, much more in the true Newport tradition than the world-famous tennis week. In a way, the "National" had been somewhat like a vast lazy-bird hatched in the nest of a gold-finch; the Horse Show was of pure Newport gold-finch stock, without a trace of the changeling about it. To the end, it was a family affair.

Flashy professional dealers did show their horses; but it was always easy to cope with them and keep them in their appointed place. Most of them had begun their careers as grooms; and the handling of grooms was a simple task for people who could tool a four-in-hand of tricky thoroughbreds.

Like all fashionable summer resorts, Newport fairly reeked of horse-flesh; but somehow the lovely summer season there did not seem the time for reckless exertion in the saddle. In Newport, one didn't see the Hunt go streaming by, with the pink coats turning the country-side into an old English sporting print. The men and women rode occasionally, followed by a groom at a discreet distance; but that was merely to give themselves and their horses a bit of routine exercise. For a time, polo was very popular, when Larry and Monty Waterbury and the Whitney boys were young; the vogue of polo, however, did not endure for long. The horse in Newport served for the most part between the shafts of a carriage; his primary rôle was to draw his owners about the streets, whisking them as swiftly as possible through a day crowded with social activities and getting them home at last from some big party in the early hours of the morning.

The horse was not a mere transportation facility, though; he was an integral and spectacular part of the general show, as important as his mistress's Paris gowns and jewels in the lavish parade of fashion. No fifteen-thousand-dollar Rolls-Royce of the twentieth century can convey such an impression of fabulous extravagance as did the Newport turn-outs of the eighteen-nineties. The afternoon was the best time to have a look at them. Soon after the elaborate and formal luncheon was over, the rubber-tired wheels would start spinning noiselessly down the driveways of Newport. Between the huge grilled gates of the Breakers, Mrs. Cornelius Vanderbilt's carriage would emerge, make a neat turn into Ochre Point Avenue and go whirling away toward Bellevue Avenue. Her sister-in-law, Mrs. Willy K. Vanderbilt, might be leaving Marble House at the same moment, the hoofs of her horses clacking on the marble paving-stones of the driveway. Through the gates of Beechwood Mrs. Astor's carriage would roll. The ladies were devoting themselves to the immensely solemn business of leaving cards. People could identify the carriages from a quick glance at the liveries; it was a part of one's cultural background then to be "up" on such matters. The Vanderbilt coachmen and footmen wore maroon coats, Mrs. Astor's blue.

The traffic on Bellevue Avenue and around the Ocean Drive never degenerated into a jam, nor were there any speed limits in those days to be boastfully broken. There was plenty of room between the carriages; and the pace, though brisk, was unhurried. The entire fifteen-mile circuit of the afternoon drive was a sort of horse-show ring where the summer colony exhibited themselves and their equipages; the competition was just as keen as at the Casino, too, though there was no distribution of blue, red, yellow, and white ribbons at the close of the daily event and no prize money for the footmen to pocket. Every entry in the unofficial show was of a pristine splendor. The ensemble was perfect, down to the last minute detail—the short manes braided just so, not a hair of a clubbed tail out of place, every crinkled rosette in its time-honored position. The horses' hides had the deep rich gleam of old oak or walnut or mahogany; the material of the liveries and cushions was so dense and soft that it was difficult to imagine the nap ever wearing off; the white breeches of the men on the box were just as immaculate as the long kid gloves of the ladies sitting behind them. No brand new patent-leather pumps ever had quite the lacquered glisten, the black dazzle of the servants' boots, or the leather trimmings of the carriages. The polish, the sheen, the blinding high-lights of the phaëtons and victorias on a sunny afternoon in Newport must have been a strain on the naked eye. There was something almost toylike about the vehicles, too, as if nothing crudely life-size could have that particular bright enameled finish; they looked as if they had emerged, not from stables but from special cupboards just off the ladies' boudoirs. The imaginative onlooker could almost picture the maid, after she had laid out the mistress's costume for the afternoon, taking the lid off the big white box that contained the carriage, the coachmen and the horses themselves, whisking away yards and yards of tissue paper from around them and lifting them out in a cloud of fragrant sachet.

The sober writer of history, turning his back on such fanciful flights, must needs record the fact that the horses and carriages did come out of stables; and the grandiose scale of life in Newport is nowhere more apparent than in those stables. Most of them were on Coggeshall Avenue, below the hill along which Bellevue Avenue runs; only a few stables were to be found on the grounds of the estates themselves. In *The Social Ladder*, Mrs. Van Rensselaer makes the preposterous statement that even the biggest Newport palaces had only about half an acre or an acre of land around them. The truth is that a ten-acre lot was about the average size; but, considering the formal driveways and broad terraces and sunken gardens, an enormous stable would have bulked too large on the scene. So Coggeshall Avenue became the official Newport Mews. To walk along Coggeshall Avenue to-day is to revisit a past as dead as the Rome of the Cæsars. Not that those prodigious piles of ivy-covered brick and stone, some of them the size of railroad terminals, have been abandoned by their owners; at present they are the garages of the Newport estates. But nothing can be more chilly and comfortless than a passing glimpse, through wide-open stable doors, of a half dozen automobiles in cold silent possession of a place that once swarmed and reverberated with life. Where a noisy tribe of grooms and ostlers used to sweat and curse, one or two men lounge about in their dark chauffeurs' uniforms, smoking their idle cigarettes. Instead of the aroma of hay and the hot pungent whiffs of horse, there is only the chemical smell of gasoline. The modern chauffeur is often a Frenchman or Italian whose youth was spent in a Renault or Fiat factory; to a man of that sort, the horse must seem as mythical a creature as the Centaur. But there are a few of the old family coachmen still left in Newport who, in the transitional days when the motor-car was young, were trained in the new art of driving behind a wheel. Given the title of head chauffeur, they accepted it with dignity but without enthusiasm. Their allegiance to the past remained unshaken.

One of these men, a fellow as round and rubicund as Pickwick, turned the old carriage-house into a sort of museum; and he was never so happy as on the occasions when he could show a party of pilgrims over his shrine. Everything was shipshape in that carriage-house, just as it had been before the motor-car was ever heard of. The four-in-hand, the landau, and the brougham all looked brand-new, with their glistening black bodies and vermilion wheels. "The real old English vermilion," he would say with just a touch of condescension. In one corner stood the quaint church-wagon, stolid and sober and with black wheels; evidently the old English vermilion was considered too frivolous for the Sabbath. It was a spacious age indeed that kept in its stables carriages designed for the sole purpose of conveying the family to divine service and back. It would have fitted into the general pattern of those days if families had had their private hearses, to be handed down from generation to generation.

"No 'orses 'ere for years and years," the homesick man would complain. "The young ones we sold when automobiles came to stay; the old ones we shot or put out to grass till they died. It's terrible quiet in the old place now, ain't it?"

A story the man loved to tell was of a skittish young mare that, breaking out of her stall one night, had a madcap romp all by herself in the corridor. He had been awakened in his room upstairs by the thunder of her galloping hoofs. Getting her back to bed had required diplomacy, keen knowledge of female wiles and a good deal of brute strength into the bargain. That corpulent old ex-groom was an incorrigible romantic. He did not scorn to enlarge upon the paternal affection he had felt for the mare when, safe in her stall again, she had burrowed her moist warm muzzle into the palm of his hand and begged for a little petting. The automobiles in his charge had no nerves to soothe; they never ramped out of their stalls at midnight to spoil his sleep. But then—and this was the fatal flaw in their mechanical perfection—they didn't have hot insinuating noses that poked themselves into a man's hands and from there straight into his susceptible heart.

"Oh, those days," he often mourned, "those days when Fatty Bates was young!"

To this day, Charlie Bates remains a tender recollection to many people in Newport. He has become the great legendary figure of the early Horse Shows at the Casino. Fatty was unique, a rare combination of showman and clown; a cherubic pudge out of the comic strips, but with something in him of the wizardry and romance of Falstaff. As a boy, he had been adored by the whole Rhode Island countryside; spoiled by his wealthy parents, he had run wild from the cradle. He had a prize vegetable garden that he tended religiously; he would be up before dawn, picking his finest egg-plants and tomatoes, and loading them into his pony-cart. Then he would be off to hawk his choice wares. The vegetable peddling was really just a pretext: after brief consultations with the cooks in the big Newport houses, he would dash around to the stables on Coggeshall Avenue for long man-to-man talks with the grooms. At ten, he was as horsy as a veteran coachman of fifty. No one ever prepared himself for his life work more thoroughly than Fatty. At an age when most boys are cramming for their college-entrance examinations, he was already the owner of a string of famous horses.

He was a great comedian and the idol of the Newport gallery. The box-holders appreciated his skill and were amused by his pranks; but he was worshiped by the ragamuffins who, after scaling the board-fence and ducking between the legs of the policemen, crowded around the gates into the ring. Fatty always put on his most spectacular act during the four-in-hand class. A magnificent driver, he could control four powerful horses and play a merry game at the same time. Jamming down the brakes of his drag, he would pretend to be climbing a steep hill. The animals would labor and sweat; yelling at the top of his lungs, Bates would flourish and crack his whip. At last the four-in-hand would reach the top of the imaginary hill; then Fatty would take a handkerchief of many colors out of his pocket, mop his baby face and loll back in his seat while his liveried bugler brayed out "Tally Ho."

Fatty was still a young man when the moment came for the bugle to sound "Taps" for him instead of the triumphant "Tally Ho." He had swelled to such a vast bulk that neither his short legs nor his stout heart could stand the strain any longer. Even in death, he was still able to startle and amuse an audience: his coffin, the mourners at his funeral discovered, was built as a perfect cube!

Mrs. J. Borden Harriman says of Bates in *From Pinafores to Politics*: "He was a twin to Dickens's Fat Boy. His tan box coat was cut so that he looked like the Liberty Bell. In a two-wheeled gig, he made the corner on one wheel. More than once I saw him turn completely over. How I wish he were alive to-day!"

Apart from the incorrigible Fatty, the Horse Show had a distinct formality about it; the people of Newport seemed more than ever to be hermetically sealed inside their own protective zone of air. The whole scene, the box-enclosure and the ring itself, had a special brightness and clarity, as if it had been enclosed in a big unbreakable crystal ball. Mullaly and his orchestra were brought over from the Horse-Shoe Piazza to the grand-stand for those three September days; and the waltzes, threading through the chatter, sounded like music being drowned out by the voices of the guests at a private party in somebody's drawing-room. The prices at the Horse Show were rather high for the Casino: a hundred dollars for a front box for the three days, seventy-five dollars for a back box. Since it was an afternoon affair, the gowns were more elaborate than for the morning matches of tennis week—the trains longer, the murmur of silken linings more pronounced. There was a greater display of jewels, too.

Even the snubs at the Horse Show had a sharper incisiveness than usual. For example, there was the case of the lovely but very pushing new-comer who had managed somehow or other to "sub-let" a front box from a family in mourning. One afternoon she sat alone in her box. As the other box-holders swept past in the aisle behind her, she deliberately accosted them one by one with a charming nod and the plaintive question, "Are you coming to my party to-night?" The fact that the invitations had all gone unanswered should have warned her that her cause was already lost; but, though she looked as defenceless and appealing as Greuze's maiden weeping over her broken pitcher, she happened to be a cool and level-headed young woman. To catch a few people off guard, to startle them into acceptance, would have struck her as a good day's work. She failed, however, to hook even one unwary victim. Her party was to take place at Berger's; and Berger's open-air dancing pavilion was situated directly behind the grand-stand, not twenty feet away from her box. All that afternoon, as she sat so conspicuously isolated at the Casino, the clatter and bustle of preparation at Berger's could be heard plainly by the gallery at the Horse Show; and the orders of Berger himself to his waiters, delivered in stentorian tones, were carried to every ear as if through a megaphone.

At last the lady left her box and drifted away, still casting nods and bright smiles among the stony outraged glares. A few moments later, she and Carl Berger were going the rounds of the dancing pavilion. The people in the back row of the grand-stand could hear her congratulating him in her soft but confident voice. Yes, the flowers were beautiful, all the decorations were just as she had wanted them. "I think it will be a lovely party," she said, her head bloody but unbowed. The struggles of that particular lady, it must be added, came to a unique and fortunate conclusion. Five years later, having divorced her husband and remarried in the interim, she was again sitting in a front box at the Casino, the wife of the most resounding catch in the entire summer colony.

If the snubs had a keen edge peculiar to the occasion, so had everything else at the Horse Show. The weather had a good deal to do with it, that magnificent September weather of Newport. Autumn always seemed to come blustering along just in time for the Horse Show. The air usually had a tang and a sparkle to it; big banks of white clouds would go shouldering across the blue sky, making a swift race of sunshine and shadow over the ring; as the afternoon wore on, women would put on their fur wraps and snuggle into them. It was a world of clear silhouettes, hard outlines, and ringing sounds. Even the leaves on the Casino trees would stand out with the definiteness of stenciling. The season was drawing to its close; the scattering to Hot Springs or White Sulphur, or to the country-houses on Long Island and up the Hudson, was imminent. The box enclosure resembled a noisy rookery, a last place of assemblage before the annual dispersal. A clean, metallic autumn sky always seems to have a gonglike reverberance; to be the perfect sounding-board for the chatter of migratory birds as they prepare to take flight. During those September afternoons, the people of Newport drew together in eager friendliness, forgetting the cliques and quarrels of the summer in an impressive farewell demonstration of family solidarity.

Alfred and Reginald Vanderbilt out in the ring, showing the famous horses from the Oakland Farm and Sandy Point Farm stables, were naturally the focal point of interest for their relatives and friends in the boxes. Those two brothers, playing year after year their friendly game of rivalry, never in their careers stepped out of character. It might be more accurate to say that they never stepped *into* character; they always seemed to be doing their level best to preserve a discreet incognito, or even a blank anonymity, behind their horses' tails. Once in a great while, they would be caught exchanging little amused grins; otherwise they stuck severely to the job of showing off their animals to the best advantage.

The two men were a picturesque study in contrasts: Alfred lean and swarthy and saturnine, with fine tragic eyes and a bitter mouth; Reggie so stout and rosy, his general attitude that of the sleek self-assured epicure. His eyes, oriental in cut like all the Vanderbilt eyes, had none of the brooding unhappiness in them that Alfred's betrayed even when he was a boy; he looked out from under his slanted upper lids with a twinkling joviality.

The gala years of the Newport show were the years
when the Vanderbilt boys were in their twenties; Alfred
was married to the former Elsie French then, and Reginald's wife was the former Cathleen Neilson. The ladies'
phaëton class, driven by ladies, was always something of
a sensation in its well-bred way. Mrs. Alfred Vanderbilt
was very tall and gracious and willowy; a word much used
in those days was "willowy." With her masses of auburn
curls and her hazel eyes, she had a striking resemblance
to Marie Antoinette as Vigée Le Brun painted her. Mrs.
Reggie was dark and frail and restless, with big intense
black eyes and a very white skin. They were typical figures
out of an Edith Wharton novel, perfect models for Wen-
zell. Indeed, a few slight alterations would have turned
Elsie French Vanderbilt into the Lily Bart of *The House
of Mirth*. She had the same "rustling grace," the air "of a
dryad subdued to the conventions of the drawing-room."
And Mrs. Reggie looked Bertha Dorset to the life. In her
phaëton, her lace-clad figure "detached itself with exaggerated slimness against the dusky upholstery"; and her
pale face "seemed the mere setting of her eyes, of which
the visionary gaze contrasted curiously with her self-
assertive tone and gestures."

From her box, the mother of Alfred and Reginald
watched the brilliant horsemanship of her sons and their
wives with a polite detachment that masked a tremendous pride. Mrs. Cornelius Vanderbilt was a diffident,
plain little woman, little indeed to the point of tininess.
She dressed simply, she shunned the spot-light and she
never indulged in an unnecessary gesture or a superfluous
word. She had none of the drive and sweep of her tempestuous sister-in-law, Mrs. Willy K. In her youth, she had
taught Sunday School; and all her life she would have fitted well into a plain parish-house setting. For all her shy
aloofness, however, she was a very admirable and a very
great lady indeed; neither the immense château on Fifth

Avenue and Fifty-Seventh Street nor the colossal Breakers could dwarf that diminutive figure.

Those years when the Vanderbilt boys and their wives "stole" the show were soon over. Alfred and Reggie continued to exhibit their horses and win their blue ribbons and championship ribbons; but after their first marriages had ended in the drab divorce courts, much of the old gaiety and exhilaration went out of the performance. Instead of Mrs. Alfred Vanderbilt and Mrs. Reginald Vanderbilt whirling around the ring in their phaëtons, Mrs. French Vanderbilt and Mrs. Neilson Vanderbilt sat in their boxes as mere spectators. Professional horsewomen—Belle Beach and the ravishing Mrs. Rasmussen—guided the phaëtons of Oakland and Sandy Point Farms. After the brief and brilliant prelude, the story of the Vanderbilts at the Newport Horse Show became a vaguely depressing one; and nobody who witnessed the last act of all will ever forget it. Alfred Vanderbilt had been dead for some years then. Mrs. French Vanderbilt had become Mrs. Paul Fitzsimmons; Mrs. Neilson Vanderbilt was Mrs. Sidney Jones Colford. Reggie was still on hand, judging classes, making himself generally indispensable. Occasionally he would leave the ring and saunter over to the box where his mother presided with all her old quiet dignity. Standing below the box-enclosure, with only his head and massive shoulders visible above the rail, he would chat with her casually and affably for a few minutes. Her expression, as she sat forward in her chair with her head bent, showed only a grave intentness on what he was saying. The effort it cost her must have been great; for it was obvious to everybody in the Casino during the three days of that show that Reginald Vanderbilt was a marked man. The whole audience, like a Greek chorus, was whispering lugubriously, "He's *doomed!*" As a matter of fact, he came very close to dying in harness, right there in the ring; four days after the show closed, he died in his bed at Sandy Point Farm.

Other picturesque figures elbow their way through one's memories of those years. There were the dealers, of course, lounging about the white fence of the oval ring and muttering to one another, "There ain't any real competition any more." According to them, the Vanderbilts were killing the show, if they hadn't "kilt" it already. The dealers and their henchmen always stayed at a French pension kept by Henri and Adelaide Desfossez. The piazza of the Desfossez House during the Horse Show was peopled by a motley throng: big showy men in loud waistcoats; their bony shambling sons, who rode "the old man's" horses by day and spent the nights in carouses and brawls; and a crew of brazenly pretty women, shrill as parrots, with the most beautiful figures and the smartest habits imaginable. The Desfossez couple took great pride in having under their roof these camp-followers of the Horse Show. Nothing was too good for them, neither truffles nor the rarest Strasbourg pâté de foie gras. They usually left a scattering of bad checks behind them, but Henri and Adelaide forgave.

Besides the hard-boiled dealers, there were the professional horsewomen who, though they "rode" for the rich, had more or less the status of guests; they sat in the boxes between classes and were treated with a sort of blurred unfocused friendliness. Mrs. Beach and her daughter Belle were the best known of this type; and when the Beaches entered a box, the eyes of the hostess actually *did* focus on them in cordial recognition. Mrs. Beach was the possessor of a pleasantly homely face; Belle's face was so fantastic in its ugliness that it somehow transcended mere ugliness. There was a sort of beguiling charm to that little wizened countenance, like the mummy of an infant monkey framed in the fuzzy blond wool of her hair; but whatever the flaws in Belle's face, she had the most exquisite figure ever seen in a horse-show ring. Swaying in her side-saddle, incredibly slender and graceful, she was one of the unforgettable pictures of the age.

Everybody liked the Beaches; earning a hard and precarious livelihood from horses, they yet were never just "horsy." They were stimulating, well-bred, and thoroughly intelligent.

One day in New York, a friend heard that Mrs. Beach was dying; at once, he hurried uptown to her apartment to pay his last respects. It happened to be the week of the Horse Show in the old Madison Square Garden. Belle was riding for some millionaire; but she and her mother had decided, just for the lark of it, to enter Belle's own little mare in one class.

The anxious friend, when he arrived at the apartment, was permitted to see Mrs. Beach for a few moments. "And how *are* you?" he asked with a somewhat inane cheeriness. "I'm happy—so happy," she sighed. "Just see what Belle's darling baby has gone and done!" She waved a hand at the wall above her bed. An ebony crucifix hung there; over the arm of the cross a blue ribbon had been draped. The mare had won first prize the evening before!

Probably that exploit of Belle's darling baby helped to bring about Mrs. Beach's recovery; at any rate, in three months she was in the saddle again, her seat as secure as ever. She lived on, indeed, for twelve more years. By that time, the day of the professional horsewoman was sadly on the wane. Belle struggled on alone for some time, dogged by poverty and crippled by arthritis. When she committed suicide, the papers devoted a few scant lines, at the bottom of the page, to her obituary.

For a while, Belle's principal rival at Newport was the adorable Mrs. Rasmussen; but the professional career of Mrs. Rasmussen was of brief duration. She soon married

Walter Hanley, a rich Providence brewer, and became the possessor of a big stable of her own. She never won for herself the slightest social recognition; so far as Newport was concerned, the minute she slipped out of her saddle she also slipped out of existence. Nonetheless, when she rode her celebrated Driftwood Blaze around the Newport ring, she always carried everything before her. To lovers of the old Horse Show, the words "Driftwood Blaze, Mrs. Hanley up" bring back the whole vivid spectacle as nothing else could.

Mrs. Hanley was very small, with a tidy compactness of outline and the swagger of a jockey. Her skin didn't seem to be mere human flesh. It looked more like some very rare kind of porcelain, translucent and rosy; and she had the face, not of a woman but of an enchanting little boy in all the pristine glory and vivid health of his fifth or sixth year on earth. Her smile was boyish, too; a frank square smile it was, a flash of the strongest, whitest teeth out of her young face.

The Horse Show ended, on the third afternoon, with the championship class for saddle horses. There was no daylight-saving then and the September twilight would be coming on. The air would be getting really chilly, with a slight premonitory tingle of frost in it. The women in the boxes wrapped their furs more closely about them. Out in the ring, the horses went through their aristocratic paces. A groom in a buff uniform would step out of the thatched summer-house at the center of the ring; with a rigid forefinger to his hat, he would relay to the riders the orders of the judges. At his signal, the men and women in the saddle would urge their horses into a trot or a gallop, or rein them up smartly to a walk.

Called back into the center of the ring at last, the competitors were lined up for the final inspection. There was a certain polite tension in the air, but not very much.

Reginald Rives and Frank Sturgis and Reginald Vanderbilt, as they strolled about and jotted down their notes and chatted amiably, were not the sort of judges to freeze an exhibitor's blood, even in a championship class. Certainly Mrs. Hanley never betrayed any perturbation as she leaned out of her saddle to say a few words to the dignified and courtly Rives. When Reggie Vanderbilt, beaming up at her, made some amusing sally, she would burst into a hearty jovial laugh. Under her, Driftwood Blaze would be behaving with exemplary correctness. Occasionally she touched him lightly with her whip or stroked the famous blaze on his forehead with her gauntleted hand. Once in a while, she gave the whole lovely ensemble of herself and her horse a swift glance of keen appraisal—to make sure that the animal's four feet were planted just so, that the folds of her habit-skirt were properly arranged, that her small boot had exactly the right toe-hold in the stirrup.

When the inevitable moment of her triumph arrived and the tri-colored ribbon had been fastened to the horse's head, Mrs. Hanley was always the most surprised and delighted little chap imaginable. Three times around the ring she and Driftwood Blaze would gallop, while the gallery clapped its kid-gloved hands and pounded with its sticks. Then the gate swung open and through it disappeared the handsome beast and his angelic mistress.

With a subdued scraping of chairs, the men of the orchestra got to their feet for the playing of the Star Spangled Banner. Then, out in the ring, the bugler in buff sounded Taps. The Horse Show and the Newport season were over in "a Driftwood Blaze of glory," as somebody once remarked on the way out of the Casino grounds in the sharp autumnal dusk.

Virginia Woolf

———◆◀◉▶◆———

"1907"

from *The Years*

"1907" is a chapter from Virginia Woolf's novel, THE YEARS, which traces the story of an English family, the Pargiters, from 1880 to 1937, the year in which the book was first published.

$\mathcal{I}$t was midsummer; and the nights were hot. The moon, falling on water, made it white, inscrutable, whether deep or shallow. But where the moonlight fell on solid objects it gave them a burnish and a silver plating, so that even the leaves in country roads seemed varnished. All along the silent country roads leading to London carts plodded; the iron reins fixed in the iron hands, for vegetables, fruit, flowers travelled slowly. Heaped high with round crates of cabbage, cherries, carnations, they looked like caravans piled with the goods of tribes migrating in search of water, driven by enemies to seek new pasturage. On they plodded, down this road, that road, keeping close to the kerb. Even the horses, had they been blind, could have heard the hum of London in the distance; and the drivers, dozing, yet saw through half-shut eyes the fiery gauze of the eternally burning city. At dawn, at Covent Garden, they laid down their burdens; tables and trestles, even the cobbles were frilled as with some celestial laundry with cabbages, cherries and carnations.

All the windows were open. Music sounded. From behind crimson curtains, rendered semi-transparent and sometimes blowing wide, came the sound of the eternal waltz— After the ball is over, after the dance is done—like a serpent that swallowed its own tail, since the ring was complete from Hammersmith to Shoreditch. Over and over again it was repeated by trombones outside public houses; errand boys whistled it; bands inside private rooms where people were dancing played it. There they sat at little tables at Wapping in the romantic Inn that overhung the river, between timber warehouses where barges were moored; and here again in Mayfair. Each table had its lamp; its canopy of tight red silk, and the flowers that had sucked damp from the earth that noon relaxed and spread their petals in vases. Each table had its pyramid of strawberries, its pale plump quail; and Martin, after India, after Africa, found it exciting to talk to a girl with bare shoulders, to a woman iridescent with green beetles' wings in her hair in a manner that the waltz condoned and half concealed under its amorous blandishments. Did it matter what one said? For she looked over her shoulder, only half listening, as a man came in wearing decorations, and a lady, in black with diamonds, beckoned him to a private corner.

As the night wore on a tender blue light lay on the market carts still plodding close to the kerb, past Westminster, past the yellow round clocks, the coffee stalls and the statues that stood there in the dawn holding so stiffly their rods or rolls of paper. And the scavengers followed after, sluicing the pavements. Cigarette ends, little bits of silver paper, orange peel—all the litter of the day was swept off the pavement and still the carts plodded, and the cabs trotted, indefatigably, along the dowdy pavements of Kensington, under the sparkling lights of Mayfair, carrying ladies with high headdresses and gentlemen in white waistcoats along the hammered dry roads which looked in the moonlight as if they were plated with silver.

"Look!" said Eugénie as the cab trotted over the bridge in the summer twilight. "Isn't that lovely?"

She waved her hand at the water. They were crossing the Serpentine; but her exclamation was only an aside;

she was listening to what her husband was saying. Their daughter Magdalena was with them; and she looked where her mother pointed. There was the Serpentine, red in the setting sun; the trees grouped together, sculptured, losing their detail; and the ghostly architecture of the little bridge, white at the end, composed the scene. The lights—the sunlight and the artificial light—were strangely mixed.

". . . of course it's put the Government in a fix," Sir Digby was saying. "But then that's what he wants."

"Yes . . . he'll make a name for himself, that young man," said Lady Pargiter.

The cab passed over the bridge. It entered the shadow of the trees. Now it left the Park and joined the long line of cabs, taking people in evening dress to plays, to dinner-parties, that was streaming towards the Marble Arch. The light grew more and more artificial; yellower and yellower. Eugénie leant across and touched something on her daughter's dress. Maggie looked up. She had thought that they were still talking politics.

"So," said her mother, arranging the flower in front of her dress. She put her head a little on one side and looked at her daughter approvingly. Then she gave a sudden laugh and threw her hand out. "D'you know what made me so late?" she said. "That imp, Sally . . ."

But her husband interrupted her. He had caught sight of an illuminated clock.

"We shall be late," he said.

"But eight-fifteen means eight-thirty," said Eugénie as they turned down a side street.

All was silent in the house at Browne Street. A ray from the street lamp fell through the fanlight and, rather capriciously, lit up a tray of glasses on the hall table; a top hat; and a chair with gilt paws. The chair, standing empty, as if waiting for someone, had a look of ceremony; as if it stood on the cracked floor of some Italian ante-room. But all was silent. Antonio, the manservant, was asleep; Mollie, the housemaid, was asleep; downstairs in the basement a door flapped to and fro—otherwise all was silent.

Sally in her bedroom at the top of the house turned on her side and listened intently. She thought she heard the front door click. A burst of dance music came in through the open window and made it impossible to hear.

She sat up in bed and looked out through the slit of the blind. Through the gap she could see a slice of the sky; then roofs; then the tree in the garden; then the backs of houses opposite standing in a long row. One of the houses was brilliantly lit and from the long open windows came dance music. They were waltzing. She saw shadows twirling across the blind. It was impossible to read; impossible to sleep. First there was the music; then a burst of talk; then people came out into the garden; voices chattered, then the music began again.

It was a hot summer's night, and though it was late, the whole world seemed to be alive; the rush of traffic sounded distant but incessant.

A faded brown book lay on her bed; as if she had been reading. But it was impossible to read; impossible to sleep. She lay back on the pillow with her hands behind her head.

"And he says," she murmured, "the world is nothing but . . ." She paused. What did he say? Nothing but thought, was it? she asked herself as if she had already forgotten. Well, since it was impossible to read and impossible to sleep, she would let herself *be* thought. It was easier to act things than to think them. Legs, body, hands, the whole of her must be laid out passively to take part in this universal process of thinking which the man said was the world living. She stretched herself out. Where did thought begin?

In the feet? she asked. There they were, jutting out under the single sheet. They seemed separated, very far away. She closed her eyes. Then against her will something in her hardened. It was impossible to act thought. She became something; a root; lying sunk in the earth; veins seemed to thread the cold mass; the tree put forth branches; the branches had leaves.

"—the sun shines through the leaves," she said, waggling her finger. She opened her eyes in order to verify the sun on the leaves and saw the actual tree standing out there in the garden. Far from being dappled with sunlight, it had no leaves at all. She felt for a moment as if she had been contradicted. For the tree was black, dead black.

She leant her elbow on the sill and looked out at the tree. A confused clapping sound came from the room where they were having the dance. The music had stopped; people began to come down the iron staircase into the garden which was marked out with blue and yellow lamps dotted along the wall. The voices grew louder. More people came and more people came. The dotted square of green was full of the flowing pale figures of women in evening dress; of the upright black-and-white figures of men in evening dress. She watched them moving in and out. They were talking and laughing; but they were too far off for her to hear what they were saying. Sometimes a single word or a laugh rose above the rest, and then there was a confused babble of sound. In their own garden all was empty and silent. A cat slid stealthily along the top of a wall; stopped; and then went on again as if drawn on some secret errand. Another dance struck up.

"Over again, over and over again!" she exclaimed impatiently. The air, laden with the curious dry smell of London earth, puffed in her face, blowing the blind out. Stretched flat on her bed, she saw the moon; it seemed immensely high above her. Little vapours were moving across the surface. Now they parted and she saw engravings chased over the white disc. What were they, she wondered—mountains? valleys? And if valleys, she said to herself half closing her eyes, then white trees; then icy hollows, and nightingales, two nightingales calling to each other, calling and answering each other across the valleys. The waltz music took the words "calling and answering each other" and flung them out; but as it repeated the same rhythm again and again, it coarsened them, it destroyed them. The dance music interfered with everything. At first exciting, then it became boring and finally intolerable. Yet it was only twenty minutes to one.

Her lip raised itself, like that of a horse that is going to bite. The little brown book was dull. She reached her hand above her head and took down another book from the shelf of battered books without looking at it. She opened the book at random; but her eye was caught by one of the couples who were still sitting out in the garden though the others had gone in. What were they saying, she wondered? There was something gleaming in the grass, and, as far as she could see, the black-and-white figure stooped and picked it up.

"And as he picks it up," she murmured, looking out, "he says to the lady beside him: Behold, Miss Smith, what I have found on the grass—a fragment of my heart; of my broken heart, he says. I have found it in the grass; and I wear it on my breast"—she hummed the words in time to the melancholy waltz music—"my broken heart, this broken glass, for love—" she paused and glanced at the book. On the fly-leaf was written:

"Sara Pargiter from her Cousin Edward Pargiter."

". . . for love," she concluded, "is best."

She turned to the title-page.

"The Antigone of Sophocles, done into English verse by Edward Pargiter," she read.

Once more she looked out of the window. The couple had moved. They were going up the iron staircase. She watched them. They went into the ballroom. "And suppose in the middle of the dance," she murmured, "she takes it out; and looks at it and says, 'What is this?' and it's only a piece of broken glass—of broken glass. . . ." She looked down at the book again.

"The Antigone of Sophocles," she read. The book was brand-new; it cracked as she opened it; this was the first time she had opened it.

"The Antigone of Sophocles, done into English verse by Edward Pargiter," she read again. He had given it her in Oxford; one hot afternoon when they had been trailing through chapels and libraries. "Trailing and wailing," she hummed, turning over the pages, "and he said to me, getting up from the low armchair, and brushing his hand through his hair"—she glanced out of the window—"'my wasted youth, my wasted youth.'" The waltz was now at its most intense, its most melancholy. "Taking in his hand," she hummed in time to it, "this broken glass, this faded heart, he said to me . . ." Here the music stopped; there was a sound of clapping; the dancers once more came out into the garden.

She skipped through the pages. At first she read a line or two at random; then, from the litter of broken words, scenes rose, quickly, inaccurately, as she skipped. The unburied body of a murdered man lay like a fallen tree-trunk, like a statue, with one foot stark in the air. Vultures gathered. Down they flopped on the silver sand. With a lurch, with a reel, the top-heavy birds came waddling; with a flap of the grey throat swinging, they hopped—she beat her hand on the counterpane as she read—to that lump there. Quick, quick, quick with repeated jerks they struck the mouldy flesh. Yes. She glanced at the tree outside in the garden. The unburied body of the murdered man lay on the sand. Then in a yellow cloud came whirling—who? She turned the page quickly. Antigone? She came whirling out of the dust-cloud to where the vultures were reeling and flung white sand over the blackened foot. She stood there letting fall white dust over the blackened foot. Then behold! there were more clouds; dark clouds; the horsemen leapt down; she was seized; her wrists were bound with withies; and they bore her, thus bound—where?

There was a roar of laughter from the garden. She looked up. Where did they take her? she asked. The garden was full of people. She could not hear a word that they were saying. The figures were moving in and out.

"To the estimable court of the respected ruler?" she murmured, picking up a word or two at random, for she was still looking out into the garden. The man's name was Creon. He buried her. It was a moonlight night. The blades of the cactuses were sharp silver. The man in the loincloth gave three sharp taps with his mallet on the brick. She was buried alive. The tomb was a brick mound. There was just room for her to lie straight out. Straight out in a brick tomb, she said. And that's the end, she yawned, shutting the book.

She laid herself out, under the cold smooth sheets, and pulled the pillow over her ears. The one sheet and the one blanket fitted softly round her. At the bottom of the bed was a long stretch of cool fresh mattress. The sound of the dance music became dulled. Her body dropped suddenly; then reached ground. A dark wing brushed her mind, leaving a pause; a blank space. Everything—the music, the voices—became stretched and generalised. The book fell on the floor. She was asleep.

"It's a lovely night," said the girl who was going up the iron steps with her partner. She rested her hand on the balustrade. It felt very cold. She looked up; a slice of yellow light lay round the moon. It seemed to laugh round it. Her partner looked up too, and then mounted another step without saying anything for he was shy.

"Going to the match tomorrow?" he said stiffly, for they scarcely knew each other.

"If my brother gets off in time to take me," she said, and went up another step too. Then, as they entered the ballrooom, he gave her a little bow and left her; for his partner was waiting.

The moon which was now clear of clouds lay in a bare space as if the light had consumed the heaviness of the clouds and left a perfectly clear pavement, a dancing ground for revelry. For some time the dappled iridescence of the sky remained unbroken. Then there was a puff of wind; and a little cloud crossed the moon.

There was a sound in the bedroom. Sara turned over. "Who's that?" she murmured. She sat up and rubbed her eyes.

It was her sister. She stood at the door, hesitating. "Asleep?" she said in a low voice.

"No," said Sara. She rubbed her eyes. "I'm awake," she said, opening them.

Maggie came across the room and sat down on the edge of the bed. The blind was blowing out; the sheets were slipping off the bed. She felt dazed for a moment. After the ballroom, it looked so untidy. There was a tumbler with a toothbrush in it on the wash-stand; the towel was crumpled on the towel-horse; and a book had fallen on the floor. She stooped and picked up the book. As she did so, the music burst out down the street. She held back the blind. The women in pale dresses, the men in black and white, were crowding up the stairs into the ballroom. Snatches of talk and laughter were blown across the garden.

"Is there a dance?" she asked.

"Yes. Down the street," said Sara.

Maggie looked out. At this distance the music sounded romantic, mysterious, and the colours flowed over each other, neither pink nor white nor blue.

Maggie stretched herself and unpinned the flower that she was wearing. It was drooping; the white petals were stained with black marks. She looked out of the window again. The mixture of lights was very odd; one leaf was a lurid green; another was a bright white. The branches crossed each other at different levels. Then Sally laughed.

"Did anybody give you a piece of glass," she said, "saying to you, Miss Pargiter . . . my broken heart?"

"No," said Maggie, "why should they?" The flower fell off her lap onto the floor.

"I was thinking," said Sara. "The people in the garden . . ."

She waved her hand at the window. They were silent for a moment, listening to the dance music.

"And who did you sit next?" Sara asked after a time.

"A man in gold lace," said Maggie.

"In gold lace?" Sara repeated.

Maggie was silent. She was getting used to the room; the discrepancy between this litter and the shiny ballroom was leaving her. She envied her sister lying in bed with the window open and the breeze blowing in.

"Because he was going to a party," she said. She paused. Something had caught her eye. A branch swayed up and down in the little breeze. Maggie held the blind so that the window was uncurtained. Now she could see the whole sky, and the houses and the branches in the garden.

"It's the moon," she said. It was the moon that was making the leaves white. They both looked at the moon which shone like a silver coin, perfectly polished, very sharp and hard.

"But if they don't say O my broken heart," said Sara, "what do they say, at parties?"

Maggie flicked off a white fleck that had stuck to her arm from her gloves.

"Some people say one thing," she said, getting up, "and some people say another."

She picked up the little brown book which lay on the counterpane and smoothed out the bedclothes. Sara took the book out of her hand.

"This man," she said, tapping the ugly little brown volume, "says the world's nothing but thought, Maggie."

"Does he?" said Maggie, putting the book on the washstand. It was a device, she knew, to keep her standing there talking.

"D'you think it's true?" Sara asked.

"Possibly," said Maggie, without thinking what she was saying. She put out her hand to draw the curtain.

"The world's nothing but thought, does he say?" she repeated, holding the curtain apart.

She had been thinking something of the kind when the cab crossed the Serpentine; when her mother interrupted her. She had been thinking, Am I that, or am I this? Are we one, or are we separate—something of the kind.

"Then what about trees and colours?" she said, turning round.

"Trees and colours?" Sara repeated.

"Would there be trees if we didn't see them?" said Maggie.

"What's 'I'? . . . 'I' . . ." She stopped. She did not know what she meant. She was talking nonsense.

"Yes," said Sara. "What's 'I'?" She held her sister tight by the skirt, whether she wanted to prevent her from going, or whether she wanted to argue the question.

"What's 'I'?" she repeated.

But there was a rustling outside the door and their mother came in.

"Oh, my dear children!" she exclaimed, "still out of bed? Still talking?"

She came across the room, beaming, glowing, as if she were still under the influence of the party. Jewels flashed on her neck and her arms. She was extraordinarily handsome. She glanced round her.

"And the flower's on the floor, and everything's so untidy," she said. She picked up the flower that Maggie had dropped and put it to her lips.

"Because I was reading, Mama, because I was waiting," said Sara. She took her mother's hand and stroked the bare arm. She imitated her mother's manner so exactly that Maggie smiled. They were the very opposite of each other —Lady Pargiter so sumptuous; Sally so angular. But it's worked, she thought to herself, as Lady Pargiter allowed herself to be pulled down onto the bed. The imitation had been perfect.

"But you must go to sleep, Sal," she protested. "What did the doctor say? Lie straight, lie still, he said." She pushed her back onto the pillows.

"I am lying straight and still," said Sara. "Now"—she looked up at her—"tell me about the party."

Maggie stood upright in the window. She watched the couples coming down the iron staircase. Soon the garden was full of pale whites and pinks, moving in and out. She half heard them behind her talking about the party.

"It was a very nice party," her mother was saying.

Maggie looked out of the window. The square of the garden was filled with differently tinted colours. They seemed to ripple one over the other until they entered the angle where the light from the house fell, when they suddenly turned to ladies and gentlemen in full evening dress.

"No fish-knives?" she heard Sara saying.

She turned.

"Who was the man I sat next?" she asked.

"Sir Matthew Mayhew," said Lady Pargiter.

"Who is Sir Matthew Mayhew?" said Maggie.

"A most distinguished man, Maggie!" said her mother, flinging her hand out.

"A most distinguished man," Sara echoed her.

"But he is," Lady Pargiter repeated, smiling at her daughter whom she loved perhaps because of her shoulder.

"It was a great honour to sit next him, Maggie," she continued. "A great honour," she said reprovingly. She paused, as if she saw a little scene. She looked up.

"And then," she resumed, "when Mary Palmer says to me, Which is your daughter? I see Maggie, miles away, at the other end of the room, talking to Martin, whom she might have met every day of her life in an omnibus!"

Her words were stressed so that they seemed to rise and fall. She emphasised the rhythm still further by tapping with her fingers on Sally's bare arm.

"But I don't see Martin every day," Maggie protested.

"I haven't seen him since he came back from Africa." Her mother interrupted her.

"But you don't go to parties, my dear Maggie, to talk to your own cousins. You go to parties to—"

Here the dance music crashed out. The first chords seemed possessed of frantic energy, as if they were summoning the dancers imperiously to return. Lady Pargiter stopped in the middle of her sentence. She sighed; her body seemed to become indolent and suave. The heavy lids lowered themselves slightly over her large dark eyes. She swayed her head slowly in time to the music.

"What's that they're playing?" she murmured. She hummed the tune, beating time with her hand. "Something I used to dance to."

"Dance it now, Mama," said Sara.

"Yes, Mama. Show us how you used to dance," Maggie urged her.

"But without a partner—?" Lady Pargiter protested. Maggie pushed a chair away.

"Imagine a partner," Sara urged her.

"Well," said Lady Pargiter. She rose. "It was something like this," she said. She paused; she held her skirt out with one hand; she slightly crooked the other in which she held the flower; she twirled round and round in the space which Maggie had cleared. She moved with extraordinary stateliness. All her limbs seemed to bend and flow in the lilt and the curve of the music; which became louder and clearer as she danced to it. She circled in and out among the chairs and tables and then, as the music stopped, "There!" she exclaimed. Her body seemed to fold and close itself together as she sighed "There!" and sank all in one movement on the edge of the bed.

"Wonderful!" Maggie exclaimed. Her eyes rested on her mother with admiration.

"Nonsense," Lady Pargiter laughed, panting slightly. "I'm much too old to dance now; but when I was young; when I was your age—" She sat there panting.

"You danced out of the house onto the terrace and found a little note folded in your bouquet—" said Sara, stroking her mother's arm. "Tell us that story, Mama."

"Not tonight," said Lady Pargiter. "Listen—there's the clock striking!"

Since the Abbey was so near, the sound of the hour filled the room; softly, tumultuously, as if it were a flurry of soft sighs hurrying one on top of another, yet concealing something hard. Lady Pargiter counted. It was very late.

"I'll tell you the true story one of these days," she said as she bent to kiss her daughter good-night.

"Now! Now!" cried Sara, holding her fast.

"No, not now—not now!" Lady Pargiter laughed, snatching away her hand. "There's Papa calling me!"

They heard footsteps in the passage outside, and then Sir Digby's voice at the door.

"Eugénie! It's very late, Eugénie!" they heard him say.

"Coming!" she cried. "Coming!"

Sara caught her by the train of her dress. "You haven't told us the story of the bouquet, Mama!" she cried.

"Eugénie!" Sir Digby repeated. His voice sounded peremptory. "Have you locked—"

"Yes, yes, yes," said Eugénie. "I will tell you the true story another time," she said, freeing herself from her daughter's grasp. She kissed them both quickly and went out of the room.

"She won't tell us," said Maggie, picking up her gloves. She spoke with some bitterness.

They listened to the voices talking in the passage. They could hear their father's voice. He was expostulating. His voice sounded querulous and cross.

"Pirouetting up and down with his sword between his legs; with his opera hat under his arm and his sword between his legs," said Sara, pummelling her pillows viciously.

The voices went further away, downstairs.

"Who was the note from, d'you think?" said Maggie.

She paused, looking at her sister burrowing into her pillows.

"The note? What note?" said Sara. "Oh, the note in the bouquet. I don't remember," she said. She yawned.

Maggie shut the window and pulled the curtain but she left a chink of light.

"Pull it tight, Maggie," said Sara irritably. "Shut out that din."

She curled herself up with her back to the window. She had raised a hump of pillow against her head as if to shut out the dance music that was still going on. She pressed her face into a cleft of the pillows. She looked like a chrysalis wrapped round in the sharp white folds of the sheet. Only the tip of her nose was visible. Her hip and her feet jutted out at the end of the bed covered by a single sheet. She gave a profound sigh that was half a snore; she was asleep already.

Maggie went along the passage. Then she saw that there were lights in the hall beneath. She stopped and looked down over the bannister. The hall was lit up. She could see the great Italian chair with the gilt claws that stood in the hall. Her mother had thrown her evening cloak over it, so that it fell in soft golden folds over the crimson cover. She could see a tray with whisky and a soda-water syphon on the hall table. Then she heard the voices of her father and mother as they came up the kitchen stairs. They had been down in the basement; there had been a burglary up the street; her mother had promised to have a new lock put on the kitchen door but had forgotten. She could hear her father say:

". . . they'd melt it down; we should never get it back again."

Maggie went on a few steps upstairs.

"I'm so sorry, Digby," Eugénie said as they came into the hall. "I will tie a knot in my handkerchief; I will go directly after breakfast tomorrow morning. . . . Yes," she said, gathering her cloak in her arms, "I will go myself, and I will say, 'I've had enough of your excuses, Mr. Toye. No, Mr. Toye, you have deceived me once too often. And after all these years!' "

Then there was a pause. Maggie could hear soda-water squirted into a tumbler; the chink of a glass; and then the lights went out.

The Marchioness of Bath

"BEFORE THE SUNSET FADES"

$\mathcal{T}$he purpose of this book is to recall the days of elegance at Longleat, before the sunset fades, before the moths of war and depression devour the last remaining shreds of a domestic tapestry which can never be replaced.

A phase of social history which has now disappeared in this country is the backstairs life of a large country house. At its zenith between 1880 and 1914, it never returned to its full splendour after the first World War.

Some of the old servants who still remember Longleat in its halcyon days have told me how a large country house, such as this, was managed fifty years ago. The intricate hive which buzzed so busily below stairs led a complete social life of its own; and its ritual and etiquette make a fascinating study. It was governed by the hierarchy of the steward's room, the heads of which were the house steward and the housekeeper.

Today Longleat is no longer used as a family home. The empty kitchens which once gleamed with burnished copper are almost as sad to see as the silent nurseries which have missed the care and attention of a whole generation of children.

Fifty years ago the Longleat staff numbered 43 and was composed of the following:

176

One House Steward
One Butler
One Under Butler
One Groom of the Chambers
One Valet
Three Footmen
One Steward's Room Footman
Two Oddmen
Two Pantry Boys
One Lamp Boy

One Housekeeper
Two Lady's Maids
One Nurse
One Nursery Maid
Eight Housemaids
Two Sewing Maids
Two Still Room Maids
Six Laundry Maids

One Chef
Two Kitchen Maids
One Vegetable Maid
One Scullery Maid
One Daily Woman

In those days the kitchen staff led their own life apart from the rest of the household. They ate in the kitchen, and the daily duty of preparing breakfast absolved them from attending early morning prayers.

The French chef was Gaillard, a friend of the royal chef at Buckingham Palace. When the family were in London he would go to the Palace to lend a hand at any big dinner party; in return the Palace chef came to the house in Berkeley Square, where he prepared his own specialties, pedestals and statuettes of semolina to decorate the sweets.

Charcoal was used for much of the cooking at Longleat, while the large joints were roasted on spits which were turned mechanically over an open fire. In the kitchen courtyard there was a fish still, an artificial pond in which the pike and trout from the Longleat waters were placed to cleanse them of the taste of mud.

Every week three sheep of different species were butchered for the household, one Southdown, one Westmorland, and one Brittany, the last being used exclusively for small cutlets.

Every morning the chef wrote out the menus on a broad slate and took them upstairs for the approval of Lady Bath. The battery of pots and pans was cleaned and polished with ale, soft soap and silver sand.

Apart from the indoor servants, fourteen others were employed in the stables. These included a coachman, a second coachman, a carriage groom, a steel boy (whose duty was to burnish the bits and metal parts of the harness) and a "tiger," a small boy in livery who sat upright on the box of the carriage, his arms folded stiffly across his chest. (This domestic post was not known until the early part of the last century. It is recorded that the composer Alexander Lee, when a boy, "entered the service of Lord Barrymore as 'tiger,' being the first of the class of servants known by that name.") I imagine that these little boys, most of whom must have been pink and cherubic, were given this fierce-sounding name on the same analogy as a tall, fat man is often called "Tiny." The "tiger's" other duty was to lead the ponies of the children of the house when they went out riding. In the stables there was a fully equipped blacksmith's shop, and once a fortnight

the village blacksmith and his lad came from Horningsham
to shoe the horses at Longleat.

When the family moved to Berkeley Square, and later
to Grosvenor Square, for the London season, seventeen
of the staff accompanied them, together with eleven horses
and five stablemen. In the mews behind the Grosvenor
Square house there were stables and a coach house, with
rooms above for the coachmen and the grooms.

The yellow state coach which was used at that time now
stands in the hall at Longleat, accompanied by the coachman's uniform, a six-tiered cape fastened from neck to
hem with silver crested buttons, and a three-cornered hat
trimmed with silver braid. The coach was only used for
state occasions such as a coronation, a ball at Buckingham
Palace, a levee, a presentation, or the opening of Parliament.

At Longleat the housekeeper and the house steward presided over the steward's room table at which the head
butler, the cook, the lady's maids, the valets and the
groom of the chambers used to eat. The remainder, the liveried servants and the under maids, had their meals in the
servants' hall where the second butler and the head laundry maid ranked the highest. The housekeeper had her
own sitting room where she received the steward's room
for tea.

A strange ritual took place over the midday meal in the
servants' hall. The under servants first trooped in and remained standing at their places until the upper servants
had filed in in order of domestic status. After the first
course the upper servants left in the following manner.
When the joint, carved by the house steward, had been
eaten and second helpings offered, it was ceremoniously
removed by the steward's room footman who carried it
out with great pomp, followed by the upper servants who

then retired to the steward's room for the remainder of their meal; while the housemaids and sewing maids scurried off with platefuls of pudding to eat in their own sitting rooms. This seems to have been the recognised custom of most large houses at that time.

At midday there was either a joint, chickens or a goose, followed by a pudding and cheese; in the evening, a four-course dinner. Callers at the back door stayed long enough to drink a glass or two of Longleat-brewed ale, and leather flagons of this brew, with plates of bread and cheese, were always left standing on the servants' hall table for anyone to help himself.

Twice a week, on Tuesdays and Thursdays, dances were held in the servants' hall. A pianist was engaged from the neighbouring town of Warminster and a buffet supper was produced by the kitchen and still room staff. The outside servants also attended these dances, as well as the unmarried grooms and gardeners who lived in a hostel close to the house, known as the "bothy." I like to think of those still room maids and housemaids discarding their printed chintz dresses and muslin caps for their evening finery, prinking in front of their mirrors before going down to the hall to dance with the "bothy" boys. The housekeeper would keep an eagle eye on the younger maids, noticing whom they danced with and reprimanding the overfrivolous.

The housekeeper superintended all the feminine departments of the house. She checked the laundry with the head housemaid, grumbled at the laundry maids for any fault in their work, gave out the stores once a week, and found work and repairs for the sewing maids to do. In the still room she performed feats of alchemy, distilling rose water from dark damask roses, producing pot-pourri from an old family recipe, preserving fruits, making jam, candying peel, bottling morello cherries in brandy, drying lavender to keep the linen cupboard sweet, and forever harrying the still room maids.

The short spiral staircase which winds its way from the housekeeper's room to the still room seems to me to be haunted by the jingling sound of the clustered keys which the housekeeper wore at her waist; and the smell of the old still room itself—that delicious combination of hot bread, biscuits, coffee and herbs—my mouth waters as I think of it today.

Many of the old household account books have been preserved at Longleat, including the dispensary books containing detailed records of the invalid delicacies and remedies, many of them prepared in the still room, which were given to the sick of the neighbourhood. I am struck by the imagination and thoughtfulness shown in these books. The food is by no means dull invalid food, but seems to have varied according to the individual's needs and taste. It is fascinating to follow the course of an illness through the dispensary book, by the gifts made to the patient.

Enormous quantities of port wine were given away weekly, and some received bottles of gin or whisky.

A large amount of beef tea for the sick and poor must have been made every day at Longleat. I find an entry of 1875: "Feb.–March. Mrs. Miller 5 lbs. of mutton." I imagine that it must have been for the use of the whole family during a period of unemployment or sickness of the wage-earner.

The third Marchioness of Bath wrote a charming little book in 1829 on how to be a good cottager. It starts with detailed instructions on the art of brewing. She is very strongly critical of tea-drinking as a habit. She says that tea "besides being good for nothing, has badness in it because it is well known to produce want of sleep, in many cases, and in all cases to shake and weaken the nerves."

She works out a sum to prove that tea-drinking would cost a cottage family £10 a year, and do them nothing but harm, whereas home-brewed beer would cost them £7 5s. od. and benefit them in every way. The book instructs on bread-making, keeping cows, pigs, bees, geese, fowls, rabbits, goats and ewes, making candles, rush lighters, mustard, dresses, household goods and fuel, and the sowing of Swedish turnip seed. She gives some simple cooking recipes, drinks for fever and illness, and gargles made from herbs.

She writes eloquently on the subject of bread-making and says "Every woman, high or low, ought to know how to make bread. If she do not, she is unworthy of trust and confidence."

Every Christmas there was a Grand Servants' Ball given in the dining room, to which the local tradesmen who served the house were also invited. The custom was for the Marquess of Bath to open the Ball with the housekeeper, while the Marchioness danced with the house steward. The Lancers was always the second dance.

When I first came to Longleat, as the wife of the son of the house, I was partnered in the first dance by the butler, and in the Lancers by the head groom, a charming bandy-legged little gnome who steered me through the figures of the dance with skill and command.

On Christmas morning all the under maids came up to see Lady Bath, who presented each one with the traditional gift of a dress length.

On Christmas night, whatever the weather might be, the maids went out to dance in the courtyard. On the

There were hansom cabs at the corner of Fifth Avenue and Fifty-ninth Street, New York, in 1902, but there were a good many more there then than there are today. The Plaza Hotel was built on this site in 1904.

In 1903 horse cars still carried passengers around New York and other American and European cities. These were photographed in New York City's Union Square.

The Easter Parade on Fifth Avenue, about 1905. The scene is the corner of Forty-eighth Street. The Collegiate Church of St. Nicholas, seen on the left, has been replaced by the very modern Esso Building.

The gentleman at the controls of this early automobile is demonstrating the steering mechanism of his vehicle at the first automobile show, held at Madison Square Garden, New York, in 1900. The lady at his left appears to be less confident of the car's powers.

© BROWN BROTHERS

Eleanora Sears, who is one of America's most famous sportswomen, and Blanche Oelrichs photographed while driving in the fashionable summer colony at Newport, Rhode Island.

© BROWN BROTHERS

The elegant James Hazen Hyde, shown here with the Countess de Rougemont, gave a magnificent "Eighteenth Century Costume Fete" at Sherry's in New York, on January 31, 1905, a ball which was said to have cost the young vice president of the Equitable Life Assurance Society between $100,000 and $200,-000. Before the end of 1905, Hyde was forced to sell his interest in the Equitable for $2,500,000. He sailed for France where he lived until 1945.

Although women were not granted the right to vote in the United States or Europe until after World War I, the suffragette was a familiar figure of the Edwardian era on both sides of the Atlantic. The English leader, Emmeline Pankhurst, was probably the most famous suffragette of this period. In this country, the prominent society woman, Mrs. O. H. P. Belmont, took up the cause. This picture was taken in 1912 at the headquarters of women voters in Cleveland, Ohio. Belle Sherwin, president of the organization, holds the flag.

The heights of fashion for a warm summer afternoon at Newport, Rhode Island, in 1910.

An imperial family gathering in London in 1907. The reigning king of England, Edward VII, stands at the far right; his handsome queen, Alexandra, in the center. The Queen of Spain, who before her marriage had been Victoria of Battenburg, is seated at the right, and Kaiser Wilhelm II of Germany, Edward's cousin, stands at Alexandra's right.

Theodore Roosevelt, president of the United States from 1901 until 1909, photographed in 1903 at his summer home, the famous Sagamore Hill in Oyster Bay, Long Island.

Mlle. Modiste, which opened in New York on Christmas night, 1905, was one of the greatest successes of its leading lady, Fritzi Scheff, and of the composer, Victor Herbert. Miss Scheff was constantly called upon to sing the hit song, "Kiss Me Again," for the rest of her long career, and she became so weary of it that she left orders that the song should not be played at her funeral.

David Belasco's *The Girl of the Golden West*, starring Blanche Bates, was a stage hit of 1905. Later the play served as the basis for an opera written by Giacomo Puccini. Romances set in the American West were very popular at the turn of the century. The gentlemanly cowboy became a national hero. Owen Wister's *The Virginian* sold 30,000 copies within five weeks in 1902 and placed high on best seller lists for two years. "Hopalong Cassidy" made his first appearance in a novel by Clarence Mulford in 1908.

Rotten Row, Hyde Park, London, which, as James Bone says (see "Twilight of the Horse"), "was for the horse lover one of the sights of Europe."

Tree Day, which Wellesley College celebrates every year in May, is typical of the graceful pageants that most American women's colleges hold in the spring when the carefully landscaped campus grounds are at their height. The building at the right was destroyed by a spectacular fire in March of 1914. This picture was taken in the spring of 1902.

A number of artists were inspired by the terrible story of the sinking of the *Titanic*, the British luxury liner which ran into an iceberg on its maiden voyage in April of 1912. The *Titanic* carried to their deaths many famous Americans of the era, including John Jacob Astor and Mr. and Mrs. Isadore Straus. Later that month there was a memorial concert at the Metropolitan Opera House in which Caruso, Mary Garden and Lillian Nordica sang. There was a program designed by Charles Dana Gibson.

A section of the grounds of Blenheim Palace, near Oxford, seat of the Dukes of Marlborough, and the richest private house in England. Sir Winston Churchill was born in the Palace in 1874. During the early part of the reign of Edward VII, the Duchess of Marlborough was the American heiress, Consuelo Vanderbilt, who had been married to the Duke with great fanfare in New York in 1895. They separated in 1907.

The enchanting Maude Adams was one of the greatest of the Edwardian era's theater stars. She was probably best known for her interpretations of leading roles in James M. Barrie's *Peter Pan* and *The Little Minister.*

The model and actress, Evelyn Nesbit, became a central figure in one of the Edwardian period's most spectacular murder trials in 1906, when her wealthy and jealous husband, Harry Thaw, shot and killed the celebrated architect, Stanford White, during the performance of a musical play in Madison Square Roof Garden. Thaw, whose family at the time was reputed to be worth some $40,-000,000, was freed in 1915 after a series of trials and appeals and periods spent in asylums.

These fashionable young ladies, described as "daughters of the Tuxedo Smart Set," are all dressed up for the horse show held every year at the wealthy resort town, Tuxedo Park, New York.

Crowds leaving the tennis grounds at Newport Casino after one of the championship matches. The United States national championship matches were held annually at Newport from the 1880's until 1915, when the scene was shifted to Forest Hills, New York.

The Fur Salon at Marshall Field & Company, Chicago, then as now one of the world's leading department stores, photographed about 1900.

Oriental rugs were an almost essential part of the decor in any well-decorated Edwardian home. Marshall Field & Company in 1906 offered a wide selection.

New York's Waldorf-Astoria has long been one of the world's fashionable hotels, and the Waldorf has always had a "Peacock Alley." This photograph was taken when the Waldorf stood at the corner of Fifth Avenue and Thirty-fourth Street where the Empire State Building is now.

Skating has always been one of Central Park's popular attractions. The open country in the background is now the busy residential street, Central Park West.

rough paving stones, in their thin dresses, they would bob around in the cold, while the gentry watched them from the windows above.

Carol singers came from Horningsham who accompanied themselves on hand bells, and a troop of mummers clowned their way through one of the Christmas plays of the locality which date back to Elizabethan days.

Whenever there was a big house party, for shooting or at Christmas, the life of the steward's room was conducted with strict formality. A visiting servant ranked on the same scale as his master or mistress, and his place at table was arranged accordingly. If, for example, a Duke came to stay, his valet would have the honour of arming-in the housekeeper and would be seated at her right; in the same way, the maid of a visiting royalty would go in to dinner on the arm of the hierarchical head, the house steward. Should a visiting servant fail to bring evening dress, he or she would not be allowed to dine in the steward's room but would have to eat in the servants' hall.

The shooting-party luncheons were elaborate affairs. A marquee was put up in the woods where the shoot was being held, and here was served the two-course luncheon, sent out in hay boxes from the kitchens.

I have been looking at menu cards of the Edwardian era. When there were big house parties, six and sometimes seven courses were served for dinner.

The fifth Marchioness of Bath, whose name was Violet, had enchanting menu cards engraved with her monogram and a violet.

Although these meals seem sumptuous compared with those we eat today, they were not always so magnificent. Some visitors who were invited to luncheon at Longleat with the fourth Marquess and Marchioness were surprised to find that there was only boiled mutton followed by a rice pudding. Lord and Lady Bath explained that they were going to France in three days' time, and so they were eating plain food in order to prepare and strengthen their digestive systems for foreign food and the hazards of a Channel crossing.

The normal day at Longleat began with prayers before breakfast, at which the whole family appeared. The staff entered the chapel in single file in order of precedence. The village clergyman officiated. At the morning service every Sunday the maid servants wore their best dresses and little black bonnets tied with ribbons under the chin. One morning, the water from the ponds flooded the chapel and hassocks had to be arranged as stepping-stones down the aisle so that the servants could leave without getting their feet wet.

None of the younger maids was allowed out after dark except to visit her home in Horningsham, the village which lies at the gates of Longleat and which once provided many members of the staff.

The under maids generally had to share bedrooms. The present china cupboard was Bishop Ken's bedroom when he lived at Longleat for twenty years.

Fanny Burney in one of her letters from Longleat describes this room, which must have then been used as a guest room. She writes that it was hung with red velvet, and the housekeeper told her that Bishop Ken came back there to try on his shroud. This room was turned into the china cupboard when a terrified housemaid refused to sleep there any longer because of the visitations of the good bishop.

The footman's uniform which is now shown at Longleat was designed in the eighteenth century. The coat of mustard yellow was worn with a black waistcoat trimmed with silver braid, knee breeches and heavy silk stockings elaborately clocked. State occasions demanded a black hat shaped like an admiral's, braided with silver and decked with one large crested button.

When big house parties were held, the footmen who waited at table wore their hair powdered. The first footman was considered to be the Lady's footman. It was he who stood behind her chair, and any chore that the Lady's maid required to have done for her mistress was his responsibility. When she went out driving he would sit on the box with the coachman—or in later days with the chauffeur—would open and shut the door for her and wrap the fur rug round her knees. If she had dinner in her room, he would carry up her tray.

The third footman was the nursery footman, at the beck and call of the nannies. He usually became a hero of the children and the flirt of the nursery maids. One of these maids once became engaged to the groom of the chambers. The horrified housekeeper said that she could not imagine where they had met. The children however knew that their tryst was the nursery sink; it was here that they met every day to carry on their courting.

The duty of the groom of the chambers was to care for the reception rooms, see that the writing tables were properly equipped, collect the letters for the post, deliver notes and messages, look after the fires and attend to the comforts and needs of the visitors. In the days of the fourth Marquess there was also a courier, who made all the necessary arrangements for journeys and who travelled with the family.

Our grandparents must have led extremely protected and cossetted lives. My husband's grandmother had her loose-change coins washed every day. The valets ironed their gentlemen's boot ribbons; and the morning papers were toasted and ironed before appearing on the breakfast table.

The kitchen gardens lie behind the pleasure grounds, three quarters of a mile away. Each morning an old man, specially appointed for the task, loaded a hand barrow with punnets of whatever fruit was in season, baskets of hot-house grapes, carnations and vegetables which he would wheel up to the house.

A housemaid's work must have been made very arduous by the constant carrying of hot-water jugs, and the laying out and clearing away of the hip baths, which were placed in the bedrooms in front of the fire. There must have been a far greater feeling of comfort in the cosy sight of a copper hot-water jug nestling in a warm white towel, and reflecting the bright lights of a blazing fire than there is in the ugly modern luxury of hot and cold water laid on in the bedrooms.

A housemaid had to change from her morning print dress into a black one with white cap and apron at five o'clock to draw the bedroom curtains and light the fires. Dressed in her print she made the early morning calls. When I think of these happy country-house awakenings I feel a wave of nostalgia, and hear in imagination the noise of curtains being pulled back to let in a shaft of early morning sunshine, which rests on the morning tea tray. The tea set is violet-patterned and there is a plate of wafer-thin bread and butter.

The butler was far too grand a figure to roll up his sleeves and work in his own pantry; and in the dining room he would serve only the wine and the more imposing dishes. Even the house steward would always knock at the pantry door out of respect for the butler.

The house steward appeared in the dining room only to ensure that all was running smoothly. He was also in sole charge of the household accounts.

There is a wage book which dates from 1883–1916. When looking through this I was surprised to find that

Albert Gaillard, the French chef, was paid as much as £130
a year in 1883. Mrs. Potts, the housekeeper, received the
wage of £60 a year. A night watchman received only 15*s.*
a week, and a needlewoman 6*s.* a week.

An odd entry recurs regularly from 1853 to 1861: "To
Mary Morgan for sweeping chimneys." I have heard of
children being employed in this capacity before the good
Lord Shaftesbury came to their rescue, but never of a
woman chimney sweep.

Life at that time must have been very pleasant for the
head servants; and although the under servants were kept
strictly in their place and had little liberty, it must on the
whole have been a merry crowd below stairs. All the old
servants with whom I have discussed that aspect of Longleat life sadly shake their heads as they say: "Those were
the days."

William Meade Prince

———◆◄◆►◆———

Selection from

The Southern Part of Heaven

This is a chapter from Mr. Prince's book, THE SOUTHERN
PART OF HEAVEN, memoirs of his childhood at the turn of
the century in Chapel Hill, North Carolina. At that time
Chapel Hill was a small college town of twelve hundred
inhabitants, including the six hundred students attending
the University of North Carolina.

*U*nfortunately, I have always had a criminal streak, and despite such instances of righteousness as the case of Dr. Kluttz and the fifth caramel, it has got me in trouble more than once. I do not like to think that my criminal streak was larger than that of most little boys: I believe I was about average in resistance to temptation, but little boys, I feel, are born into this tempting world under a great handicap, that of arriving here already little thugs and potential burglars. I have no explanation to offer as to why these evil tendencies are peculiar to my sex; perhaps little girls have them, too, but if so they conceal or stifle them better than little boys. I agree whole heartedly with that part of the old nursery rhyme which claims that little girls are constructed of sugar and spice, et al, but I go even farther than the jingle in my analysis of the ingredients of little boys. Little boys are public enemies and dangers to the community.

The first overt act of my criminal career, insofar as I can recollect (it even antedated the purloining of my friend's marbles, in Richmond), occurred in the somewhat opaque days before we came to Chapel Hill, when we lived in Roanoke and my chief interest in life was Dad's red setter, Rab. In fact, it is one of the only three things of that hazy period which I clearly remember. I remember Rab's silky, sanguine coat and his magnificent head and drooling jaws, and a night Dad took me out on a back porch somewhere (it must have belonged to the house in which we lived, though I have no recollection of the house) while he called and whistled to Rab, who was hidden from sight out in the impenetrable and mysterious darkness. I remember being a little afraid of the black void and imagining the sinister things which might be out there where Rab was.

The second of these three memories is Miss Daisy Wills. I remember her house, all right; it had a lot of gingerbread and jigsaw cornices on it, and a round, towerlike projection with a cupola which hung over the street below, and was a part of Miss Daisy's boudoir. And I remember vividly that Mother took me with her, calling on Miss Daisy, because they were great friends, and Miss Daisy, being not quite dressed, called down to us to come up to her room with the round alcove . . . and Miss Daisy was in her unimagined undergarments. What struck me forcibly and made a lasting and indelible impression upon my youthful consciousness was Miss Daisy's drawers—voluminous affairs of white with ruffles on the bottom. Miss Daisy walked around the room in them, her midriff and superstructure (which was really super) enclosed in a long laced corset, which was just as novel and interesting an article to me as the drawers. I had never seen, and never did see, my mother thus arrayed. This was the important moment in my life when I became aware of the hitherto unsuspected fact that ladies have legs. Miss Daisy was not brazen or even immodest in this display before a gentleman; she just failed to realize the powers of perception and the deep appreciation of the gentleman. I couldn't have been much more than three years old, an age at which children are not supposed to see things, or if they do, remember them. But somehow in bold relief, and starched ruffle detail, the picture formed upon my infant brain, and there it has stuck for more than half a century.

I have never before told anyone about Miss Daisy Wills' drawers.

Third, and clearest of all these three Roanoke recollections, is my stealing of the candy—the first indication I believe I could have given of the evil impulses which dominated me. I said I could remember nothing of the house in which we must have lived, but this is not altogether true: I do remember a fireplace, in awful detail. The mantel was an awesome thing of filigree and gingerbread, with several shelves and levels and projections, and the hearth below it was laid with small and glistening tiles of a green-and-brownish mottled, or curdled, design, quite horrible. These tiles were very slick and smooth and gleaming, baked enamel, probably. Anyway they were hideous things. These nauseating tiles continued up the sides and across the top of the fireplace opening, framed by the malignant mantel. Close on each side of the fireplace sat a light and fragile gilt chair which appeared to be constructed of small golden balls, backed against the mantel frame, purely for decorative purposes and not under any conditions for use, as one was fairly sturdy and the other broken and propped and held together insecurely. It was never worth your while to investigate and find out which was good and which was bad; you just never sat on either.

It all made a hard and brittle and jiggly ensemble. It was of that period of decoration which included the cozy corner and the portieres of glass beads which tinkled as they were thrust aside. I am proud to say that my house never included either of the last named; I would remember if it had, as I was envious of other more ostentatious abodes which boasted them.

There must have been some candy eating, for Mother put two or three pieces of candy in a little china dish and placed it on one of the higher shelves of the mantel out of harm's, and my, way, and said it was for next time.

Shortly thereafter I found the room unoccupied, and temptation was too great. I mounted one of the gilt chairs, the safe, sound one, I was sure, and greedily grasped the little china dish from off the shelf. The chair collapsed in splinters and a shower of little gilt balls, and down I crashed upon the hard, unyielding tiles. The little china dish was smashed to smithereens and one sharp sliver cut me badly between my eyebrow and the eye, just above the ball. I yelled and bled upon the cold and hideous tiles. I don't remember any punishment—I was too badly hurt— but the scar has been with me ever since. I came very close to collaborating with a black patch the rest of my life. This was my first lesson in the consequences of right and wrong, but did I profit by it? Did I learn the poor returns one gets from crime? No.

There was the time in Chapel Hill when I unlawfully entered the pantry and feloniously attempted to appropriate the powdered sugar. I was indirectly steered into the doing of this deed by Mother's cookies, and when I went after the cookies I had no thought of powdered sugar. (The name confectioners' sugar was unknown; we had no confectioners.) Gastronomy has always led to my undoing; my moral fibre, where my stomach is concerned, is weak; and Mother made the best cookies that were ever baked.

Mother was really not any great shakes as a cook— that is a regular cook of regular food—and I am not one to bring up the things that Mother Used to Make, other than her cookies. This lack of culinary skill was not to her discredit; always there was a slavey in the kitchen, that was an accepted fact of life and one you took for granted. Everybody had a cook. Even genteel poverty, if such was your lot, was not genteel unless you had a cook. Not that we were at all poverty-stricken; we did all right. But it was just that any Southern lady of the period, even though she be as poor as Job's turkey, had as soon be caught over a hot cook stove in the kitchen as without her corset cover. What cooking she did was Art—superfluous, of course, but tending toward the finer things—cookies or fudge or some exotic, fancy, chafing dish creation, or putting up preserves or pickles. And desserts. All ladies were experts in desserts. They were theoretical authorities on cooking, but they seldom did the work.

Mother had a wonderful cookbook called *Housekeeping in Old Virginia*, published in Richmond some years after the Civil War. It was a collection of recipes gathered and donated by Virginia ladies in the lean days when the wolf was scratching at their doors, the object of which was to prove that even in such hard times as those one could concoct palatable dishes from poor and makeshift ingredients. There was a foreword to that effect. However, a recipe might start out like this: From the springhouse fetch one qt. sweet cream, into which slowly stir one bottle best Madeira, or: Melt 2 lbs. fresh sweet butter in saucepan for the basting of the pheasant . . . Stuff like that! Mother seldom tried to use any of the recipes. We have the book now, but my wife never uses it; we keep it only as a quaint reminder of what slim rations our sturdy forebears got along on.

Where Mother got her cookie recipe I do not know, but the result would indicate it came straight from Heaven. She made these cookies—tea cakes, she called them—fairly often, and she made not just a pan or so, she made 'em wholesale! Our pantry, where the cookies rested after their ordeal by fire, was large as pantries go, but the cookies filled it. There was a broad workbench or counter around three sides, with shelves above, and on brown paper on this counter Mother spread her cookies, thin and brown and hot, straight from the oven, to crisp and cool. Afterward she filled crocks and tin boxes with them, and the pantry door was locked. I don't like to think that

Mother distrusted me; the fact is the appetites of the entire family, where tea cakes were concerned, were unrefined. Mars' Phil and Mars' Pike could each have eaten a bushel at a sitting, if he could have got them, and of course there was no limit to my capacity. Mother liked them pretty well herself, and even Grandpa ate more of them than you'd think he would.

On the day of which I speak—the one involving the powdered sugar—a fresh batch of cookies had just been laid out in the pantry, and the pantry door carelessly left unlocked. This was very reprehensible of Mother, and eventually caused me, in my innocence, great distress. I entered the unlocked pantry only to snitch a few cookies; there were so many of them a dozen or so would not be missed. I was completely innocent so far as anything beyond this was concerned. In a way, you might say I was framed, for there on the counter beside the cookies was a large jar of powdered sugar.

I was helpless in the face of powdered sugar. My passion for it was blind, unreasoning. I knew it was a luxury, a rare and costly thing we seldom used except to sprinkle tea cakes, and never just to *eat*, and yet here was a whole large jar of it! Perhaps a little of that would go unmissed, also. Guiltily, I thought I heard a board creak, a step approach, and quickly I scooped up a big handful of the snowy dust and crammed it in my mouth. . . .

It was baking soda.

Apparently that lesson did me no good, either, for under almost identical circumstances occurred the episode of Grandpa's sacramental wine. This I knew he kept in a tightly corked jug under the counter in the pantry, and that small amounts of the mysterious dark red liquid were carefully poured out into a smaller container and taken to the church on Communion Sundays where people tasted it in the solemn rite of Holy Communion. I had a great and consuming curiosity concerning this sacramental wine. I asked Mother, one day when we were together in the pantry, if I could taste it and she gave me a very definite and horrified *No!* Not under any conditions, she said, until I was confirmed and became a Communicant. I decided to beat the gun, and when my chance came I slipped into the pantry, reached down in the dimness of the windowless room and grabbed and raised the jug and took a good long swig.

And this time it was vinegar.

Old, strong vinegar. I almost burned and choked to death.

You'd think I would have learned, wouldn't you? That is why my convictions are so strong that little boys, even little boys who Work Hard and May Become President of the United States Someday, have two strikes on them from the start, and just can't help these heinous things. It took another experiment to partly make clear to me that crime is not a remunerative employment; and this digression from the straight and narrow path was really serious. I burgled the Cobbs' house.

I say "I" but it was really "we." I am not trying to shift the blame, understand—that is, not more than half of it—but I did have an accomplice, and, well, you know how easy and pleasant things are if done together. There was a boy named Loren Smith who lived one summer, with his mother, at Mr. Pickard's University Inn. For some reason all my family were still in Chapel Hill while most of my friends were vacationing, and for company I began palling around with this Loren Smith. It was not at all that he was an Evil Companion, or that I was too easily swayed by his big city sophistication (he came from Charlotte), but he did seem to find my usual and favorite pastimes uninteresting and childish, he being a trifle older than I and having had far more experience in the really enjoyable pursuits of life. Anyway, the whole Cobb family was away, and their house shut up and empty, and we took it in our heads to investigate their pantry. There again someone else's carelessness was to blame; their pantry window was unlocked.

I knew that it was wrong—I was quite a big boy then— and I am covered with confusion, telling this, but we climbed through their pantry window from the Cobbs' back porch. It seemed fairly safe to do this, as we scouted around and were sure we could not be seen; there were no other houses within eyeshot, and only the tranquil vegetable garden was in our rear. When we got inside, the pantry did not contain the epicurean treasures we had hoped, however; and we had to settle for a can of salmon (this may have been intended for the Cobbs' cat) and a jar of cherry preserves. Nothing else seemed appetizing or readily movable. After carefully closing the window, just as we found it, we repaired to the woods and consumed our booty. I can't say that it was much of a feast, as—if you have ever tasted the combination, you will agree— canned salmon and cherry preserves without benefit of bread or anything leave something to be desired. But, like stolen apples, we enjoyed it. After a while, except for occasional slight twinges of conscience, I ceased to think about it, and when the Cobb boys came home listened with interest to the tales of their adventures. Collier, in particular, had a fine story of being caught on a great long trestle he was walking across by an onrushing train, and escaping a horrible death by climbing underneath the trestle and hanging by his hands from the cross ties while the train thundered over him. I was glad the Cobbs were home again, and my transgression was practically forgotten.

And then, one day, my grandfather called me in the

study, and told me, very sadly, that Mr. Cobb had been to see him and that he knew all.

What Grandpa said was not all I suffered, either, though that hurt me very much. I really got what was coming to me, and afterwards I was made to go to Mr. Cobb all by myself and apologize most humbly and promise him never, never to do such a terrible thing again. What I could not figure out, however, was how Mr. Cobb knew that Loren Smith and I had done it. . . .

When I went fearfully to him to apologize, Mr. Cobb was fine about it. He said that it was all right and that he hoped it would be a lesson to me and that he knew boys would be boys. This had not occurred to me before, and made me feel a little better, but I told him I felt awful about it, which I did, and that I would reform, completely. He was so nice about it, and patted me on the back, that I screwed up courage to ask him how he found out. He smiled at me and said a little bird told him. I knew it wasn't a bird, and I have wondered many times who it was.

At any rate, I was cured of Unlawful Entry. The informer remained anonymous, and I had the uncomfortable feeling that should I ever do anything of the sort again, unseen eyes would see me, sure as anything. Grandpa told me gravely that even though I thought no one knew, *God* knew, always,—and that sooner or later one always reaped as he had sown. But this did not entirely clear things up, as I felt certain God had not told Mr. Cobb, personally. However, inoculations take, sometimes. Demonstrations really demonstrate, and there was one shameful instance of iniquity in which I was shown the light, forcefully, effectively, and I learned my lesson. It was the case of Edwin Black.

Edwin Black was Mrs. Black's little boy, and Mrs. Black's name and reputation were such as to cause whispering and eyebrow lifting. Even the house the Blacks lived in was a sinful-looking thing, tall and dark and bare. It stood halfway down Windy Hill, back from the road, and always I speculated with a quickened pulse as to what went on behind the broken shutters. The yard was always full of flapping sheets and garments, for Mrs. Black took in washing. This was only a blind, however, and Mrs. Black, a rawboned, knotty individual, spent long days over the washtubs only to make you think her an estimable and God-fearing woman. The truth was, Rumor said, she ran a *Blind Tiger* . . . and running a Blind Tiger, in those days, was the Ultimate Offense. She sold unlawful liquor to Our Boys, as the students were tenderly and sympathetically called, and ruined their bright young lives. I used to look at the baleful Black abode, protected by its wash lines, and wonder when the mob would form and burn it down and lynch the Blacks. Queer, quaint ideas . . . Since then, of course, many of the best friends of all of us have been Blind-Tiger-running bootleggers, and the sin seems not so terrible. In the light of later years I am inclined to make allowances for Mrs. Black: it may be that the income from her washing did not close the gap between the ends, and that to support herself and family she may have occasionally disposed of, for some slight remuneration, an extra jug or so of scuppernong or elderberry wine. But then no such charitable point of view was ours. We boys, along with our elders, thought of the Blacks as well-named outcasts, a disgrace to the community, and their Blind Tiger as a sore and festering spot in our holy habitation. I don't ever remember hearing a specific discussion of their shortcomings in my home, for Grandpa was a very charitable man and no mudslinging went on within his hearing (Mother said Mrs. Black was a fine laundress, but we used Aunt Jinny Johnson, so I had no direct evidence of this point in her favor), but nevertheless the knowledge of the Blacks' perfidy was common.

Mrs. Black's family consisted of two sons. There was no Mr. Black. The two boys were Edwin and his much older brother—whose name I have forgotten. However, I remember other details of him very clearly.

Edwin was about my age, which at that time was nine, a shy, silent boy with enormous dark eyes and a patient, frightened look. I believe now that he must have keenly felt the cloud under which he lived, as he never tried to mix with us; I don't see how he could have helped it, what with the jeers and insults shouted at him, and the rocks thrown. Not that I was any worse about this than the rest of us; we were all little stinkers, unbelievably cruel as only boys can be. I remember hearing Mother say that little Edwin had a face like a choir boy, but I had never seen a choir boy and the description meant nothing to me, and I thought only of his wickedness and the Blind Tiger which his mother ran.

It happened one day when Edwin had been delivering some wash. He emerged onto the quiet, deserted Back Street from the heavy honeysuckle hedge by the Woolens' backdoor. (They lived across from the Abernathys.) The devil prompted me, and I spoke roughly to him. I could almost smell his fear, the way they say dogs can. Self-righteously I gave him a hard shove and he dropped his empty basket and fell in the dust of the street. I don't remember whether I hit him, but that was my intention, in my blind better-than-thouness. Perhaps I didn't have time to start beating him up, for something hit *me!* Something struck and sent me headlong in the road beside the fallen Edwin. . . . It was Edwin's brother. All the things I had intended doing to Edwin, Edwin's brother did to me! And he did them well. Nobody came, nobody pulled him off, and in his righteous rage he gave me almost all that I deserved.

When I got home I would not tell my mother where I got my mauling; I was too ashamed. I could not bear her sympathy and solicitude; she thought I was an innocent little martyr beaten up by bullies, and I could not bring myself to tell her that the only bully was I. I had to take my bitter punishment alone. Thinking of it now, my face gets red and hot.

The cut mouth and the blackened eye I took home with me that day I've always kept. They are very valuable. I learned not only never to pick on somebody when his big brother may be just behind the hedge, but I learned a little, too, about man's inhumanity. That was a lesson, to my body and to my soul, which did me good.

Saki

◆◆◆◆◆

Selection from

The Unbearable Bassington

Comus Bassington, hero (if he can be so called) of Saki's novel, THE UNBEARABLE BASSINGTON, is an Edwardian dandy, the only son of a snobbish, acquisitive woman whose chief ambition is to see Comus make a rich marriage. The penniless Comus falls in love with an heiress, Elaine de Frey, but when he fails to propose, Elaine becomes engaged to his rival, Courtenay Youghal. At luncheon, in the chapter immediately preceding this one, Elaine has promised to marry Courtenay. "Saki" was the pseudonym of H. H. Munro, who was killed in World War I.

*A*fter the momentous lunch at the Corridor Restaurant, Elaine had returned to Manchester Square (where she was staying with one of her numerous aunts) in a frame of mind that embraced a tangle of competing emotions. In the first place she was conscious of a dominant feeling of relief; in a moment of impetuosity, not wholly uninfluenced by pique, she had settled the problem which hours of hard thinking and serious heart-searching had brought no nearer to solution, and, although she felt just a little inclined to be scared at the headlong manner of her final decision, she had now very little doubt in her own mind that the decision had been the right one. In fact, the wonder seemed rather that she should have been so long in doubt as to which of her wooers really enjoyed her honest approval. She had been in love these many weeks past with an imaginary Comus, but now that she had definitely walked out of her dreamland she saw that nearly all the qualities that had appealed to her on his behalf had been absent from, or only fitfully present in, the character of the real Comus. And now that she had installed Youghal in the first place of her affections he had rapidly acquired in her eyes some of the qualities which ranked highest in her estimation. Like the proverbial buyer she had the happy feminine tendency of magnifying the worth of her possession as soon as she had acquired it. And Courtenay Youghal gave

Elaine some justification for her sense of having chosen wisely. Above all other things, selfish and cynical though he might appear at times, he was unfailingly courteous and considerate towards her. That was a circumstance which would always have carried weight with her in judging any man; in this case its value was enormously heightened by contrast with the behaviour of her other wooer. And Youghal had in her eyes the advantage which the glamour of combat, even the combat of words and wire-pulling, throws over the fighter. He stood well in the forefront of a battle which however carefully stage-managed, however honeycombed with personal insincerities and overlaid with calculated mock-heroics, really meant something, really counted for good or wrong in the nation's development and the world's history. Shrewd parliamentary observers might have warned her that Youghal would never stand much higher in the political world than he did at present, as a brilliant Opposition free-lance, leading lively and rather meaningless forays against the dull and rather purposeless foreign policy of Government that was scarcely either to be blamed for or congratulated on its handling of foreign affairs. The young politician had not the strength of character or convictions that keeps a man naturally in the forefront of affairs and gives his counsels a sterling value, and on the other hand his insincerity was not deep enough to allow him to pose artificially and successfully as a leader of men and shaper of movements. For the moment, however, his place in public life was sufficiently marked out to give him a secure footing in that world where people are counted individually and not in herds. The woman whom he would make his wife would have the chance, too, if she had the will and the skill, to become an individual who counted.

There was balm to Elaine in this reflection, yet it did not wholly suffice to drive out the feeling of pique which

Comus had called into being by his slighting view of her as a convenient cash supply in moments of emergency. She found a certain satisfaction in scrupulously observing her promise, made earlier on that eventful day, and sent off a messenger with the stipulated loan. Then a reaction of compunction set in, and she reminded herself that in fairness she ought to write and tell her news in as friendly a fashion as possible to her dismissed suitor before it burst upon him from some other quarter. They parted on more or less quarrelling terms, it was true, but neither of them had foreseen the finality of the parting nor the permanence of the breach between them; Comus might even now be thinking himself half-forgiven, and the awakening would be rather cruel. The letter, however, did not prove an easy one to write; not only did it present difficulties of its own, but it suffered from the competing urgency of a desire to be doing something far pleasanter than writing explanatory and valedictory phrases. Elaine was possessed with an unusual but quite overmastering hankering to visit her cousin Suzette Brankley. They met but rarely at each other's houses and very seldom anywhere else, and Elaine for her part was never conscious of feeling that their opportunities for intercourse lacked anything in the way of adequacy. Suzette accorded her just that touch of patronage which a moderately well-off and immoderately dull girl will usually try to mete out to an acquaintance who is known to be wealthy and suspected of possessing brains. In return Elaine armed herself with that particular brand of mock humility which can be so terribly disconcerting if properly wielded. No quarrel of any description stood between them and one could not legitimately have described them as enemies, but they never disarmed in one another's presence. A misfortunate of any magnitude falling on one of them would have been sincerely regretted by the other, but any minor discomfiture would have produced a feeling very much akin to satisfaction. Human nature knows millions of these inconsequent little feuds, springing up and flourishing apart from any basis of racial, political, religious or economic causes, as a hint perhaps to crass unseeing altruists that enmity has its place and purpose in the world as well as benevolence.

Elaine had not personally congratulated Suzette since the formal announcement of her engagement to the young man with the dissentient tailoring effects. The impulse to go and do so now overmastered her sense of what was due to Comus in the way of explanation. The letter was still in its blank unwritten stage, an unmarshalled sequence of sentences forming in her brain, when she ordered her car and made a hurried but well-thought-out change into her most sumptuously sober afternoon toilette. Suzette, she felt tolerably sure, would still be in the costume that she had worn in the Park that morning, a costume that aimed at elaboration of detail, and was damned with overmuch success.

Suzette's mother welcomed her unexpected visitor with obvious satisfaction. Her daughter's engagement, she explained, was not so brilliant from the social point of view as a girl of Suzette's attractions and advantages might have legitimately aspired to, but Egbert was a thoroughly commendable and dependable young man, who would very probably win his way before long to membership of the County Council.

"From there, of course, the road would be open to him to higher things."

"Yes," said Elaine, "he might become an alderman."

"Have you seen their photographs, taken together?" asked Mrs. Brankley, abandoning the subject of Egbert's prospective career.

"No; do show me," said Elaine, with a flattering show of interest; "I've never seen that sort of thing before. It used to be the fashion once for engaged couples to be photographed together, didn't it?"

"It's very much the fashion now," said Mrs. Brankley assertively, but some of the complacency had filtered out of her voice.

Suzette came into the room, wearing the dress that she had worn in the Park that morning.

"Of course, you've been hearing all about the engagement from mother," she cried, and then set to work conscientiously to cover the same ground.

"We met at Grindelwald, you know. He always calls me his Ice Maiden because we first got to know each other on the skating-rink. Quite romantic, wasn't it? Then we asked him to tea one day, and we got to be quite friendly. Then he proposed."

"He wasn't the only one who was smitten with Suzette," Mrs. Brankley hastened to put in, fearful lest Elaine might suppose that Egbert had had things all his own way. "There was an American millionaire who was quite taken with her, and a Polish count of a very old family. I assure you I felt quite nervous at some of our tea-parties."

Mrs. Brankley had given Grindelwald a sinister but rather alluring reputation among a large circle of untravelled friends as a place where the insolence of birth and wealth was held in precarious check from breaking forth into scenes of savage violence.

"My marriage with Egbert will, of course, enlarge the sphere of my life enormously," pursued Suzette.

"Yes," said Elaine; her eyes were rather remorselessly taking in the details of her cousin's toilette. It is said that nothing is sadder than victory except defeat. Suzette began to feel that the tragedy of both was concentrated in the creation which had given her such unalloyed gratification till Elaine had come on the scene.

"A woman can be so immensely helpful in the social way to a man who is making a career for himself. And I'm so glad to find that we've a great many ideas in common. We each made out a list of our idea of the hundred best books, and quite a number of them were the same."

"He looks bookish," said Elaine, with a critical glance at the photograph.

"Oh, he's not at all a bookworm," said Suzette quickly, "though he's tremendously well-read. He's quite the man of action."

"Does he hunt?" asked Elaine.

"No, he doesn't get much time or opportunity for riding."

"What a pity!" commented Elaine. "I don't think I could marry a man who wasn't fond of riding."

"Of course that's a matter of taste," said Suzette stiffly; "horsey men are not usually gifted with overmuch brains, are they?"

"There is as much difference between a horseman and a horsey man as there is between a well-dressed man and a dressy one," said Elaine judicially; "and you may have noticed how seldom a dressy woman really knows how to dress. As an old lady of my acquaintance observed the other day, some people are born with a sense of how to clothe themselves, others acquire it, others look as if their clothes had been thrust upon them."

She gave Lady Caroline her due quotation marks, but the sudden tactfulness with which she looked away from her cousin's frock was entirely her own idea.

A young man entering the room at this moment caused a diversion that was rather welcome to Suzette.

"Here comes Egbert," she announced, with an air of subdued triumph; it was at least a satisfaction to be able to produce the captive of her charms, alive and in good condition, on the scene. Elaine might be as critical as she pleased, but a live lover outweighed any number of well-dressed straight-riding cavaliers who existed only as a distant vision of the delectable husband.

Egbert was one of those men who have no small talk, but possess an inexhaustible supply of the larger variety. In whatever society he happened to be, and particularly in the immediate neighbourhood of an afternoon-tea table, with a limited audience of womenfolk, he gave the impression of someone who was addressing a public meeting, and would be happy to answer questions afterwards. A suggestion of gaslit mission-halls, wet umbrellas, and discreet applause seemed to accompany him everywhere. He was an exponent, among other things, of what he called New Thought, which seemed to lend itself conveniently to the employment of a good deal of rather stale phraseology. Probably in the course of some thirty odd years of existence he had never been of any notable use to man, woman, child, or animal, but it was his firmly-announced intention to leave the world a better, happier, purer place than he had found it; against the danger of any relapse to earlier conditions after his disappearance from the scene, he was, of course, powerless to guard. 'Tis not in mortals to ensure succession, and Egbert was admittedly mortal.

Elaine found him immensely entertaining, and would certainly have exerted herself to draw him out if such a proceeding had been at all necessary. She listened to his conversation with the complacent appreciation that one bestows on a stage tragedy, from whose calamities one can escape at any moment by the simple process of leaving one's seat. When at last he checked the flow of his opinions by a hurried reference to his watch, and declared that he must be moving on elsewhere, Elaine almost expected a vote of thanks to be accorded him, or to be asked to signify herself in favour of some resolution by holding up her hand.

When the young man had bidden the company a rapid business-like farewell, tempered in Suzette's case by the exact degree of tender intimacy that it would have been considered improper to omit or overstep, Elaine turned to her expectant cousin with an air of cordial congratulation.

"He is exactly the husband I should have chosen for you, Suzette."

For the second time that afternoon Suzette felt a sense of waning enthusiasm for one of her possessions.

Mrs. Brankley detected the note of ironical congratulation in her visitor's verdict.

"I suppose she means he's not her idea of a husband, but he's good enough for Suzette," she observed to herself, with a snort that expressed itself somewhere in the nostrils of the brain. Then with a smiling air of heavy patronage she delivered herself of her one idea of a damaging counterstroke.

"And when are we to hear of your engagement, my dear?"

"Now," said Elaine quietly, but with electrical effect; "I came to announce it to you but I wanted to hear all about Suzette first. It will be formally announced in the papers in a day or two."

"But who is it? Is it the young man who was with you in the Park this morning?" asked Suzette.

"Let me see, who was I with in the Park this morning? A very good-looking dark boy? Oh no, not Comus Bassington. Someone you know by name, anyway, and I expect you've seen his portrait in the papers."

"A flying-man?" asked Mrs. Brankley.

"Courtenay Youghal," said Elaine.

Mrs. Brankley and Suzette had often rehearsed in the privacy of their minds the occasion when Elaine should come to pay her personal congratulations to her engaged cousin. It had never been in the least like this.

On her return from her enjoyable afternoon visit Elaine found an express messenger letter waiting for her. It was from Comus, thanking her for her loan—and returning it.

"I suppose I ought never to have asked you for it," he wrote, "but you are always so deliciously solemn about money matters that I couldn't resist. Just heard the news of your engagement to Courtenay. Congrats to you both. I'm far too stony broke to buy you a wedding present so I'm going to give you back the bread-and-butter dish. Luckily it still has your crest on it. I shall love to think of you and Courtenay eating bread-and-butter out of it for the rest of your lives."

That was all he had to say on the matter about which Elaine had been preparing to write a long and kindly-expressed letter, closing a rather momentous chapter in her life and his. There was not a trace of regret or upbraiding in his note; he had walked out of their mutual fairy-land as abruptly as she had, and to all appearances far more unconcernedly. Reading the letter again and again, Elaine could come to no decision as to whether this was merely a courageous gibe at defeat, or whether it represented the real value that Comus set on the thing that he had lost.

And she would never know. If Comus possessed one useless gift to perfection it was the gift of laughing at Fate even when it had struck him hardest. One day, perhaps, the laughter and mockery would be silent on his lips, and Fate would have the advantage of laughing last.

James Bone

———◆◆◆◇◆◆◆———

"TWILIGHT OF THE HORSE"

from *London Echoing*

$\mathcal{T}$he whole appearance of the London street suffered a change more sudden and more drastic in Edward the Seventh's short reign than any change in a generation in London's long history. When he was crowned the horse was as necessary and pervading a part of the capital as it had been at any time since Boadicea had driven her team across Londinium. When Edward's reign ended the horse bus had almost vanished and the hansom cab and fourwheeler lingered as curiosities while the cart-horse and van horse were a dwindling remnant of their old strength. The two world wars, particularly, of course, the last with its petrol scarcity, led to revivals in work-horse traffic but never to the horse's return to bus or charabanc or cab.

At King Edward's Coronation the horse was supreme. True, the early motor cars had been relieved in 1896 of the necessity of a chaperon with a red flag, and experimental motor buses had appeared, but the horse-bus driver's saucy remark to the engineers working on the stranded motor bus, 'Didn't I tell you to take it 'ome— and now ye can't!' was thought to cover the situation for good. Hyde Park was then for the horse-lover one of the sights of Europe. Thousands of victorias and landaus and family coaches with sleek horses, coachmen and footmen in livery and cockade, took the air; and the Row at its proper times had its battalions of riders which included Mr. Cunninghame Graham and many children who seemed to have come out of John Leech's albums. Four-in-hands met on appointed days and drove in a stately way to Richmond or Ascot, but these were revivals not survivals. Hansoms, glossy black for three-quarters of the year and in summer with a gay tasselled trapping on top, pervaded the town. These summer trappings were generally made by the drivers' wives as the Venetian gondola cabin-covers are made by the wives of the gondoliers, and one often wondered if that set Disraeli's mind to his famous image of the hansom as the London gondola.

Tattersall's flourished and Mr. Soapy Sponge and the world of fashion attended there. Donkeys, which seem now to have vanished from the earth and Guildford market, enlivened the poorer streets and songs about them roared through music halls. Lord Lonsdale himself made awards to the owners of the best-looking donkeys. Lord Rothschild presented on his birthday a brace of pheasants or partridges from his big shoots to every London busdriver, and the bus-drivers wore his colours on their whips that day. On boat-race day they sported dark blue or light blue on their whips according to their fancy. On St. Patrick's Day Irish hansom cabmen had a flick of green ribbon on their whips and nosegays of shamrocks. Householders laid down straw in front of their houses when there was serious illness there and the buses were walked past. An appeal was made for it to be done when Arnold Bennett lay dying in his Baker Street flat. I remember seeing the buses drop piously to a walk as they passed the lit-up church of St. Clement Danes at evening service.

The establishment of the railways in Victorian times, even the London underground railway and the Tuppenny Tube, had not seriously affected anything beyond outer suburban traffic. People still went by horse bus to Streatham and Greenwich and Hampstead. At the foot of Haverstock Hill your Hampstead bus increased its horse power by a 'unicorn' which there was harnessed ahead of the

pair 'oss and led the team up the hill. Arriving in the end
at the Bird in Hand Tavern in the Hampstead High
Street, the 'unicorn' received a handful of shrimps and
then trotted downhill past the Sir Richard Steele and the
Haverstock to his post near the Adelaide to await his next
task.

The first electric motor bus was licensed in 1897 and
the first petrol-driven bus in 1899. These were only experiments, but in 1904 the London General Omnibus Company established a regular service and in 1911 it with-
drew its last horse bus which moved between Moorgate
Street and London Bridge (how I remember my admiration
when I first sat next a bus-driver who lit his segar with one
match and one hand one blowy day driving across London
Bridge!). The last regular horse bus in town ran, I think,
from Somerset House to Waterloo in 1916.

Even after the last London General horse bus made its
last journey some other bus companies still held their
horses. The Associated Omnibus Company ran their dark
green 'Favourites' from The Monster at Pimlico to The Angel at Islington, threading the narrows of Chancery Lane,
and their 'Royal Blues' plied up Bond Street ultimately to
reach King's Cross, while their yellow buses trotted to
Camden Town. They vanished in 1912 and with them
went a yet more picturesque cavalcade of the road. Tillings till then ran a four-in-hand bus from Balham to the
City every secular morning. It was a satisfactory sight as it
trotted over London Bridge at half-past nine of a morning
—four spirited horses, the bus loaded with the nearest
George the Fifth's London had to the Cheerybles and
Linkinwaters and the drivers were of the ripest type. The
passengers were a sort of family party who knew one another well and the right things to say on a four-in-hand on
a frosty morning. Those passengers petitioned Tillings to
continue the service, but that was not to be. 'Old Tom,'

the driver, drove on for a bit on the Clapham-Richmond route and then vanished. When did the last horse bus stop? No record has come down to us when the last public sedan chair was withdrawn. (One survived at the service of an aged lady in Hampton Court's stony passages long after Victoria's reign.) I think 1916 saw London's last horse bus and when it went the middle-aged felt suddenly much older, for its survival was like something on the stretched elastic of time and when it snapped their epoch seemed shrunken and remote. With the horse bus we parted sharply with the last animate link with Dickens's London.

A last scene in the departure of the bus horse echoes in my memory. Their occupation gone, the London General's horses were sold in the Harrow Road repository, about a hundred and fifty horses a day. The sale was a strange one and the attendance included many types of men that one thought could hardly survive beyond the bus horse era. Many old bus-drivers could be discerned, their knobby hands still wearing their useful stained gloves, and their faces marked and patched by the weather without and the internal toll paid by their cramped bodies. With them were thinner, more active, and even horsier men, the horsekeepers and stable hands, and a few compulsorily retired hansom-cab drivers, a melancholy group in shabby clothes of a buckish cut. One of them wore a high-waisted yellow coat, belcher tie, curly tall hat, dog-skin gloves and brown gaiters, but everything was dirty and out of gear, and his bold handsome face had a raffish, dangerous look. Seedy men with a horsey cut of a meaner kind stood about raking the tan with their boots and spitting to keep off the bad luck that was already upon them. Some of these carried coils of rope over their shoulder, not to hang themselves with in the empty stables when the last of the horses had gone, but to lead them home for the purchasers.

Everyone seemed to have got up too early that morning to have time for a shave, except a score of broad, comfortably dressed men in blue melton coats who looked like town horse dealers, and the same number of flashier publicans and tradesmen, and about a dozen other placeless men, who did most of the bidding. The horses were run along the hall with a 'Hi! Mind your backs,' the groom running beside them with a short whip, which he used unobtrusively with a back-hand flick under the horse's belly, causing unexpected shows of spirit. The sun streamed through the dirty skylight at the far end, and it was curious to see the heavy palpable bus horse as it reached the dust-laden beams become pale and insubstantial as a ghost or a memory, the memory it was so soon to be.

The hansom cab lingered much longer, indeed a magnate of the Cable and Wireless Company had a smart one in the last years of the Second War when petrol restrictions were at their worst, and elderly Londoners would cock their ears as they heard the old clip-clop, clip-clop, jingle jingle, arising on the streets again. But in 1912 there were only four hundred of them in London of the 7600 that pervaded the town at the turn of the century. Half a dozen stragglers were on the cab rank opposite the Café Royal in Regent Street in the 'twenties, and later and on rainy nights a hansom would wait outside the Garrick Club in Covent Garden, in case Sir Squire Bancroft thought of driving home to Albany.

The drivers were a stiff-necked, sporting class of men, and had they accepted the taximeter they might have made a long fight of it as the Paris *fiacres* drivers did, but prudence was not their style. 'Toss you for the fare—double or quits!' was a challenge they rarely refused. Some of them learnt to drive motor cabs but most of them went down, so to speak, with their whips flying; a few became what they affected most to despise—a gardener! In cabmen's quarrels 'gardener' was the utmost term of contempt. This derived from the days when the family coachman was ill or had a day off and the gardener drove the carriage and wasn't so good at it. One recalls a fracas with whips in Fetter Lane between two hansom-cab drivers just because the one had called to the other 'Ga on—gardener!'

'Clarences' mechanical power, 19' was how motor cabs first humbly appeared in 1905 in the London statistics. Five years later the hansoms were 2000 and the taxicabs no longer 'Clarences' were 6397. In 1912 a hansom cab was added to the London Museum. One wonders if hansom cabmen—there were 400 of them still driving—came to look at it and scratched their heads! It must have seemed a very palpable hint! There would be sad faces in the snugs in Gray's Inn Road in that year.

Builders of private hansom cabs, once as proud of their 'gondolas' as Fyfe's or Herreshoff's were of their yachts, were closing their shops or turning to motor cars. In 1907, in Birmingham, where Joseph Aloysius Hansom was born, a big hansom-cab builder failed in his business and London's best builder had only one cab in his showroom and no orders for a month. Queen Victoria herself bought one in 1887, but history alas! tells us absolutely nothing of Her Majesty driving in it, nor, for the matter of that, does Sir Maximilian Beerbohm! King Edward, when Prince of Wales, used his own hansom habitually between 1880 and 1890, and many grandees, lords and commoners kept their own hansoms into this century, some even illicitly drove them. Premier Lord Rosebery was the last well-known man in London to sport a cabriolet. There is a story of a French fashionable man visiting London in the 'nineties who recorded his complete impressions of London to a friend in these words, 'I love hansom cabs and they are still playing "Dorothy"!'

The best and the worst of what was once the pride of London were sold off in their hundreds as 'scrap,' even those private beauties that had cost two hundred pounds only a few years before. Thirty shillings apiece was the usual price, their elegant shiny bodywork for firewood, the shafts and wheels for traps and vans, the springs for tradesmen's carts.

The horse bus and the hansom had one thing in common that made the London street more human and more public than it has ever been since their passing. In the bus, the driver and the outside passengers sat high and free over the street, able to see all that went on around them. It was like a seat in a circus or on a grandstand as you sat and had your entertainment through the changing streets. True, there was the rain at times, but there were also the sky and the great buildings and the monuments before you. A swarm of buses with crowded tops held up by the policeman's orchestral hand gave an impressive seated audience for an incident—the passing by of a great visitor or a coster's donkey-cart upset. Crossing the street before such a hold-up you felt the eye of London was upon you, as one has never felt it since.

With the hansom, the driver on his high perch presided over the street, but the fare, or better the fares—for to the young of those days the advantage of the hansom was there was no room for a chaperon—sat high and looked over the horse at the happenings of the street and felt themselves part of it which no one can feel in a taxicab even with the top open. How Piccadilly used to glitter in those days as you looked down or up its gentle hills as the cavalcades pranced before you with the mansions and hotels and shops painted for the season and the window boxes of flowers all ablowing! The passing of the hansom was a peculiar loss, the tall, delicately poised carriage, shining black, with the driver commanding cab and horse from his lofty seat, and the slender whip rising high above all, was one of the most decoratively satisfying things that London has ever produced. It was like an invention from the beautiful attenuated art of Whistler, who always brought a hansom into his lithographs when he could. Its praises have been sung by many a cunning writer. Without the hansom Stevenson's *New Arabian Nights* would lose much of its haunting London flavour. Richard Le Gallienne's couplet, too, is haunting as a poetic young man's conception of hansoms at night in the Strand when he first came to town:

> Like dragon-flies the hansoms hover
> With jewelled eyes to catch the lover.

But even after the motor bus was pulsating over all the London streets the most urgent and dramatic of our street services still held to the horse. Not till 1911 was all the Fire Brigade changed to motor traction. I think I can remember the very moment when the need for transition was publicly manifested. It was one afternoon and the fire engine drawn by two fiery horses had swung round from Theobald's Road into Southampton Row. The firemen, still buttoning their tunics, shouted their 'Hi-hi-hi', their bell was ringing madly and the horses were rushing at full speed. A grand sight! The traffic drew in to either side of the road and stopped to leave a clear way, but there were so many vehicles that the motor bus I was travelling in had some way to go to reach an empty space at the street side. The driver accelerated hard and on we went. But when we reached a clear berth what was happening? The cries of 'Hi-hi-hi!' and the ringing of the bell were hardly heard. The conductor looked back and took a historic decision. He rang his bell signalling right ahead, the motor bus rushed on leaving the fiery horses and the shouting firemen and the Victorians' last effort far behind. After that the horsepower was in the engines.

The King still drives to open Parliament in the gilded royal coach with its tall horses, and at the last Coronation one seems to remember that the Speaker's coach re-emerged, but owing to its weight and the absence of brakes and the presence of inclines in the Processional Way, it had to take a lonely detour for part of the route.

But only in one proud survival does the horse keep its old supremacy in London City. That is, of course, with the Lord Mayor's coach which will surely be drawn by its six horses as long as that 'mighty carbuncle of valour and worth' still reigns at the Guildhall. The shadow of the motor car, oddly enough, first fell on the Lord Mayor's Show in 1896 just after the red flag attendance had been abolished when a motor car astoundingly appeared in the Procession. But it was nearly a generation after that before the worshipful liverymen and their beadles drove in state in worshipful motor cars.

The most unlikely survival of all horse transport was the Royal Mail Coach to Brighton which took the road at night until the June of 1905. Few people knew of it for it carried no passengers, only Post Office parcels. This old arrangement lingered on in the Post Office economy because it was cheaper up to that time to carry the parcels by coach instead of by rail. Let me repeat from what I wrote at the time about the mail coach's last journey to Brighton for, as it happened, I was on it.

It was the best of nights for the last run of the Brighton Mail Coach, being Derby night in June in King Edward's third year when the old life of the road was flooding back into its empty channels and every decent inn on the southward roads had its string of waiting horses and coaches and traps. On the morrow a new motor van was to take up the run. We rattled down the cobbled yard in the Dickensian region of Guy's Hospital, near London Bridge, that was then the parcels department of the Post Office, with hardly an official word of farewell, and out into the swarming Borough High Street at ten minutes to ten, in a desperate downpour of rain. Charabancs,

slap-up four-in-hands, donkey-carts, and all manner of
traps were straggling to London Bridge; the driver bore
along very carefully until we swung into the Brixton Road
and soon we had left the main stream of the Epsom traffic.

The big coach, with the tarpaulin over the hampers on
its roof making a shape rather like a haystack, moved up
the hill very nicely; you looked down on a tramway car-
line with a horse on each side of it, and heard the steady
patter of hoofs and movement of the chains. They were
old stagers who had served for years on the same road, and
the coachman trusted them. Streatham slipped past,
then the electric-lit Common and stucco-faced Norwood.
The driver and the guard talked together of the places
they passed, recalling incidents that were to assist their
midnight conversation for the last time. The guard
pointed out the duck pond in which the coach had found
itself one foggy night ten years ago; a turn of the road
here recalled the driver's memory to the second time he
had driven the coach, when he had had the misfortune to
topple it over. He had been a 'temporary driver' on the
coach for some fifteen years, but his main business was
with the Tunbridge Wells Coach. The guard, a polite, responsible man, had seen seventeen years of the Brighton
road.

We had now left our first team at the Old Windsor Cas-
tle at Croydon ('James Selby's stage,' said the driver) and
were seeing the last of the electric street cars and the
lights of London. The rain had ceased, and the night was
dark, with a few stars. The villages lay quite dark, and
there was no sound on the road but the patter of hoofs
and the roll and creak of the coach. After the rain the
scent of hawthorn came keenly from the roadside mixed
with fainter scents of lilac and laburnum. Our five noble
lamps glimmered on the moving quarters of the horses and
blanched the hedges. From the high box seat one looked
down on the grey trail of the road and the dark country

and breathed in the fresh May night, and agreed with the driver in his views on motor cars. Who could smell haw-thorn from a train or a motor car? Our route lay by Hor-ley, Crawley, Cuckfield and Hassocks. We were scheduled to cover it in seven hours, including half-an-hour stop-pages, and this had been kept so exactly that people on the route had revived the custom of setting their watch by the appearance of the coach.

At Horley we stopped at the cross-roads beside the old Chequers Inn. As it was the last night the women-folk of the horse-minders were waiting in a sad little body be-side the local van to say goodbye to the driver. As we waited the Brighton up-coach came thundering in with its lights shining and horses very fresh and sportive after their twelve-mile stage. The two great coaches, the relays of horses, and the little group of women and ostlers gathered together at the dark cross-roads formed as picturesque a sight as the road could show in its palmiest days, but al-ready it seemed a thing of the past. 'Good nights' and 'Farewells' were shouted to the up-coach, to which our coachman had transferred himself, and it sped away into the darkness.

Our new coachman was telling how Brighton had turned out to see the last of the up-coach and had sung 'Auld Lang Syne,' and this had been repeated at the villages on the route. His coat had only two buttons, for his admir-ers had cut off the others, and also the tab of his collar and other little things, as relics. This coachman, as it could easily be gathered, was a great figure on the road. His ap-pearance recalled an older type than the crop-headed driver of our time. He had a tall, portly figure which he carried with an air, his hair was rather long, with a slight curl, such as one sees in pictures of 'Corinthians,' his clean-shaven face was of one pink tone, and altogether he was as hearty-looking a man as one could wish to sit be-side; and he handled his cattle like an artist. He was proud of the fact that he never used his whip and asked me to mark how he took his horses up a steep hill with only a word or two, bringing them to the top exactly as they began it. He accepted the question what his whip was for as distinctly a poser, and then smiled and said that you must have a whip, and, holding the whip at an angle, the lash wrapped round the middle, he added slowly, 'Com-plete.'

He was particularly fond of one of his horses called Nigger, which, like most horses, had a curious personality of his own; he carried his head like the knight on the chessboard, and had an odd quick high action, raising his knees to an absurd height. You thought no horse could keep it up for a mile, but Nigger pranced on without a break for his ten-mile stage. I was told that Nigger did not like anyone to speak to his driver, and he seemed very fidgety during the conversation. The coachman described the kind of punishments he considered suitable to anyone who used a whip on Nigger. With Nigger were Daisy, Nobby and Old Mary, a grand team, and at one bit the coachman—this being the last night—'set 'em alight,' and we had a touch of the great days, racing along for ten minutes at something like sixteen miles an hour, and for twenty minutes at twelve miles, which, with a three-ton coach and load, was something to talk about. He spoke of James Selby's memorable run of the 104 miles to Brighton and back in seven hours fifty seconds, and of Lord Lonsdale's great twenty miles in fifty-five minutes on Lowfield Heath. The coachman pointed out that road.

It was now daylight, and we had heard the first thrush piping her morning song. (Whoever heard the morning song of a thrush from a train or motor?) The sun was bright when we crossed the South Downs and drew down towards Brighton. Famous old coaching and pugilist inns like the rambling King's Head, and a host of other relics of the Regency days and the reign of fancy, old manor-houses, like Cuckfield House, the original of 'Rockwood,' crazy fragrant villages and windmills sunk behind us, and we could feel the breath of the sea in the distance. Aged shepherds and cottagers hobbled to the doors, people waited at cross-roads, and early farmers drew up as the great red coach raced along the road for the last time. 'Goodbye, Mr. Garnham—goodbye; farewell to you!' The coachman made his replies with his whip. He was of the third generation of coachmen, and could perhaps express himself best through his whip.

In the excitement of the night the guard had forgotten his horn, so only our wheels and horse-hoofs raised the echoes as we ran into Brighton, where another company were gathered to see the end of the last run of the Brighton Mail Coach.

The last hoof-sounds of the Brighton Mail Coach were heard on the road in 1905. Forty years after, hoofs still beat on the London streets and in the Second War there were more of them than a decade before, for horses were drummed up from all parts to help in the petrol shortage, though harness and stables were hard to find. Enough horse vans and carts survived, however, to produce a glimmer of the old parade of horses and vehicles on Easter Monday revivals in Regent's Park. At the Lord Mayor's Show cart-horses still pull the weighty gilded coach; the Mounted Police can still find nothing so good and high and mobile as the horse for their work in crowds; Hyde Park has still a few morning riders where squadrons of horsemen used to thump and scamper along and rein up to form equestrian avenues when Victoria drove down the Row. But the Twilight of the Horse is fading fast out of the London scene. In another generation a horse may only be something the average Londoner hears about from a tipster, or sees in the television of a race!

Gene Fowler

------◄─●─►------

"THE UNSINKABLE MRS. BROWN"

from *Timber Line*

$\mathcal{M}$rs. Margaret Tobin Brown encountered the hoots of her Western sisters. But she hoisted herself by the bootstraps of heroism into huge *Denver Post* headlines.

Molly Brown was as naïvely colorful as she was brave. She mistook her own enormous zest for a symptom of artistic ability, her ingenuous thirst for human relationship as evidence of social grace. She was received abroad by titled big-wigs because of her lack of worm-eaten sophistication. That selfsame lack barred her from the portals of a Denver society that was as hidebound as it was provincial.

This vital Amazon lived a novel of Eulenspiegel dimensions. Her father was old Shaemus Tobin. Molly liked to fancy her sire an Irish peer, but he was in fact a tin-roof Celt of the Missouri River bottoms. Old Shaemus was a man more ready of song than of cash, red-haired and tempestuous.

A cyclone occasioned Molly's birth two months before the laws of nature warranted such an event. The mother, father and two sons had skurried into a cellar while the twister tucked their shanty under its arm and raced like a monstrous half-back over a gigantic field.

Old Shaemus fashioned a crude incubator for the seven-months baby, then collected a new supply of scantlings and tin cans for another shanty. The mother died and Shaemus borrowed a goat as Molly's wet nurse.

Molly's premature arrival on earth was in key with her aggressive temperament, but the frailty of the tiny infant in no way augured a maturity of power and red-headed vigor. She grew up in the river bottoms near Hannibal, Missouri, hated house work—particularly that of a shanty— and spent all her days hunting in winter and fishing in summer.

When she was twelve years Molly became acquainted with Mark Twain. Mr. Clemens, too, had been fishing. He at once saw her for what she was, a female *Huckleberry Finn*. He admired her flaming red pigtails, her almost fierce blue eyes, and invited her to fish from his rowboat. She delightedly gave up her home-made raft to angle from the bow of the author's punt.

Mr. Clemens found that Molly didn't have the most remote idea that she was a girl. She could whistle like a calliope, and before Mr. Clemens could gather his celebrated wits together, she had disrobed completely and dived overboard, with an absence of mock modesty that characterized her entire life. She engaged in porpoise-like maneuvers, laughing and shouting and blowing water, but came to grief. Her head got stuck in the mud, and Mr. Clemens pulled her out, half drowned.

She looked like some weird clay model as he began scraping mud from her eyes. He helped her on with her garments, and from that day, Mark Twain was Molly's god.

When Molly was fifteen, she concluded that the shanties of Hannibal held no promise of adventure. She and her brothers packed a single carpet bag and ran away from home. They traveled by stagecoach to Colorado, arriving in the gold camp of Leadville.

She did not know how to cook—nor did she wish to learn that art—but went to work as a "pot-walloper" in the cabins of miners. She washed their dishes, rearranged the bedding on their bunks, and sometimes acted as nurse for sour-dough prospectors. She and her brothers pitched a discarded tent at the end of State Street, a noisy avenue of honeytonks, saloons with long bars and gambling hells.

The rigors of the mining camp only strengthened the body and courage of this illiterate hoyden. Three weeks after her arrival she met and married John J. Brown, called "Leadville Johnny" by intimates at the Saddle Rock Saloon in Harrison Street.

Leadville Johnny was thirty-seven years old, as homely as a hippopotamus—although not so fat—unlettered, open-fisted, and had red hair. He seldom was in funds, but when luck infrequently came his way was foremost among the belly-up-to-the-bar boys. Homely or not, he had a way with the dance-hall girls.

In less than two months after his marriage to fifteen-year-old Molly, Leadville Johnny struck pay dirt. He was offered three hundred thousand dollars *cash* for his claim. He accepted, imposing but one condition.

"Pay me off in thousand-dollar bills," he said. "I want to take it home and toss it into the lap of the prettiest gal in this here camp."

He came bellowing into the cabin, did a bear dance with his young wife, then gave her the money, all of it. He found it necessary to explain at length just how much money three hundred thousand dollars was—a genuine fortune! Her mind did not go beyond a silver dollar at most.

"I wanted you to see it; to hold it," he said. "That's why I didn't put it in a safe. But you got to hide it, even if it is all yours."

"Where?" asked Molly.

"You figure that out, honey. It's yours. I'm goin' down to celebrate at the Saddle Rock."

He kissed her and was gone to receive the back-slap-pings of Saddle Rock pals. In an hour he had forgotten he was a rich man; he was having such a good time of it. He stayed at the saloon until early morning and was brought home by two of his intimates. He was sober enough to make two requests. One was that the "boys" would not disturb his pretty young wife; the other that they fetch some kindling and start a fire.

"I'm freezin' plumb to death," said Leadville Johnny.

The boys put him on a bunk, then made a fire. Molly, rousing from deep sleep, had an uneasy feeling. She sniffed as the new fire sent wisps of smoke through crev-ices of the stove. She felt the mounting heat. Then she screamed. She got up, while her husband's pals retreated hastily from the cabin. She scorched her fingers on the stove lids. She couldn't find a lifter and used a steel-pronged fork instead. She almost set herself and the cabin on fire. She delved among the burning sticks, but it was too late. Of all places, she had hidden the money in the stove, and now her fortune had gone up the flue; three hundred thousand dollars floating in the Leadville morn-ing sky.

Johnny rallied somewhat and announced that he was freezing to death. Then he wanted to know if his wife was freezing, too. If so, she should come sleep beside him. For half an hour she wept, yammered and howled in his ear. When it did penetrate his haze that the money had been burned, he sat up and said:

"Don't you worry a bit, honey, I'll get more. Lots more." Then he reiterated the fact—or fancy—that he was freezing plumb to death.

Molly began to shower kisses on Leadville Johnny's red head, his face and lips. It appears that she had not been screaming and wailing because of the lost fortune, but from fear that her husband would be angry.

When Johnny sobered up next morning, he actually *laughed* about the loss. "It just goes to show how much I think of you," he said. "There's plenty more."

"Lots of men would be mad," she said.

Leadville Johnny slapped his chest grandly. "Mad? I'll show you how mad I am. As soon as I get a drink into me, I'll go right out and get a bigger and better claim. Where'd you put that bottle, honey?"

Fantastic as it may seem, Leadville Johnny went out that very afternoon and located "The Little Johnny," one of the greatest producers of gold in Colorado history. It is estimated that he took twenty million dollars from this bonanza.

"Nope," he said to the men who had bought his other property, "I won't sell this one."

"There's another three hundred thousand if you do," his bidders said.

"Nope, let's have a drink instead."

"Why won't you sell?"

He slapped his chest. "I don't trust chimneys. It's safer in the ground."

The meaning of money began to dawn on Molly. It was the commencement, critics said, of her progress from Leadville to lorgnettes. The Browns moved "up the hill," where mine owners and bankers had mansions. Leadville Johnny went the limit in building a house for his bride. As a climactic touch, he laid concrete floors in every room of the house, and embedded silver dollars, edge to edge, in the cement surfaces!

Leadville now was not big enough to hold Molly. She had heard of Denver society, of the gay balls and salons.

"Denver it is, then," said Johnny. "Just name the thing you want, and Big Johnny (slapping his chest) and Little

Johnny (pointing in the direction of his claim) will get it for you."

The Browns built a mansion in Pennsylvania Avenue, Denver's Capitol Hill, where the *élite* resided. Leadville Johnny contemplated paving this place with *gold pieces*, but was dissuaded. He compromised by having two huge lions made by a cemetery sculptor. The lions were placed flanking the doorway.

The new mansion was a "show place," where rubberneck—"Seeing Denver"—buses paused and tourists stared while a spieler narrated the drama of the Little Johnny. Inside its stone halls, conniving spongers and fake grand dukes partook of the Brown bounty. But so inexhaustible were the Little Johnny's veins that the attacks of these leeches were hardly felt.

The town's preening dowagers would have none of this red-headed upstart from the hills. Not one of them—their own husbands but once removed from the pick-handle and the stope—was kind enough to advise Molly in her social adolescence. Still in her teens, unschooled and impetuous, how was she to know the emptiness of display?

She hired the largest orchestras, gave the costliest balls, drove the finest horses, but met with snobbery. She often attended, uninvited, the social functions of her neighbors. Indeed, she became such a nuisance as a "gate crasher" that the ladies decided to crush her.

As part of a cat-like hoax, Molly was solicited to write a dissertation on Denver society. This she did, laboring at a desk inlaid with gold from the Little Johnny shaft. Her husband admitted his inability to judge literary works, but said he guessed she knew what she was doing.

"As for me," said Leadville Johnny, "I'd rather be back this minute at the Saddle Rock."

Molly's "article" appeared in a magazine owned and edited by Polly Pry. The effort was published, word for word, as written by Mrs. J. J. Brown. She was very proud of it until the whole of the city's upper crust began heaving with merriment. The new author's misspellings, fantastic verbiage and artless philosophies were there for all to see.

At last conscious of her ignorance, and shamed by her social shortcomings, Molly left town. Johnny said he guessed he'd stay home.

"I never knowed how to spell and never claimed to," he said, "and as far as society is concerned, I ain't aimin' that low. Good-bye, honey, and don't forget the name of our bank. It's all yours."

Denver saw nothing of Mrs. Brown for nearly eight years, and heard little. It was something of a sensation, then, when she returned to the city, gowned in Parisian creations. More, the word spread that Molly had two French maids, with whom she conversed fluently in their native language. Indeed, during seven and a half years in European capitals, she had become proficient in five languages—she who had left town unable to spell in English!

There were other incredible surprises for the hometowners. Molly had made friends with the Divine Sarah Bernhardt, had received stage lessons, and even contemplated playing the Bernhardt rôle in *L'Aiglon*. She had received instruction in painting and singing and had appeared with some success in a charity concert in London and had sung aboard an ocean liner on the voyage from Southampton to New York City.

The hardest blow to her critics, however, was the fact that celebrities and titled foreigners made the Brown home their headquarters while visiting Denver.

But despite her education in the polite arts, Molly

Brown's real nature was manifest at all times. She permitted herself the luxury of forthright speech, and, if in the mood, used slang and cursed like a pit boss. Her detractors, still unable to stomach her social ambitions, described her as "eccentric."

"Sure I'm eccentric," she said. "But I have a heart as big as a ham."

When Leadville Johnny refused to "gad about" in Europe and elsewhere, they separated. But he never shut her off from his great purse. He still loved and wanted her to have a good time. All he desired for himself was privacy and the privilege of sitting with his shoes off in the parlor.

Mrs. Brown acquired a seventy-room house and estate near New York City. She entertained the Astors and other Eastern notables—all of which agonized her Denver scoffers.

In April of 1912, the home town which had refused flatly to receive Molly as a social equal, passionately acclaimed her as its very own celebrity. The *S. S. Titanic* had gone down, and Molly had been its heroine.

Suddenly her virtues were sung in nearly every paragraph of a front-page layout in the *Post*. She became known as "The Unsinkable Mrs. Brown." The New York press called her "The Lady Margaret of the *Titanic*."

Now that Mrs. Brown had received the accolade in alien fields, her townsmen's praises resounded like songs in a beer stube.

The tardy cheers for Mrs. Brown were in keeping with the psychology of the provinces. Similarly, Eugene Field had been tolerated as an amiable prankster, a thistle-down jingler and something of a sot during his Denver interlude. Then, his fame having been certified abroad, and death having corroborated his genius, Denver was the first of cities to rear a monument to his memory.

Perhaps it was an instinctive feeling for another free

and generous soul that led Mrs. Brown to purchase Field's old Denver home and set it aside, a shrine for children.

Mrs. Brown was thirty-nine years old when she left Liverpool for New York on the *Titanic's* maiden voyage. Instead of a girlish slimness, she now was ruggedly and generously fleshed. Nevertheless, she still bubbled with a seldom-varying vitality.

She sang in the ship's concert and was popular with the traveling notables despite her growing eccentricities. She amused some and terrified others with pistol-feats, one of which consisted of tossing five oranges or grapefruits over the rail and puncturing each one before it reached the surface of the sea.

Although she spent great sums on clothes, she no longer paid attention to their detail or how she wore them. And, when she traveled, comfort, and not a desire to appear *chic*, was her primary consideration.

So, when Molly decided to take a few turns of the deck before retiring, she came from her cabin prepared for battle with the night sea air. She had on extra-heavy woolies, with bloomers bought in Switzerland (her favorite kind), two jersey petticoats, a plaid cashmere dress down to the heels of her English calfskin boots, a sportsman's cap, tied on with a woolen scarf, knotted in toothache style beneath her chin, golf stockings presented by a seventy-year-old admirer, the Duke Charlot of France, a muff of Russian sables, in which she absent-mindedly had left her Colt's automatic pistol—and over these frost-defying garments she wore a sixty-thousand-dollar chinchilla opera cloak!

If anyone was prepared for Arctic gales, Mrs. Brown was that person. She was not, however, prepared for a collision with an iceberg.

In fact, she was on the point of sending a deck steward

below with her cumbersome pistol when the crash came.

In the history of that tragedy, her name appears as one who knew no fear. She did much to calm the women and children. Perhaps she was overzealous, for it is recorded that she refused to enter a lifeboat until all other women and their young ones had been cared for, and that crew members literally had to throw her into a boat.

Once in the boat, however, she didn't wait for approval —she seized command. There were only five men aboard, and about twenty women and children.

"Start rowing," she told the men, "and head the bow into the sea."

Keeping an eye on the rowers, she began removing her clothes. Her chinchilla coat she treated as though it were a blanket worth a few dollars. She used it to cover three small and shivering children. One by one she divested herself of heroic woolens. She "rationed" her garments to the women who were the oldest or most frail. It was said she presented a fantastic sight in the light of flares, half standing among the terrified passengers, stripped down to her corset, the beloved Swiss bloomers, the Duke of Charlot's golf stockings and her stout shoes.

One of the rowers seemed on the verge of collapse. "My heart," he said.

"God damn your heart!" said The Unsinkable Mrs. Brown. "Work those oars."

She herself now took an oar and began to row. She chose a position in the bow, where she could watch her crew. Her pistol was lashed to her waist with a rope.

The heart-troubled rower now gasped and almost lost his oar. "My heart," he said. "It's getting worse!"

The Unsinkable one roared: "Keep rowing or I'll blow your guts out and throw you overboard! Take your choice."

The man—who really *did* have a fatty condition of the heart—kept rowing. Mrs. Brown sprouted big blisters on her hands. But she didn't quit. Then her palms began to bleed. She cut strips from her Swiss bloomers and taped her hands. She kept rowing. And swearing.

At times, when the morale of her passengers was at its lowest, she would sing.

"The God damned critics say I can't sing," she howled. "Well, just listen to this . . ."

And she sang from various operas.

"We'll have an Italian opera now," she said at one time. "Just let anyone say it's no good."

She kept rowing.

And so did the others. They knew she *would* throw anyone overboard who dared quit, exhaustion or no exhaustion.

She told stories. She gave a history of the Little Johnny. She told of the time she hid three hundred thousand dollars in a camp stove, and how it went up the flue.

"How much is three hundred thousand dollars?" she asked. "I'll tell you. It's nothing. Some of you people—the guy here with the heart trouble that I'm curing with oars —are rich. I'm rich. What in hell of it? What are your riches or mine doing for us this minute? And you can't wear the Social Register for water wings, can you? Keep rowing, you sons of bitches, or I'll toss you all overboard!"

When they were picked up at sea, and everyone was praising Mrs. Brown, she was asked:

"How did you manage it?"

"Just typical Brown luck," she replied. "I'm unsinkable."

And ever afterward she was known as "The Unsinkable Mrs. Brown."

Perhaps because it is the thing most lacking, heroism lifts anyone above caste. *Still*, the Denver social tabbies would not admit Mrs. Brown to their select functions. But now she no longer cared. She went in for thrills.

She took world tours and explored far places, always meeting adventure half way. Once she almost perished in a monsoon in the China seas. At another time she was in a hotel fire in Florida. But the Unsinkable one was Unburnable as well. She rescued four women and three children from that fire.

In France she was given a Legion of Honor ribbon, with the rank of chevalier, in recognition of her charities in general and her work in establishing a museum for the relics of Sarah Bernhardt in particular.

She now was legally separated from old Leadville Johnny. But still he had not tied the purse strings. Molly could go where she wanted and do what she wanted. It was his way. As for him, he stayed in the parlor with his shoes off, or bent the elbow a bit with old-time pals. The Little Johnny continued to pour out gold as from a cornucopia.

Although her husband was a mine owner, Mrs. Brown always took the side of labor, and sent food, clothing and money to the families of strikers.

During the World War she contributed heavily for the welfare of soldiers and for the hospitalization of wounded warriors of the Allied arms. If she had been hooted by a handful of social snobs in her home town, she now received the prayers of thousands of soldiers. The Allied nations awarded her all the medals it was possible for a civilian woman to receive. She was recipient of personal congratulations and the thanks of kings and princes.

After the war she took another of her world tours. When reporters met her in New York, she said:

"I'm getting to be more of a lady every day. In Honolulu I learned to play the uke. In Siam I mastered the native dances. In Switzerland I learned how to yodel. Want to hear me?"

And she astonished the customs guards by breaking into Alpine melody.

Rumors were circulated that the aged Duke of Charlot was planning to marry her—old Leadville Johnny having died in his stocking feet—and Mrs. Brown confirmed the report. Forty-eight hours later she declared the romance ended.

"Me marry *that* old geezer?" she said. "Never! Give me every time the rugged men of the West. The men of Europe—why, in France they're only perfumed and unbathed gallants; in England, only brandy-soaked British gents. Pooh! Pooh! Pooh! And a bottle of rum."

In keeping with his character, Leadville Johnny, a multimillionaire, *left no will.* There was an unpretty fight now. The Unsinkable Mrs. Brown was left floating with little financial ballast. Her eccentricities were cited; her charities construed as loose business affairs. She was awarded the life-income on one hundred thousand dollars annually.

"Just to think," she said with a gay smile, "and I burned up three times that much in one bonfire."

Mrs. Margaret Tobin Brown died in October, 1932. Apoplexy was the cause. She had been singing in her town apartment at the Barbizon Club, in East Sixty-third Street, New York City, then became dizzy and faint.

She was buried at Hempstead, Long Island, in surroundings that she loved almost as well as she had loved her Colorado hills.

Sir Osbert Sitwell

"BETWEEN SEASONS"

from *The Scarlet Tree*

The following excerpt from "Between Seasons" is taken from a chapter of THE SCARLET TREE, the second of Sir Osbert Sitwell's four volumes of memoirs. THE SCARLET TREE covers the period 1899 to 1909, the year that the author left Eton. The coming-out party described took place at Renishaw Hall, ancestral home of the Sitwell family, which is situated near Scarborough in Yorkshire, England.

$\mathcal{N}$ow the Edwardian Carnival was at its height, but my immediate family took little part in it. Every spring, we would go abroad, and my father and mother now would usually pay a second visit to Italy in the autumn. My father never went elsewhere, neither to Spain, nor Portugal, nor Holland, nor Morocco, nor to any of the other countries that, it might have been supposed, would interest him, except France—that is to say, Paris, as a stopping place en route for Italy—and Germany. Russia he had visited as a young man, to attend the Coronation of the Tsar Alexander III, but he seldom spoke of his travels there, except to commend the double-gauge railway. It was Italy that appealed to him and he kept to the track he had made for himself.

In the world outside, the era of the Stock Exchange was in full swing. The institution now set every standard. Musical Comedy filled the theaters devoted to it, and this was its peak, the age of *The Merry Widow*. This play, first produced at Daly's on June 8, 1907, ran for over two years, during which time its music, by Franz Lehár, served as background to every meal in a restaurant, every dance, and every garden party that was given. . . . I remember being taken to see this piece during an exeat from Eton in the autumn of 1907: we sat in the stage box, and so I was able to watch the expressions of the members of the audience,

242

reproducing in their own fashion the sentiment and humor that came to them from the stage.

> I'm going to Maxim's
> Where fun and frolic gleams;
> The girls all laugh and greet me;
> They will not trick or cheat me.

Copyright MCMVII by Chappell & Co. Ltd.

reflected the current ennui with the responsibilities of life to perfection; how marvelous, many of those seated in the theater felt, to be able to say that, and to cast away your cares in this manner. And as, later, the banal, but in a way charming, waltz sounded out, and Miss Lily Elsie came down the stairs to her prince, and as the glare from the stage fell on those in the front rows of the stalls, on the stiff white shirts, flashing studs, white waistcoats, and self-indulgent faces, brown or white, on the noses, hooked or snub, and gleaming, pouchy eyes, of these members of the Cosmopolitan Bourgeoisie, I can recall contemplating them and wondering whether it were possible that in the future such entertainments or such an audience would—or could—be considered as being typical of their epoch, or providing a clue to it, in the same way that we looked back, past our fathers, to *La Vie Parisienne* or *Die Fledermaus*. I decided, then, that to adopt such a view would be to overrate both entertainment and spectators—but I was wrong. It held a suitably designed mirror to the age, to the preference for restaurant to palace, for comfort to beauty, and to the idealization of Mammon. Mammon underlay the smudgy softness and superficial prettiness of the whole performance, as the skull supports the lineaments of even the youngest and freshest face. . . . Nor was it only to the stockbroker that *The Merry Widow* appealed. So popular was it that, at its farewell performance, at the end of

July, 1909, the theater was besieged all day, the earliest
arrival taking his stand at half-past five in the morning.
. . . But even then the piece had not finished its career.
It was revived frequently, and eventually entangled itself
with history by becoming Hitler's favorite entertainment:
curious that he who so hated the Stock Exchange, and saw
himself as ordained to destroy it, should thus share its
tastes.

Apart from a visit about once a year to one of the trivial
but popular musical comedies of the day, my father seldom visited the theater. Even at that, he preferred the native brand to the Austrian. His real dislike of music helped
him, it may be, to enjoy these entertainments, and I think
the experience of being able, indeed of finding himself
obliged, to laugh at the same jokes as the rest of the audience allowed him to feel to a certain, even agreeable degree, fashioned of the same clay. . . . Besides, in medieval
times—and they were drawing nearer to him every year—
even the castellan had enjoyed watching jesters and fools.
And afterwards there had been round dances in the great
hall. . . . Such a pity to let that sort of thing die out.
. . . For the rest he disapproved of the theater, and especially of the intellectual drama. . . . As a child, therefore,
I had seldom been allowed to go to the play; but now, during my "long leave" every half, I would usually accompany
my mother or uncle. Often they would take me to see the
Follies, a celebrated company of the time, the chief or-
ganizer of which was the great Pélissier, an enormous figure of comedy; though his gift, perhaps, was more for pure
fun, without implication, than for the satire and irony at
which his devotees considered him adept. There was little
distortion—the essence of satire—in his art; only a natu-
ralistic exaggeration, as though one looked through a
magnifying glass.

In addition, at the end of my holidays, when I was pass-

ing through London on my way to Eton, my parents
would usually detail Henry to take me to a theater, and
this we would not seldom interpret as meaning a music
hall, a form of entertainment of which we were both very
fond. . . . Often he would conduct me to the Alhambra,
then still the most typical and, in its own atmospheric
way, the most beautiful of London theaters, untouched
since the 'sixties, when it had been built. The honeycomb
ceilings and stalactites were painted in blue and red, and
there was, too, a great deal of dark gilding, though obscured by the clouds of cigar and cigarette smoke that
hung under the wide, flat dome. In the background as we
entered, I caught a glimpse of the promenade, where
women in hats the size of bicycle wheels, piled up with
ostrich feathers, their faces powdered and painted in the
various shades of mauve, pink, salmon, and cyclamen that
had been contemporaneously introduced in the new vari-
eties of sweet pea—a flower which must remain as typical
of the age of *The Merry Widow* as does the camellia of the
age of crinoline and muslins—trailed the trains of their
dresses along the carpets in a haze of cheap, strong scent,
tobacco smoke, and dust. To me, these unknown but formal priestesses of primitive unrecognized rites and urgen-
cies seemed less enticing than portentous, frightening, and
of an immense age. We quickly gained our seats, and there,
from the comparative darkness, watched the figures on the
stage, consumed by and consuming the light of a world
that by the help of a label—a gesture, a mannerism, a lisp,
a laugh—they would create. Here, for example, I first saw
the minute, irresistibly grotesque figure of Little Tich,
surely a dancer of genius, as he stamped magically, with a
divine power of comedy, upon the boards; his huge boots,
half the size of himself, being shaped like skis. His whole
stunted body seemed the expression of his dance, rather
than the dance an expression of his body: as surely as the

lion was created for its leap, so Little Tich had been molded, the spectator felt, for this purpose alone, for rousing laughter out of a crowd, in the same way that a bellows fans flame out of smoldering logs.

Here, too, I first saw a ballet: in those days still billed as "The Italian Ballet," *Italian* being used to indicate the identical sort of transcendent excellence that came to be signified later by the use of *Russian* in the same connection. A ballet then always occupied the final forty or fifty minutes of such a formal variety program as still survived at the Alhambra or Empire, a lingering tradition from an earlier period. Built upon a long, humorless, and involved plot, it was executed by surprisingly large women and old men; the representatives of both sexes, indeed, seeming left over from some other era. They used a peculiarly stilted and yet coherent technique of foot, gesture, and expression; to these three means, their art, such as it was, had been confined. They aimed at no use of the body, except for heaving, panting, and showing emotion, and at little expression by the limbs. The chief male dancers were heavily mustached, a conventional stroking of these long appendages being a favorite gesture, to show either self-satisfaction or a sudden determination, according to the manner in which it was done. The chief dancer, if I remember rightly, was titled the Great Leonora . . . was it Leonora? . . . but I recall her appearance, a large, dark, flashing woman, who seemed always to be balanced on the knifelike edge of toes surprisingly small for the support of such a frame, or to be indulging in imperious, whirlwind gestures or foot stamping. The whole thing was staged in a flat and jejune manner, alternating with outbursts of a pantomime-like splendor. . . . One could not fail to be amazed at the lack of reality displayed, and I formed a great distaste for the ballet, little foreseeing the new art at that very moment being shaped in Russia out of the amor-

phous mass of time by the genius of Diaghilev, or that I,
together with those others of my generation interested in
the arts, or gifted for them, should find more pleasure in
it than in any other form of theatrical entertainment. . . .
But, after all, who could predict the soaring of a phoenix,
only just reborn—and from what dusty ashes!—who could
deduce from this banal staging before me, from this less
than mediocre dancing in front of me, or from these in-
sipid strains which now tinkled in my ears, the genius of
L'Oiseau de Feu, with its encroaching bands of ogres and
harpies, or the high tragedy of *Petrouchka*, the sweeping
lines of the music summing up the world of fire to come,
who could divine in the overstrained bodies and overloaded emotions of this pedantic and puerile survival, the
leap of Nijinsky into his momentary glare of world fame,
the doomed grace and alluring beauty of Karsavina, Lopo-
kova's humor born of limbs as well as mind, the fantastic,
inspired satire of Massine, or foretell in the antics of the
corps de ballet, quarter-trained over forty years, the vital
significance of movement in *Les Noces* or *Tricorne* . . . ?
Yet this ballet before us was own cousin to those I was to
see, sharing the same high descent.

The romantic age, it seemed, the romantic gloss, had
vanished, both in life itself and in my surroundings. . . .
Something had gone wrong, and farce, public and private,
was sweeping the boards clear for tragedy—or at any rate
for disaster. The shadow was inspissating, becoming homi-
cidal in the world at large, and material and squalid at
home. . . . Relations drifted in and out of Renishaw, but
it seemed emptier than in the years when I was a very small
boy, the guests fewer and fewer (they were to increase
again before the coming of the First World War). Partly
this was due to my father's fear that they might "disturb
his literary work," partly to his growing dread of any expense incurred save in building or altering, partly to the

fact that he had at last decided that he rather disliked some of my mother's friends, and, looking around, seemed now to have none of his own. . . . Odd! . . . Perhaps, he consoled himself, it was really better so. Friends often exercised a frivolous influence. . . . And it was more interesting to see strangers—you acquired more information from them—or to show a little kindness to those who needed it. (Really, he must ask the editor of the *Scarborough Post* to stay!) Every now and then, though, he liked to indulge in a burst of entertaining, and then the question arose, whom to entertain?

One such occasion, the biggest of its kind, is possibly worth describing. When my sister was nineteen, my father resolved that she ought to have a coming-out party. It was the correct thing to do, and though he disapproved of conventional ways as a rule, for some reason the idea appealed to him. . . . But again, *whom* to ask and what for? . . . Well, my mother could invite one or two of her relations to help her, he decided; and the party must be for the Doncaster Races. . . . Into this last decision certainly entered an element of ancestor worship, together with his individual brand of extravagance mingled with economy; because he possessed the silver badge which had belonged to his great-grandfather, one of the founders of the meeting, and which, worn in the buttonhole, would still obtain for him a free admission. Hitherto he had never worn it . . . And in any case he was determined to try the effect of one last sortie from his ivory tower, not yet completed.

Preparations—the Doncaster Races, I may remind any non-sporting reader who may happen to see this book, take place in September, usually in the second week—were of the widest scope and occupied many months. The following letter was written by the subagent to his friend the agent in June of the previous year:—

I have an enormous list of work to be done for Sir G.
Yesterday he went round and showed me what painting
and papering is to be done, and I had a warm time this
morning from 7 to 1, with 3 men, transforming the Ball-
Room into a sitting-room. I have to design a French-
window for it, to open on the lawn.

Lady Ida's room. Paint and paper; a ceiling paper with a
"faint, quiet pattern" to be put on. Patterns to be sent
Sir G. at Scarborough. Repair cornice.

Sir G.'s room. Re-cover green-baize door.

Duke's Dressing-Room. Paint and paper. A paper with
"*small* quiet pattern to suit pictures."

Tapestry-Room. Paper and paint. Paper with "pattern in
low tones" to suit tapestry.

Red Room. Paper, paint and plaster end.

Small Drawing-Room. Repair, paint and line ceiling.
"Bring out old gold tone."

General. Get mirror for *Hall-Chamber* fireplace 1'-9
inches high, similar to mirror in Duke's Room.

Hang 2 pictures in *Ball-Room.* Clean and Varnish.

Repaint windows in *Ball-Room.*

Take down all curtains and put up again in month's
time.

Ditto stair-carpets.

Have *Drawing-Room* curtains dyed dark red.

Make design for French Window in *Ball-Room.*

Paint seat outside garden-door.

Get sconces for small mirrors from abroad.

Lay water on to 3 new marble fountains.

Fix sun-dial.

Re-arrange terracotta vases. Take some away.

Syringe poison into all the worm-holes in the furniture.
I will send you a complete list soon.

I am on the look-out for a fresh job when Sir G. returns
in July!

Three weeks later, he adds a postscript to another letter to the same correspondent: "Sir G. continues to write daily."

It will be noticed that the arrangements he was making did not include the addition of another bathroom. Here we may remark, as a singular footnote to the period, but a thing in no way unusual at this date, even for so large a house, that Renishaw still possessed only one. And, in this connection, I remember Luytens complaining to me some years later, that even when he planned for rich clients new and most luxurious houses, he found the greatest difficulty in persuading them to allow a bathroom to each bedroom. . . . In other directions, continually the pace increased. By the end of August the following year, nearly everyone on the estate, and in the house, had been driven frantic. Chefs arrived. Enormous parcels were delivered every day from London. New linen was bought. All the silver plate, some of it unused for many years, was got out of the bank. Extra footmen appeared, and Major Viburne was called in to manage the whole thing as if it were an officers' mess. The running of special trains to Doncaster and back was arranged with the railway company, to convey to the races those who did not want to go by motor. Motors were hired. A Blue Hungarian Band was engaged for ten days . . . And for a full month beforehand I used to see my father, sitting later than usual at breakfast, with eight or ten small glass jam-pots— Bar-le-Duc—in front of him, labeled in French, red currant, white currant, scarlet strawberry, white strawberry, gooseberry, and so on. When I inquired what he was doing, he would reply, as one manfully executing a duty, "Just trying out the jams for the Doncaster party," for he believed in personal supervision. Like a soldier, he stuck to it, in spite of the strain on the liver: but after a few weeks, one could see that it was beginning to tell on him.

. . . Excitement mounted. And when the great day came, and every bedroom was prepared, and the thirty or so people arrived, we were amazed at the total of their combined ages. The whole point of the party had been that it was for my sister. But every single one of the guests, with the exception of my cousin Veronica and one or two others, was well stricken in years and seasoned to the world. The only young man present was a nice American, who had been faithfully retrieved for the occasion by a cousin of ours, and who was frankly puzzled at finding himself in this gallery of antiques. Altogether the party was scarcely suitable and revealed the lengthening gap between reality and things as my parents were beginning to see them.

It was a party, I suppose, none the less—but it seemed curiously impersonal to me in composition and aim. Nobody knew anyone else in the house—unless it were so intimately that to ask them to meet should have been deemed a work of supererogation—and nobody particularly wanted to know anyone else. In addition, my father detested racing, and Edith loathed it. My mother, alone, enjoyed the pointless stir and activity of it—and, of course, the opportunities it afforded for betting. The meals were long and good. (The Bar-le-Duc jams, then a novelty in England, were consumed with relish.) The Blue Hungarian Hussars, who put up at the Sitwell Arms in the village, may have puzzled and perturbed the habituals of the inn, colliers and agricultural laborers, by their sallow appearance, raven locks, and Magyar swagger. (They carried up to the house each day suitcases, containing their frogged sling-jackets and cherry-colored britches, and local opinion, until it became informed, inclined to the view that they were Indians or Armenians peddling carpets—the type of foreigner with which the neighborhood was best acquainted.) But within doors they were in constant demand, whenever racing was not in progress, playing under the gilded Tudor Rose of the Little Parlor, next the Dining Room, during every meal except breakfast, and were in continual discourse after dinner in the ballroom. Every restaurant in Europe must have been ransacked to find the repertory. "The music makes things go," said my father, "and prevents people from feeling they *have* to make conversation." (Better still, it prevented them from hearing it.) Only "The Blue Danube," a piece of which the band was fond, was here rather frowned on, being taken by some of the guests, I fear, as a reflection upon their ages. They pretended never to have heard it before. "What a delightful old-fashioned thing!" they used to exclaim. "What is it? . . . But let's have something we know, 'The Merry Widow,' or one of those delightful tunes from the Gaiety!" . . . Trains and motors ran in their ordained grooves; the garden looked its best, swooning under a special weight of flowers. It was usually only visited in the morning, when clematis and rose and honeysuckle and hollyhock glowed in the butter-colored golden haze, born of sun and morning mist—or was it from a ground frost; it was difficult to tell which, for even after hours of hot sun, the grass still remained wet, and the rose heads full of moisture—or in the late afternoon, an hour at which the whole summer seemed to return in epitome, so that it was impossible to believe that we stood on the very brink of autumn in this high country, and the scent of flowers, out-pressed by the heat, seemed to linger in the air with an unwonted persistence, while the fruit, ripening on the dark red-brick walls, appeared to shine in its own radiance and heat. The house, too, seemed to be in commotion at both ends of the day. In the morning, the housemaids and footmen struggled upstairs with old-fashioned tin baths, resembling Egyptian coffins, and hip baths like gigantic snail shells, and enormous cans of steaming-hot water, to the rooms respectively of female and male guests. Then there was a hiatus in activity at midday, when the party had left for Doncaster. Henry would enjoy a siesta: the chef would drink a bottle of wine. The gardener would come round to see to the flowers in the house. Finally, hammering would sound out again from the kitchen. . . . The party would return: baths would be carried up once more. . . . And soon there would be the procession down to dinner, down the oak staircase, across the flagged hall, through the Little Parlor. "Racing makes one very rheumatic," the guests would say to one another when their knees creaked as they descended the stairs—for it could have nothing to do with their ages.

. . . Yes, I think the party must have been adjudged a success. . . . If any doubt lay at the back of my parents' minds on this matter, the blame was allotted to Edith. "*Très difficile*," my father would say, for he reserved his rather restricted knowledge of French for the crystallization of such domestic problems. He complained that she did not play tennis—"lawn tennis," as he still called it— while my mother regretted her addiction to books. She had not "been out" long, and already she had created a bad impression elsewhere, while staying with relations, as well as having excessively startled the late Lord Chaplin, by inquiring of him, during an evening when she was placed next to him at dinner, whether he preferred Bach to Mozart. She had been hastily withdrawn from circulation and sent home. It would never do . . . Still, one could try one's best. . . . The party was nearly over.

Only Major Viburne was, as major-domo, patently a failure. Owing to what must have been high blood pressure, still further inflamed, no doubt, by his ferocious military opinions, or, again, perhaps, merely as a result of endeavoring to help my father by "trying out the jams," he began to have fits of giddiness. Especially when he was showing visitors from neighboring houses round the gardens would these attacks descend to overwhelm him, and, suddenly grasping for safety a thick post—shaped like the ragged staff held by the bear in public-house signs—up which grew climbing roses, he would spin wildly round it, unable to tell which way he was going and leading those to whom he was acting as guide in circles, much to their surprise.

"There's the Major playing 'Round and Round the Mulberry Bush' again in the garden!" Henry would remark. "He's too old for that sort of game now, if he'd only realize it. . . . The guests don't like it."

And my mother, as if he had done it on purpose, would complain that it made her feel giddy even to look at him.

Sacheverell and I, and our tutor Mr. Ragglesedge, who might have enjoyed the race meetings, were not allowed to attend them, nor the meals in the Dining Room. My brother and I feasted on scraps in our attic. . . . It seemed rather lonely, not being allowed to join in. Never being able to realize when I am not wanted, I decided one evening to bicycle through the park and meet my father —who was that day motoring back from the races—at the gates. I was wearing a best new blue suit, appropriate to the occasion. Free-wheeling blithely downhill, through a grove of trees, I paid no attention to where I was going, caught the back of the heel of a cow, which was mooching across the drive, with my front wheel and, flying with an unexpected elegance and agility over the handle bars just as my father was entering the park, landed, with torn trousers, grazed knees, and a black eye, a few yards ahead of him. It was a silly thing to have done. . . . I sensed as much in the atmosphere. I had let the side down. Further, I had ruined, unnecessarily, a new suit—a fact of which, ever and again, I was reminded during the remaining weeks of the holidays.

Gradually the music faded, the musicians, clothed soberly in black, returned to London, the guests left—many of them were never to see such a party again—Major Viburne's dizziness began to pass off, the head chef went back to London with a large check and a scalded hand, the train service relapsed to the normal, and the motors stopped breaking down and raced home. My father abandoned the life of the time as he saw it, and sped back to the gothic centuries. In addition to his never-ending studies of medieval life, he was at work on his book *On the Making of Gardens*, and continued entering notes on many and diverse subjects. I find the following jotting, under the heading "Venus," dated September of that same year: "The author of the book on classical statuary which I have been reading, does not allow for the great interest attaching to ideal types of womanhood. The Venus of Syracuse is really very beautiful. Of course, the proper place for a Venus is in a private or a public bath."

As for Venus, whether in private or public bath, she was certainly more in evidence in England than she had been for a hundred years. The goddess seemed more openly to be occupying men's thoughts. For the first time for many decades, clothes had become highly stylized again, with an elegance verging on absurdity. At Ascot, and on the lawns of garden parties, it was to be noticed that women had at last begun to shed once more the multitude of their garments, had left behind the veilings and feather boas in which we saw them wrapped at Lord's, and were now clad, skin-deep, in tight silks, were sheathed in satin, or wore slit skirts and silver anklets. For the world took its note from Musical Comedy rather than from the immense tragedies that were being prepared in the wings to replace it, and the production of *Les Merveilleuses* at Daly's in November 1906 had introduced, or at any rate popularized, Directoire dresses. The hats were gigantic now, and covered with ostrich feathers. The colors were those of young grass and leaves, the checkerings of branches against a gray sky, or rose-pink and azure-blue— they had about them a peculiar ephemerality, a butterfly-like character that was the essence of modishness. Paris had again asserted her leadership, and marched behind the smiling mask of the Entente Cordiale, to take London captive, yet London was now becoming, in her place, the pleasure center of the world.

Edmund Pearson

"THE WICKED HANSOM"

from *More Studies in Murder*

$\mathcal{I}$t was sad that hansom-cabs should fall under a blight. A curse descended upon them thirty-two years ago, come the fourth of next June. Although they were jolly, teetery-looking carriages, and more innocent than your limousines, pious folk thought of them, for many years, as chariots of sin.

The notorious hansom which disgraced all its tribe in New York was driven by Frederick Michaels, and the black hour came upon him on a fair June morning in 1904. The time was as early as half-past seven—when the wicked have usually gone to bed, and the virtuous are abroad. Michaels and his horse belonged with the good and the pure, and so they were looking for business in Columbus Circle, while the dew was still on the grass in Central Park.

A man and a girl hailed the cab. They got in; the hansom turned, I suppose, through 59th Street, and started down Fifth Avenue.

The only noise it made was the familiar cloppety-clop of the horse's hooves on the asphalt. But if Michaels had been endowed with second-sight—no, with second hearing—he would have detected the Fates, or other sinister creatures, muttering the soon-to-be notorious names of: "Miss-Nan-Patterson-and-Caesar-Young . . . Miss-Nan-Patterson-and-Caesar-Young."

And, as an accompanying chorus of doom, like the unpleasant old busybodies in a Greek tragedy, the grumbling voices of half a dozen New York clergymen, who were very shortly to be repeating the names of the man and the girl, and adding: "The-wages-of-sin-is-certainly-death . . . the-wages-of-sin-is-certainly-death."

Ann Elizabeth Patterson, a fatally beautiful lady, of twenty-two, was a native of the city of Washington. Newspapers said that three men had already died—absolutely perished and crossed the dark river—for love of her. From her sixteenth to her twentieth year she had been the wife of a railroad official named Martin, but she secured a divorce in 1903.

Her real celebrity, up to the moment she entered this hansom, lay in the fact that she was a "Floradora girl." As it is said to be a scientific fact that when "the original Floradora double sextette"—i.e., twelve persons—held a reunion in Pittsburgh, it took five hotels to accommodate them, we must inquire into Nan Patterson's exact status in that vast chorus. Good authorities say that she belonged to the second sextette, organized by Edna Wallace Hopper in 1901.

On a westbound train, before her divorce, Nan Patterson met Frank T. Young, called "Caesar." Mr. Young, an Englishman, had come to America, years earlier, to compete in track and field athletics for the Manhattan Athletic Club. He married; fell upon hard times; took up book-making at Morris Park track, where he prospered greatly—sometimes as a result of the excellent advice of his wife, who was a good judge of horses. He was said to possess $750,000. In his pocket, as he sat in the cab, were $1,820 and two tickets on the *S.S.Germanic*, sailing for Europe that morning at 10 o'clock.

The second ticket was not for Miss Patterson, but for Mrs. Young, then waiting on, or near, the ship. She was patiently and tolerantly hoping that her husband's promise to sail with her indicated the end of his affair with "that Patterson woman."

Early in the morning, Miss Patterson had been called by telephone at the St. Paul Hotel in 60th Street, where she lived with her sister and brother-in-law, the J. Morgan Smiths. Caesar Young bade her meet him at the 59th Street station of the 6th Avenue "El." This she did, and she is the only witness to most of the events which followed, for the cabman remained more aloof than the gods upon Olympus.

It was, by her account, a bibulous ride. Caesar had already been drinking when she met him. They had a drink together before taking the cab. On the way down the Avenue, Caesar discussed his old hat, and the universal opinion that he needed a new one. At Knox's in Madison Square, he alighted and bought a new hat. In Bleecker Street—they were on their way toward the pier—he demanded another drink. They had this, and when they were once more in the cab, Caesar was melancholy, affectionate, and despairing, by turns.

"Are you going to leave me? Or are you going to follow me to Europe?"

The girl replied:

"I am not going to Europe."

She went on: "When he grabbed hold of me, and kissed me roughly, I pulled away from him . . . there was a flash, and he was dead."

She added: "I never saw the pistol."

This happened in West Broadway, near Franklin Street. Michaels was at last made aware that something was going on. He drew up to the curb; a policeman came, and found Miss Patterson kissing her companion's face, as his head lay in her lap. Caesar never spoke, but died five minutes after reaching the hospital.

Whose was the pistol? Where did it come from. Which

hand pulled the trigger? No jury which tried Miss Patterson for murder ever found an answer to these questions.

The defense steadily maintained that "Caesar" Young, in profound melancholy at this separation from his sweetheart, or from a recent loss of $30,000 on the track, or from drink, or from all three causes, held the pistol under his coat and shot himself.

The prosecution's theory was that Nan Patterson had been urged to the slaughter by J. Morgan Smith, who feared that she was losing a wealthy friend. The evidence, by which they sought to bolster up this doubtful idea failed them altogether. (How would it profit her to kill him?) The ownership of the pistol was not satisfactorily traced to anybody. But for eleven months, the sob-sisters and the Sunday newspapers continued to discuss the beautiful defendant, her affairs, and her venerable father, while the country at large had a good time deploring the wickedness of New York.

Rural communities righteously thanked God that as they had no Floradora girls and no hansom-cabs, therefore they had no wayward husbands and no violent deaths.

The first trial was stopped by the illness of a juror. At the second trial the jury disagreed—6 to 6. At the third trial there was another disagreement: 7 to 5 for acquittal, and the prisoner was discharged.

Miss Patterson's subsequent career upon the stage, in Pennsylvania, was brief and unsuccessful. Her later life, as a happily married woman on the Pacific coast, has, it is said, brought her the esteem of her neighbors. It is a pleasure to record this, since, if I may venture an opinion, she deserved an acquittal. The government's theory that she plotted to commit the crime, seems all but destroyed by the fact that the meeting, that morning, was not the result of her arrangement.

We know the fate of some of the participants in that

early morning drive down the Avenue. The horse, in the natural course of things, would be dead. But where are the cabman and the hansom itself? Properly stuffed and mounted they could well form an important exhibit in the Museum of the City of New York. As one of the most famous vehicles in our history, the cab deserves a place beside Boss Tweed's fire-engine, with the Tammany Tiger on it.

Harold Nicolson

"THE EDWARDIAN WEEKEND"

from *Small Talk*

$\mathcal{T}$he Edwardian age will, we may presume, live in history as an age of comfort. It was not. It was an age of fevered luxury; at the same time it was an age of peculiar human ineptitude. People possessed false values, and they endeavored, fortunately without success, to impose these values upon their children. The whole glittering decade passed in an atmosphere of plethoric friction. It is time that the jade and lobster of the Edwardian epoch were exposed.

In the first place, they ate excessively and competitively. No age, since that of Nero, can show such unlimited addiction to food. People were called by their valets at eight-thirty. These silent but hostile men would arrive bearing in their left hand a neat brass can of shaving water, and in their right hand a neat brass tray of tea, toast, and Marie biscuits. The Edwardian, blinking plethoric eyes above his pink silk eiderdown, would munch the biscuits and would sip the tea. He would then adjust his teeth, adjust his hair, adjust his Afghan dressing-robe, and slouch plethoric along the passage to the bathroom. If he were staying in a rich house (and all houses in the Edwardian epoch were rich), he would find in the bathroom the scented smell of his predecessor's indulgence, the half-empty bottles ("flacons" was the word they used) which contained Hammam Bouquet of Mr. Penthalicon. The guest would pour this unguent into the bath, from which his valet would already have removed the stains, the soapsuds and the other disjecta membra of the former occupant. The water would be tepid. Edwaridan water was always tepid. The soap would also be tepid. His predecessor had left his signet ring in the soap dish. Through the smell of Hammam Bouquet would gradually pierce the smell of lavender bags and Sanitas. Disgusted and dyspeptic, the Edwardian would proceed with his bath. He shaved in it. All Edwardians, being at heart dirty folk, shaved in their baths.

When he returned to his bedroom, along the red pile carpet which marked the unending symmetry of the corridor, he would find that the windows had been slightly opened, and that his clothes had been laid ready for him upon the chintz settee. Taking a Regie cigarette from his Fabergé case he would contemplate these clothes with satisfaction. If he were a good Edwardian his shirt and collar would be all in one. A white shirt, somewhat frilled and tucked on the breast, ending in a stiff little upturned collar. Hard, expectant, circular—that collar would shortly encase his neck. Alternatively a Piccadilly collar of equal rigidity would be waiting for him on the dressing table. Black clothes; a grey silk tie; a neat turquoise pin representing a pheasant walking slowly from left to right; a white cambric handkerchief; a dab of eau-de-Cologne; his purse; his card case; the smell of Euchrisma as he brushed his hair. Then he descended down the red pile staircases, to breakfast.

Only the really improper Edwardians had breakfast in their rooms. The others met, on that Sunday morning, in the dining-room. The smell of last night's port had given place to the smell of this morning's spirits of wine. Rows of little spirit lamps warmed rows of large silver dishes. On a table to the right between the windows were grouped Hams, Tongues, Galantines, Cold Grouse, ditto Pheasant, ditto Partridge, ditto Ptarmigan. No Edwardian meal was complete without Ptarmigan. Hot or cold. Just Ptarmigan.

There would also be a little delicate rectangle of pressed beef from the shop of M. Benoist. On a further table, to the left between the doors, stood fruits of different calibre, and jugs of cold water, and jugs of lemonade. A fourth table contained porridge utensils. A fifth coffee, and pots of Indian and China tea. The latter were differentiated from each other by little ribbons of yellow (indicating China) and of red (indicating without arrière pensée, our Indian Empire). The center table, which was prepared for twenty-three people, would be bright with Malmaisons and toast-racks. No newspapers were, at that stage, allowed.

The atmosphere of the Edwardian dining-room at nine-thirty was essentially daring. A pleasant scene of confederacy and sin hung above the smell of the spirit-lamps. For had they not all been brought up to attend family prayers? And had they not all eluded that obligation? It was true, of course, that the host and hostess, with their niece, had at nine proceeded to the family chapel and heard the butler reading a short collect for the day. But the guests had for their part evaded these Victorian obligations. This corporate evasion gave to the proceedings an atmosphere of dash. There was no insincerity in the bright gaiety with which they greeted each other, with which they discussed how he or she had slept. "A little kidjiree, Lady Maude?" "Oh, thank you, Mr. Stapleton." Evidently it was all going very well.

Edwardian breakfasts were in no sense a hurried proceeding. The porridge was disposed of negligently, people walking about and watching the rain descend upon the Italian garden. Then would come whiting and omelette and devilled kidneys and little fishy messes in shells. And then tongue and ham and a slice of Ptarmigan. And then scones and honey and marmalade. And then a little melon, and a nectarine or two, and just one or two of those delicious raspberries. The men at that stage would drift (I employ the accepted term) to the smoking room.

The women would idle in the saloon watching the rain descend upon the Italian garden. It was then 10:30.

If the house possessed no private chapel (not all Edwardian houses possessed private chapels) the guests would then "assemble in the hall." There would be footmen fussing about in cockaded top-hats and long buff overcoats with gold buttons. A degree of jollity would be extracted from the process of deciding who would drive in the wagonette, who in the landau, who in the Victoria, who in the brougham. And who should walk. The latter category seized umbrellas and capes. People jingled off, clasping their prayer books and the half-crown for the offertory. From the side door the children, wide-eyed and washed, would appear with their governesses. They crossed the park to the church beyond the lodge.

With fervor would these Edwardians sing the psalms and the hymns, with reverence would they listen to the stories from the Old Testament. The smell of leather and wet mackintosh would permeate the damp little church. Every now and then an umbrella would tumble from a pew. The final benediction descended upon rows of bowed heads. The ladies' hats were rich with artificial flowers; the heads of the men were rich with the smell of Euchrisma. They walked back to luncheon under dripping trees.

The half-hour before luncheon hung a little heavy on their hands. The women would repair to their rooms and deal with their hair and faces. The men would gather in the library, where they would shortly be joined by the curate or, as the case might be, the house chaplain. A shy little man this, not knowing all these London people, not very certain how to modulate his voice. The younger men would come in later, having changed into tweeds. Great bowls of orchids and chrysanthemums were massed on the tables. There were silver vases of white roses, and cut glass vases in which the roses were red. The hostess, passing from group to group, would flick irritable emerald-laden fingers at these flowers, tugging them into different shapes. They would pass in to luncheon. The curate, hanging behind, would hang behind.

Edwardian luncheons were strained and bright. There was a theory that the good hostess should "draw her guests into conversation." This entailed a process of flinging conversational flies across the vast table and not waiting to see if the fish rose. "Colonel Westmacott, you simply must tell us about the Zambesi," and "Oh, Clara! Is it really true that dearest Evy has got to go to Nauheim?" There was a buzz of general talk. It would only be a buzz.

After luncheon they walked round the park. They did not visit the stables. Since the introduction of motors, the stables had become Victorian. The elder members of the party would drive over to Stonehenge in an open Daimler. They appeared, aged and flustered, in motoring veils of watered silk. Colonel Westmacott, in a tweed cape and spats, stumped off with Lady Moira to visit the quarries. Captain Fairfax took Miss Sinclair for a drive in his De Dion. Professor Steinholtz slept.

Tea was served in the blue gallery. There were little ginger biscuits which one could only get from Biarritz and of which one kept a store in case the King came. All Edwardian houses kept stores of things like ginger biscuits and aubergines and French patissiers and bath salts in case the King came. And he did come. He came over and over again. And on Monday morning other people would read all about it in the Morning Post. It was only, however, when the King actually did come that one went so far as to have lobster salad for tea. Otherwise one just had scones, and egg sandwiches, and paté sandwiches and cucumber sandwiches, and chocolate cake, and walnut cake, and coffee cake, and cake. Also there were little plates, with china-handled knives to match, from which people ate Tiptree jam with toast or brioches. The butler, the groom of the chambers, the under-butler and the footmen would move about offering food. But in the best houses (and most Edwardian houses were the best) the servants did not remain for tea.

After tea there would be bridge tables in the red drawing-room, and the men would not infrequently play billiards. Dinner was at half-past eight. The women would retire an hour before to change their tea-gowns for the other things which they donned to dine. The men also would change into clothes even more galling and restrictive than those they had worn all day. The guests would reassemble in the yellow saloon. The host by this time was already bored by his party, and would indicate a little irritably who was to take in whom. He held a fussy little piece of paper in his hand and would fuss from one man to another. The women, one by one, entered the room slowly, showing off their clothes. Then there would be dinner. Ptarmigan and champagne. Champagne and Ptarmigan. The hostess did not endeavor to stimulate general conversation at dinner. One only did that at luncheon. At dinner people talked, inclining their neat bodies sideways, to their neighbors. At nine-forty-five the women swept, with backward glances, from the room. The host would take his glass of port, holding it with gingerly fingers above, and move to the seat vacated by his wife. At ten-fifteen they joined the ladies in the music-gallery.

Bridge again. And at midnight, in the Holbein room, there would be devilled chicken, and more sandwiches and every form of spirit and mineral water which man or woman could desire. In the corridors upstairs the ladies-maids would hang listlessly yawning. Fires would sparkle in the grates, reflected in brass bedstead and in mirror. The pink-silk reading-lamps were lit beside the beds. Upon the night-table stood bottles of Malvern Water and of Vichy, covered dishes of sandwiches. A ribboned coverlet of swans-down would be draped across the sofa. The kettle, by the fireplace, purred.

Next morning their valets would pack their Enos and their shooting-sticks. They would return by train to London. Their carriages would meet them, horses champing bits, at the arrival platform of Paddington. In the train coming up the members of the house-party would read in the Morning Post a list of the members of the house-party. They returned to Curzon Street feeling very pleased indeed. And next Saturday it would all begin again.

Compared to the strenuous social discipline which these hardy people imposed upon themselves, our own laxity may seem a little decadent. Who among us today would really dress for church and dress for luncheon and dress for tea and dress again for dinner? Who among us would possess the endurance to relish all those meals, to relish all that tittle-tattle? Who today would care whether he was or was not invited to Upyatt Lacy or to West Warren? Who today prints or reads those lists of Saturday to Monday parties? The war has not been fought in vain. We have been released from false and exacting pretensions. We have our jumpers, our cocktails and our freedom. We can smoke pipes in Bond Street, and wear grey flannel in June. I do not regret that I was old enough to touch the fringe of Edwardian luxury. But I render thanks to Providence that I was also young enough to relish and share the wider liberties of our subsequent age. Let us be frank about it. The Edwardians were vulgar to a degree. They lacked style. They possessed only the hard glitter of their own electric light: a light which beat down pitilessly upon courtier, Ptarmigan, bridge scores, little enamel boxes, and plates and plates of food. They lacked simplicity, and their intricacies were expensive but futile. I, for one, prefer the wide circle of our simpler horizon, tumbled though it be by the waves of uncertainty. Nor, when all is said and done, can one forgive the Edwardians for their fundamental illusion. For it never dawned upon them that intelligence was of any value.

Elizabeth Robins Pennell

◆◆◆◆◆

"A PERFECT DINNER"

from *The Feasts of Autolycus—*
The Diary of a Greedy Woman

*F*ashion and art have little in common. Save for chance, they would remain always as the poles apart. The laws of the one are transitory, or the other eternal; and as irreconcilable are they in the observance. Make then your choice between them, since no man may serve two masters.

Know that if ever the noble art of cookery be wrecked, it will be upon the quicksands of Fashion. In many ways is it threatened by the passing mode, but, above all others, one danger looms up before it, grim, relentless, tragic: the more awful because, to the thoughtless, at first it seems sweet as siren's singing. It is an evil born of the love of display and of the keen competition between Fashion's votaries. For they who would pose as delicate diners, think to eclipse their rivals by number of courses and bewildering variety. How to prolong the *menu*, rather than how to perfect it, is their constant study. In excess they would emulate the banquets of the ancients, though they are too refined by far to revive the old vomitories—the indispensable antidote. Dish follows dish, conceit is piled upon conceit; and with what result? Before dinner is half over, palates are jaded, "fine shades" can no more be appreciated, every new course awakens fear of the morrow's indigestion.

Or else, pleasure is tempered by caution, a melancholy compromise; nothing is really eaten, the daintiest devices are but trifled with, and dinner is degraded into a torture fit for Tantalus. Surely, never was there a more cruel, fickle mistress than Fashion! Sad, immeasurably sad, the fate of her worshippers.

Art despises show, it disdains rivalry, and it knows not excess. A Velasquez or a Whistler never overloads his canvas for the sake of gorgeous detail. To the artist in words, superfluous ornament is the unpardonable sin. And so with the lovers of Gasterea, the tenth and fairest of the Muses. Better by far Omar Khayyam's jug of wine and loaf of bread, if both be good, than all the ill-regulated banquets of a Lucullus. Who would hesitate between the feasts of Heliogabalus and the frugal fowl and the young kid, the raisins, figs, and nuts of Horace?

It matters not how many courses between oysters and coffee Fashion may decree, if, turning your back upon her and her silly pretensions, you devise a few that it will be a privilege for your guests to eat, a joy for them to remember. Bear in mind the master's model luncheon and its success. No *menu* could have been simpler; none more delicious. The table was laid for three, a goodly number, for all the slurs cast upon it. At each plate were "two dozen oysters with a bright golden lemon; at each end of the table stood a bottle of Sauterne, carefully wiped all except the cork, which showed unmistakably that it was long since the wine had been bottled." After the oysters roasted kidneys were served; next, truffled *foie gras*; then the famous *fondue*, the beautiful arrangement of eggs beaten up with cheese, prepared over a chafing-dish at table, stimulating appetite by all the delights of anticipation. Fruit followed, and coffee; and last, two liqueurs," one a spirit, to clear, and the other an oil, to soothe." Be not content to read, but go and do likewise!

Imagine a dinner planned on the same pattern, and the conventional banquet of the day soon will seem to you the monstrosity it is. Observe two all-important rules and you may not wander far wrong. One is to limit the number of courses; the other to serve first the substantial dishes, then those that are lighter, first the simpler wines, afterwards those of finer flavours.

The *hors d'oeuvre*, however, is an exception. If too substantial it would defeat its end. It must whet the appetite, not blunt it. In its flavour must its strength lie; at once keen and subtle, it should stimulate, but never satisfy. An anchovy salad touches perfection; the anchovies—the boneless species from France—the olives skilfully stoned, the capers in carefully studied proportions, the yellow of the egg well grated, the parsley, chopped fine, must be arranged by an artist with a fine feeling for decorative effect, and the dressing of oil, vinegar, pepper, and salt, poured gently over the design so as not to destroy the poetry of line and colour. A crisp Vienna roll, with sweet fresh butter, makes an excellent accompaniment, but one to be enjoyed in moderation.

Crème Soubise is the soup to follow. Thick, creamy, onion-scented, the first spoonful enchants, and a glamour is at once cast over dinner and diners. Sufficing in itself, it needs neither Parmesan nor toast to enhance its merits. Like a beautiful woman, unadorned it is adored by the most.

Admirably, it prepares the way for oysters, deftly scalloped, with shallots and fragrant *bouquet garni* to lend them savour, and bread crumbs to form a rich golden-brown outer covering. If not unmindful of the eye's pleasure, you will make as many shells as there are guests serve the purpose of a single dish.

Without loitering or dallying with useless *entrées*, come at once to the one substantial course of the pleasant feast —and see that it be not too substantial. Avoid the heavy, clumsy, unimaginative joint. Decide rather for idyllic *Tour-*

nedos aux Champignons; the fillet tender and *saignant,* as
the French say, the mushrooms, not of the little button
variety, suggesting tins or bottles, but large and black and
fresh from the market. Rapture is their inevitable sauce:
rapture too deep for words. To share the same plate
pommes soufflées may be found worthy.

None but the irreverent would seek to blur their impressions by eating other meats after so delectable a dish. Order, rather, a vegetable salad, fresh and soothing: potatoes,
cauliflower, carrots, celery, a suspicion of garlic, and a
sprinkling of parsley. Eat slowly; foolish is the impatient
man who gallops through his pleasures in hot haste.

And now, be bold, defy convention, and do away with
sweets. After so tender a poem, who could rejoice in the
prose of pudding? But "a last course at dinner, wanting
cheese, is like a pretty woman with only one eye." Therefore, unless you be blind to beauty, let cheese be served.
Port Salut will do as well as another; neither too strong
nor too mild, it has qualities not to be prized lightly.

Fruit is the sweet envoy to the Ballade of Dinner. And
of all winter's fruits, the fragrant, spicy little Tangerine
orange is most delicious and suggestive. Its perfume alone,
to those who have dined discreetly, is a magic pass to the
happy land of dreams. Conversation rallies, wit flashes,
confidences are begotten over walnuts and almonds, and
so, unless in surly, taciturn mood—as who could be after
so exquisite a dinner?—let these have a place upon your
menu.

See that your wines are as perfect of their kind as your
courses. Too many would be a dire mistake. A good Sauterne, a light Burgundy will answer well if "of the first
quality." Cheap, or of a poor vintage, they will ruin the
choicest dish.

Upon coffee, too, much depends. It must be strong, it
must be rich, it must be hot. But strength and richness

may not be had unless it be fresh roasted and ground. Worse a hundred fold you may do than to mix Mocha with Mysore; theirs is one of the few happy unions. If romance have charm for you, then finish with a little glass of green Chartreuse—the yellow is for the feeble and namby-pamby; powerful, indeed, is the spell it works, powerful and ecstatic.

And having thus well and wisely dined, the cares of life will slip from you; its vexations and annoyances will dwindle into nothingness. Serene, at peace with yourself and all mankind, you may then claim as your right the true joys of living.

Edith Wharton

---◆◆◆---

"EXPIATION"

from *The Descent of Man*

I can never," said Mrs. Fetherel, "hear the bell ring without a shudder."

Her unruffled aspect—she was the kind of woman whose emotions never communicate themselves to her clothes—and the conventional background of the New York drawing-room, with its pervading implication of an imminent tea-tray and of an atmosphere in which the social functions have become purely reflex, lent to her declaration a relief not lost on her cousin Mrs. Clinch, who, from the other side of the fireplace, agreed, with a glance at the clock, that it *was* the hour for bores.

"Bores!" cried Mrs. Fetherel impatiently. "If I shuddered at *them*, I should have a chronic ague!"

She leaned forward and laid a sparkling finger on her cousin's shabby black knee. "I mean the newspaper clippings," she whispered.

Mrs. Clinch returned a glance of intelligence. "They've begun already?"

"Not yet; but they're sure to now, at any minute, my publisher tells me."

Mrs. Fetherel's look of apprehension sat oddly on her small features, which had an air of neat symmetry somehow suggestive of being set in order every morning by the housemaid. Someone (there were rumours that it was her cousin) had once said that Paula Fetherel would have been very pretty if she hadn't looked so like a moral axiom in a copy-book hand.

278

Mrs. Clinch received her confidence with a smile. "Well," she said, "I suppose you were prepared for the consequences of authorship?"

Mrs. Fetherel blushed brightly. "It isn't their coming," she owned—"it's their coming *now*."

"Now?"

"The Bishop's in town."

Mrs. Clinch leaned back and shaped her lips to a whistle which deflected in a laugh. "Well!" she said.

"You see!" Mrs. Fetherel triumphed.

"Well—weren't you prepared for the Bishop?"

"Not now—at least, I hadn't thought of his seeing the clippings."

"And why should he see them?"

"Bella—*won't* you understand? It's John."

"John?"

"Who has taken the most unexpected tone—one might almost say out of perversity."

"Oh, perversity—" Mrs. Clinch murmured, observing her cousin between lids wrinkled by amusement. "What tone has John taken?"

Mrs. Fetherel threw out her answer with the desperate gesture of a woman who lays bare the traces of a marital fist. "The tone of being proud of my book."

The measure of Mrs. Clinch's enjoyment overflowed in laughter.

"Oh, you may laugh," Mrs. Fetherel insisted, "but it's no joke to me. In the first place, John's liking the book is so—so—such a false note—it puts me in such a ridiculous position; and then it has set him watching for the reviews —who would ever have suspected John of knowing that books were *reviewed*? Why, he's actually found out about the Clipping Bureau, and whenever the postman rings I hear John rush out of the library to see if there are any yellow envelopes. Of course, when they *do* come he'll bring them into the drawing-room and read them aloud to everybody who happens to be here—and the Bishop is sure to happen to be here!"

Mrs. Clinch repressed her amusement. "The picture you draw is a lurid one," she conceded, "but your modesty strikes me as abnormal, especially in an author. The chances are that some of the clippings will be rather pleasant reading. The critics are not all union men."

Mrs. Fetherel stared. "Union men?"

"Well, I mean they don't all belong to the well-known Society-for-the-Persecution-of-Rising-Authors. Some of them have even been known to defy its regulations and say a good word for a new writer."

"Oh, I dare say," said Mrs. Fetherel, with the laugh her cousin's epigram exacted. "But you don't quite see my point. I'm not at all nervous about the success of my book —my publisher tells me I have no need to be—but I *am* afraid of its being a *succès de scandale*."

"Mercy!" said Mrs. Clinch, sitting up.

The butler and footman at this moment appeared with the tea-tray, and when they had withdrawn, Mrs. Fetherel, bending her brightly rippled head above the kettle, continued in a murmur of avowal, "The title, even, is a kind of challenge."

" 'Fast and Loose,' " Mrs. Clinch mused. "Yes, it ought to take."

"I didn't choose it for that reason!" the author protested. "I should have preferred something quieter—less pronounced; but I was determined not to shirk the responsibility of what I had written. I want people to know beforehand exactly what kind of book they are buying."

"Well," said Mrs. Clinch, "that's a degree of conscientiousness that I've never met with before. So few books fulfil the promise of their titles that experienced readers never expect the fare to come up to the menu."

" 'Fast and Loose' will be no disappointment on that score," her cousin significantly returned. "I've handled the subject without gloves. I've called a spade a spade."

"You simply make my mouth water! And to think I haven't been able to read it yet because every spare minute of my time has been given to correcting the proofs of 'How the Birds Keep Christmas'! There's an instance of the hardships of an author's life!"

Mrs. Fetherel's eye clouded. "Don't joke, Bella, please. I suppose to experienced authors there's always something absurd in the nervousness of a new writer, but in my case so much is at stake; I've put so much of myself into this book and I'm so afraid of being misunderstood . . . of being, as it were, in advance of my time . . . like poor Flaubert. . . . I *know* you'll think me ridiculous . . . and if only my own reputation were at stake, I should never give it a thought . . . but the idea of dragging John's name through the mire . . ."

Mrs. Clinch, who had risen and gathered her cloak about her, stood surveying from her genial height her cousin's agitated countenance.

"Why did you use John's name, then?"

"That's another of my difficulties! I *had* to. There would have been no merit in publishing such a book under an assumed name; it would have been an act of moral cowardice. 'Fast and Loose' is not an ordinary novel. A writer who dares to show up the hollowness of social conventions must have the courage of her convictions and be willing to accept the consequences of defying society. Can you imagine Ibsen or Tolstoy writing under a false name?" Mrs. Fetherel lifted a tragic eye to her cousin. "You don't know, Bella, how often I've envied you since I began to write. I used to wonder sometimes—you won't mind my saying so?—why, with all your cleverness, you hadn't taken up some more exciting subject than natural history;

but I see now how wise you were. Whatever happens, you will never be denounced by the press!"

"Is that what you're afraid of?" asked Mrs. Clinch, as she grasped the bulging umbrella which rested against her chair. "My dear, if I had ever had the good luck to be denounced by the press, my brougham would be waiting at the door for me at this very moment, and I shouldn't have had to ruin this umbrella by using it in the rain. Why, you innocent, if I'd ever felt the slightest aptitude for showing up social conventions, do you suppose I should waste my time writing 'Nests Ajar' and 'How to Smell the Flowers'? There's a fairly steady demand for pseudo-science and colloquial ornithology, but it's nothing, simply nothing, to the ravenous call for attacks on social institutions—especially by those inside the institutions!"

There was often, to her cousin, a lack of taste in Mrs. Clinch's pleasantries, and on this occasion they seemed more than usually irrelevant.

"'Fast and Loose' was not written with the idea of a large sale."

Mrs. Clinch was unperturbed. "Perhaps that's just as well," she returned, with a philosophic shrug. "The surprise will be all the pleasanter, I mean. For of course it's going to sell tremendously; especially if you can get the press to denounce it."

"Bella, how *can* you? I sometimes think you say such things expressly to tease me; and yet I should think you of all women would understand my purpose in writing such a book. It has always seemed to me that the message I had to deliver was not for myself alone, but for all the other women in the world who have felt the hollowness of our social shams, the ignominy of bowing down to the idols of the market, but have lacked either the courage or the power to proclaim their independence; and I have fancied, Bella dear, that, however severely society might punish me for revealing its weaknesses, I could count on the sympathy of those who, like you"—Mrs. Fetherel's voice sank—"have passed through the deep waters."

Mrs. Clinch gave herself a kind of canine shake, as though to free her ample shoulders from any drop of the element she was supposed to have traversed.

"Oh, call them muddy rather than deep," she returned; "and you'll find, my dear, that women who've had any wading to do are rather shy of stirring up mud. It sticks—especially on white clothes."

Mrs. Fetherel lifted an undaunted brow. "I'm not afraid," she proclaimed; and at the same instant she dropped her tea-spoon with a clatter and shrank back into her seat. "There's the bell," she exclaimed, "and I know it's the Bishop!"

It was in fact the Bishop of Ossining, who, impressively announced by Mrs. Fetherel's butler, now made an entry that may best be described as not inadequate to the expectations the announcement raised. The Bishop always entered a room well; but, when unannounced, or preceded by a Low Church butler who gave him his surname, his appearance lacked the impressiveness conferred on it by the due specification of his diocesan dignity. The Bishop was very fond of his niece Mrs. Fetherel, and one of the traits he most valued in her was the possession of a butler who knew how to announce a bishop.

Mrs. Clinch was also his niece; but, aside from the fact that she possessed no butler at all, she had laid herself open to her uncle's criticism by writing insignificant little books which had a way of going into five or ten editions, while the fruits of his own episcopal leisure—"The Wail of Jonah" (twenty cantos in blank verse), and "Through a Glass Brightly; or, How to Raise Funds for a Memorial Window"—inexplicably languished on the back shelves of a publisher noted for his dexterity in pushing "devotional goods." Even this indiscretion the Bishop might, however, have condoned, had his niece thought fit to turn to him for support and advice at the painful juncture of her history when, in her own words, it became necessary for her to invite Mr. Clinch to look out for another situation. Mr. Clinch's misconduct was of the kind especially designed by Providence to test the fortitude of a Christian wife and mother, and the Bishop was absolutely distended with seasonable advice and edification; so that when Bella met his tentative exhortations with the curt remark that she preferred to do her own housecleaning unassisted, her uncle's grief at her ingratitude was not untempered with sympathy for Mr. Clinch.

It is not surprising, therefore, that the Bishop's warmest greetings were always reserved for Mrs. Fetherel; and on this occasion Mrs. Clinch thought she detected, in the salutation which fell to her share, a pronounced suggestion that her own presence was superfluous—a hint which she took with her usual imperturbable good humour.

II

LEFT alone with the Bishop, Mrs. Fetherel sought the nearest refuge from conversation by offering him a cup of tea. The Bishop accepted with the preoccupied air of a man to whom, for the moment, tea is but a subordinate incident. Mrs. Fetherel's nervousness increased; and knowing that the surest way of distracting attention from one's own affairs is to affect an interest in those of one's companion, she hastily asked if her uncle had come to town on business.

"On business—yes—" said the Bishop in an impressive tone. "I had to see my publisher, who has been behaving rather unsatisfactorily in regard to my last book."

"Ah—your last book?" faltered Mrs. Fetherel, with a sickening sense of her inability to recall the name or nature of the work in question, and a mental vow never again to be caught in such ignorance of a colleague's productions.

"'Through a Glass Brightly,'" the Bishop explained, with an emphasis which revealed his detection of her predicament. "You may remember that I sent you a copy last Christmas?"

"Of course I do!" Mrs. Fetherel brightened. "It was that delightful story of the poor consumptive girl who had no money, and two little brothers to support—"

"Sisters—idiot sisters—" the Bishop gloomily corrected.

"I mean sisters; and who managed to collect money enough to put up a beautiful memorial window to her— her grandfather, whom she had never seen—"

"But whose sermons had been her chief consolation and support during her long struggle with poverty and disease." The Bishop gave the satisfied sigh of the workman who reviews his completed task. "A touching subject, surely; and I believe I did it justice; at least so my friends assured me."

"Why, yes—I remember there was a splendid review of it in the *Reredos!*" cried Mrs. Fetherel, moved by the incipient instinct of reciprocity.

"Yes—by my dear friend Mrs. Gollinger, whose husband, the late Dean Gollinger, was under very particular obligations to me. Mrs. Gollinger is a woman of rare literary acumen, and her praise of my book was unqualified; but the public wants more highly seasoned fare, and the approval of a thoughtful churchwoman carries less weight than the sensational comments of an illiterate journalist." The Bishop bent a meditative eye on his spotless gaiters. "At the risk of horrifying you, my dear," he added, with a slight laugh, "I will confide to you that my best chance of a popular success would be to have my book denounced by the press."

"Denounced?" gasped Mrs. Fetherel. "On what ground?"

"On the ground of immorality." The Bishop evaded her startled gaze. "Such a thing is inconceivable to you, of course; but I am only repeating what my publisher tells me. If, for instance, a critic could be induced—I mean, if a critic were to be found, who called in question the morality of my heroine in sacrificing her own health and that of her idiot sisters in order to put up a memorial window to her grandfather, it would probably raise a general controversy in the newspapers, and I might count on a sale of ten or fifteen thousand within the next year. If he described her as morbid or decadent, it might even run to twenty thousand; but that is more than I permit myself to hope. In fact I should be satisfied with any general charge of immorality." The Bishop sighed again. "I need hardly tell you that I am actuated by no mere literary ambition. Those whose opinion I most value have assured me that the book is not without merit; but, though it does not become me to dispute their verdict, I can truly say that my vanity as an author is not at stake. I have, however, a special reason for wishing to increase the circulation of 'Through a Glass Brightly'; it was written for a purpose—a purpose I have greatly at heart—"

"I know," cried his niece sympathetically. "The chantry window—?"

"Is still empty, alas! and I had great hopes that, under Providence, my little book might be the means of filling it. All our wealthy parishioners have given lavishly to the cathedral, and it was for this reason that, in writing 'Through a Glass,' I addressed my appeal more especially to the less well-endowed, hoping by the example of my heroine to stimulate the collection of small sums throughout the entire diocese, and perhaps beyond it. I am sure," the Bishop feelingly concluded, "the book would have a widespread influence if people could only be induced to read it!"

His conclusion touched a fresh thread of association in Mrs. Fetherel's vibrating nerve-centres. "I never thought of that!" she cried.

The Bishop looked at her enquiringly.

"That one's books may not be read at all! How dreadful!" she exclaimed.

He smiled faintly. "I had not forgotten that I was addressing an authoress," he said. "Indeed, I should not have dared to inflict my troubles on any one not of the craft."

Mrs. Fetherel was quivering with the consciousness of her involuntary self-betrayal. "Oh, uncle!" she murmured.

"In fact," the Bishop continued, with a gesture which seemed to brush away her scruples, "I came here partly to speak to you about your novel. 'Fast and Loose,' I think you call it?"

Mrs. Fetherel blushed assentingly.

"And is it out yet?" the Bishop continued.

"It came out about a week ago. But you haven't touched your tea and it must be quite cold. Let me give you another cup."

"My reason for asking," the Bishop went on, with the bland inexorableness with which, in his younger days, he had been known to continue a sermon after the senior warden had looked four times at his watch—"my reason for asking is, that I hoped I might not be too late to induce you to change the title."

Mrs. Fetherel set down the cup she had filled. "The title?" she faltered.

The Bishop raised a reassuring hand. "Don't misunder-

stand me, dear child; don't for a moment imagine that I
take it to be in any way indicative of the contents of the
book. I know you too well for that. My first idea was that
it had probably been forced on you by an unscrupulous
publisher—I know too well to what ignoble compromises
one may be driven in such cases! . . ." He paused, as
though to give her the opportunity of confirming this con-
jecture, but she preserved an apprehensive silence, and he
went on, as though taking up the second point in his sermon—"Or, again, the name may have taken your fancy
without your realising all that it implies to minds more
alive than yours to offensive innuendoes. It is—ahem—
excessively suggestive, and I hope I am not too late to
warn you of the false impression it is likely to produce
on the very readers whose approbation you would most
value. My friend Mrs. Gollinger, for instance—"

Mrs. Fetherel, as the publication of her novel testified,
was in theory a woman of independent views; and if in
practice she sometimes failed to live up to her standard, it
was rather from an irresistible tendency to adapt herself
to her environment than from any conscious lack of moral
courage. The Bishop's exordium had excited in her that
sense of opposition which such admonitions are apt to
provoke; but as he went on she felt herself gradually
enclosed in an atmosphere in which her theories vainly
gasped for breath. The Bishop had the immense dialecti-
cal advantage of invalidating any conclusions at variance
with his own by always assuming that his premises were
among the necessary laws of thought. This method, combined with the habit of ignoring any classifications but his
own, created an element in which the first condition of
existence was the immediate adoption of his standpoint;
so that his niece, as she listened, seemed to feel Mrs. Gollinger's Mechlin cap spreading its conventual shadow over
her rebellious brow and the *Revue de Paris* at her elbow

turning into a copy of the *Reredos*. She had meant to assure her uncle that she was quite aware of the significance of the title she had chosen, that it had been deliberately selected as indicating the subject of her novel, and that the book itself had been written in direct defiance of the class of readers for whose susceptibilities he was alarmed. The words were almost on her lips when the irresistible suggestion conveyed by the Bishop's tone and language deflected them into the apologetic murmur, "Oh, uncle, you mustn't think—I never meant—" How much farther this current of reaction might have carried her the historian is unable to compute, for at this point the door opened and her husband entered the room.

"The first review of your book!" he cried, flourishing a yellow envelope. "My dear Bishop, how lucky you're here!"

Though the trials of married life have been classified and catalogued with exhaustive accuracy, there is one form of conjugal misery which has perhaps received inadequate attention; and that is the suffering of the versatile woman whose husband is not equally adapted to all her moods. Every woman feels for the sister who is compelled to wear a bonnet which does not "go" with her gown; but how much sympathy is given to her whose husband refuses to harmonise with the pose of the moment? Scant justice has, for instance, been done to the misunderstood wife whose husband persists in understanding her; to the submissive helpmate whose taskmaster shuns every opportunity of browbeating her, and to the generous and impulsive being whose bills are paid with philosophic calm. Mrs. Fetherel, as wives go, had been fairly exempt from trials of this nature, for her husband, if undistinguished by pronounced brutality or indifference, had at least the negative merit of being her intellectual inferior. Landscape-gardeners, who are aware of the usefulness of a valley in emphasising the height of a hill, can form an idea of the account to which an accomplished woman may turn such deficiencies; and it need scarcely be said that Mrs. Fetherel had made the most of her opportunities. It was agreeably obvious to every one, Fetherel included, that he was not the man to appreciate such a woman; but there are no limits to man's perversity, and he did his best to invalidate this advantage by admiring her without pretending to understand her. What she most suffered from was this fatuous approval: the maddening sense that, however she conducted herself, he would always admire her. Had he belonged to the class whose conversational supplies are drawn from the domestic circle, his wife's name would never have been off his lips; and to Mrs. Fetherel's sensitive perceptions his frequent silences were indicative of the fact that she was his one topic.

It was, in part, the attempt to escape this persistent approbation that had driven Mrs. Fetherel to authorship. She had fancied that even the most infatuated husband might be counted on to resent, at least negatively, an attack on the sanctity of the hearth; and her anticipations were heightened by a sense of the unpardonableness of her act. Mrs. Fetherel's relations with her husband were in fact complicated by an irrepressible tendency to be fond of him; and there was a certain pleasure in the prospect of a situation that justified the most explicit expiation.

These hopes Fetherel's attitude had already defeated. He read the book with enthusiasm, he pressed it on his friends, he sent a copy to his mother; and his very soul now hung on the verdict of the reviewers. It was perhaps this proof of his general inaptitude that made his wife doubly alive to his special defects; so that his inopportune entrance was aggravated by the very sound of his voice and the hopeless aberration of his smile. Nothing, to the observant, is more indicative of a man's character and circumstances than his way of entering a room. The Bishop of Ossining, for instance, brought with him not only an atmosphere of episcopal authority, but an implied opinion on the verbal inspiration of the Scriptures and on the attitude of the Church toward divorce; while the appearance of Mrs. Fetherel's husband produced an immediate impression of domestic felicity. His mere aspect implied that there was a well-filled nursery upstairs; that his wife, if she did not sew on his buttons, at least superintended the performance of that task; that they both went to church regularly, and that they dined with his mother every Sunday evening punctually at seven o'clock.

All this and more was expressed in the affectionate gesture with which he now raised the yellow envelope above Mrs. Fetherel's clutch; and knowing the uselessness of begging him not to be silly, she said, with a dry despair, "You're boring the Bishop horribly."

Fetherel turned a radiant eye on that dignitary. "She bores us all horribly, doesn't she, sir?" he exulted.

"Have you read it?" said his wife, uncontrollably.

"Read it? Of course not—it's just this minute come. I say, Bishop, you're not going—?"

"Not till I've heard this," said the Bishop, settling himself in his chair with an indulgent smile.

His niece glanced at him despairingly. "Don't let John's nonsense detain you," she entreated.

"Detain him? That's good," guffawed Fetherel. "It isn't as long as one of his sermons—won't take me five minutes to read. Here, listen to this, ladies and gentlemen: 'In this age of festering pessimism and decadent depravity, it is no surprise to the nauseated reviewer to open one more volume saturated with the fetid emanations of the sewer—' "

Fetherel, who was not in the habit of reading aloud, paused with a gasp, and the Bishop glanced sharply at his niece, who kept her gaze fixed on the tea-cup she had not yet succeeded in transferring to his hand.

" 'Of the sewer,' " her husband resumed; " 'but his wonder is proportionately great when he lights on a novel as sweetly inoffensive as Paula Fetherel's "Fast and Loose." Mrs. Fetherel is, we believe, a new hand at fiction, and her work reveals frequent traces of inexperience; but these are more than atoned for by her pure fresh view of life and her altogether unfashionable regard for the reader's moral susceptibilities. Let no one be induced by its distinctly misleading title to forego the enjoyment of this pleasant picture of domestic life, which, in spite of a total lack of force in character-drawing and of consecutiveness in incident, may be described as a distinctly pretty story.' "

III

IT WAS several weeks later that Mrs. Clinch once more brought the plebeian aroma of heated tramcars and muddy street-crossings into the violet-scented atmosphere of her cousin's drawing-room.

"Well," she said, tossing a damp bundle of proof into the corner of a silk-cushioned bergère, "I've read it at last and I'm not so awfully shocked!"

Mrs. Fetherel, who sat near the fire with her head propped on a languid hand, looked up without speaking.

"Mercy, Paula," said her visitor, "you're ill."

Mrs. Fetherel shook her head. "I was never better," she said, mournfully.

"Then may I help myself to tea? Thanks."

Mrs. Clinch carefully removed her mended glove before taking a buttered tea-cake; then she glanced again at her cousin.

"It's not what I said just now—?" she ventured.

"Just now?"

"About 'Fast and Loose'? I came to talk it over."

Mrs. Fetherel sprang to her feet. "I never," she cried dramatically, "want to hear it mentioned again!"

"Paula!" exclaimed Mrs. Clinch, setting down her cup.

Mrs. Fetherel slowly turned on her an eye brimming with the incommunicable; then, dropping into her seat again, she added, with a tragic laugh: "There's nothing left to say."

"Nothing—?" faltered Mrs. Clinch, longing for another tea-cake, but feeling the inappropriateness of the impulse in an atmosphere so charged with the portentous. "Do you mean that everything *has* been said?" She looked tentatively at her cousin. "Haven't they been nice?"

"They've been odious—odious—" Mrs. Fetherel burst out, with an ineffectual clutch at her handkerchief. "It's been perfectly intolerable!"

Mrs. Clinch, philosophically resigning herself to the propriety of taking no more tea, crossed over to her cousin and laid a sympathising hand on that lady's agitated shoulder.

"It *is* a bore at first," she conceded; "but you'll be surprised to see how soon one gets used to it."

"I shall—never—get—used to it—" Mrs. Fetherel brokenly declared.

"Have they been so very nasty—all of them?"

"Every one of them!" the novelist sobbed.

"I'm so sorry, dear; it *does* hurt, I know—but hadn't you rather expected it?"

"Expected it?" cried Mrs. Fetherel, sitting up.

Mrs. Clinch felt her way warily. "I only mean, dear, that I fancied from what you said before the book came out—that you rather expected—that you'd rather discounted—"

"Their recommending it to everybody as a perfectly harmless story?"

"Good gracious! Is *that* what they've done?"

Mrs. Fetherel speechlessly nodded.

"Every one of them?"

"Every one."

"Whew!" said Mrs. Clinch, with an incipient whistle.

"Why, you've just said it yourself!" her cousin suddenly reproached her.

"Said what?"

"That you weren't so *awfully* shocked—"

"I? Oh, well—you see, you'd keyed me up to such a pitch that it wasn't quite as bad as I expected—"

Mrs. Fetherel lifted a smile steeled for the worst. "Why not say at once," she suggested, "that it's a distinctly pretty story?"

"They haven't said *that*?"

"They've all said it."

"My poor Paula!"

"Even the Bishop—"

"The Bishop called it a pretty story?"

"He wrote me—I've his letter somewhere. The title rather scared him—he wanted me to change it; but when he'd read the book he wrote that it was all right and that he'd sent several copies to his friends."

"The old hypocrite!" cried Mrs. Clinch. "That was nothing but professional jealousy."

"Do you think so?" cried her cousin, brightening.

"Sure of it, my dear. His own books don't sell, and he knew the quickest way to kill yours was to distribute it through the diocese with his blessing."

"Then you don't really think it's a pretty story?"

"Dear me, no! Not nearly as bad as that—"

"You're so good, Bella—but the reviewers?"

"Oh, the reviewers," Mrs. Clinch jeered. She gazed meditatively at the cold remains of her tea-cake. "Let me see,"

she said, suddenly; "do you happen to remember if the
first review came out in an important paper?"

"Yes—the *Radiator*."

"That's it! I thought so. Then the others simply fol-
lowed suit: they often do if a big paper sets the pace.
Saves a lot of trouble. Now if you could only have got the
Radiator to denounce you—"

"That's what the Bishop said!" cried Mrs. Fetherel.

"He did?"

"He said his only chance of selling 'Through a Glass
Brightly' was to have it denounced on the ground of immorality."

"H'm," said Mrs. Clinch, "I thought he knew a trick or
two." She turned an illuminated eye on her cousin. "You
ought to get *him* to denounce 'Fast and Loose'!" she
cried.

Mrs. Fetherel looked at her suspiciously. "I suppose
every book must stand or fall on its own merits," she said
in an unconvinced tone.

"Bosh! That view is as extinct as the post-chaise and
the packet-ship—it belongs to the time when people read
books. Nobody does that now; the reviewer was the first
to set the example, and the public were only too thankful
to follow it. At first they read the reviews; now they read
only the publisher's extracts from them. Even these are
rapidly being replaced by paragraphs borrowed from the
vocabulary of commerce. I often have to look twice before
I am sure if I am reading a department-store advertisement or the announcement of a new batch of literature.
The publishers will soon be having their 'fall and spring
openings' and their 'special importations for Horse-Show
Week.' But the Bishop is right, of course—nothing helps
a book like a rousing attack on its morals; and as the publishers can't exactly proclaim the impropriety of their own

wares, the task has to be left to the press or the pulpit."

"The pulpit—?" Mrs. Fetherel mused.

"Why, yes—look at those two novels in England last year—"

Mrs. Fetherel shook her head hopelessly. "There is so much more interest in literature in England than here."

"Well, we've got to make the supply create the demand. The Bishop could run your novel up into the hundred thousands in no time."

"But if he can't make his own sell—"

"My dear, a man can't very well preach against his own writings!"

Mrs. Clinch rose and picked up her proofs.

"I'm awfully sorry for you, Paula dear," she concluded, "but I can't help being thankful that there's no demand for pessimism in the field of natural history. Fancy having to write 'The Fall of a Sparrow,' or 'How the Plants Misbehave'!"

IV

MRS. FETHEREL, driving up to the Grand Central Station one morning about five months later, caught sight of the distinguished novelist, Archer Hynes, hurrying into the waiting-room ahead of her. Hynes, on his side, recognising her brougham, turned back to greet her as the footman opened the carriage door.

"My dear colleague! Is it possible that we are travelling together?"

Mrs. Fetherel blushed with pleasure. Hynes had given her two columns of praise in the *Sunday Meteor*, and she had not yet learned to disguise her gratitude.

"I am going to Ossining," she said smilingly.

"So am I. Why, this is almost as good as an elopement."

"And it will end where elopements ought to—in church."

"In church? You're not going to Ossining to go to church?"

"Why not? There's a special ceremony in the cathedral —the chantry window is to be unveiled."

"The chantry window? How picturesque! What *is* a chantry? And why do you want to see it unveiled? Are you after copy—doing something in the Huysmans manner? 'La Cathédrale,' eh?"

"Oh, no." Mrs. Fetherel hesitated. "I'm going simply to please my uncle," she said, at last.

"Your uncle?"

"The Bishop, you know." She smiled.

"The Bishop—the Bishop of Ossining? Why, wasn't he the chap who made that ridiculous attack on your book? Is that prehistoric ass your uncle? Upon my soul, I think you're mighty forgiving to travel all the way to Ossining for one of his stained-glass sociables!"

Mrs. Fetherel's smiles flowed into a gentle laugh. "Oh, I've never allowed that to interfere with our friendship. My uncle felt dreadfully about having to speak publicly against my book—it was a great deal harder for him than for me—but he thought it his duty to do so. He has the very highest sense of duty."

"Well," said Hynes, with a shrug, "I don't know that he didn't do you a good turn. Look at that!"

They were standing near the book-stall and he pointed to a placard surmounting the counter and emblazoned with the conspicuous announcement: *"Fast and Loose.* New Edition with Author's Portrait. Hundred and Fiftieth Thousand."

Mrs. Fetherel frowned impatiently. "How absurd! They've no right to use my picture as a poster!"

"There's our train," said Hynes; and they began to push their way through the crowd surging toward one of the inner doors.

As they stood wedged between circumferent shoulders, Mrs. Fetherel became conscious of the fixed stare of a pretty girl who whispered eagerly to her companion: "Look, Myrtle! That's Paula Fetherel right behind us—I knew her in a minute!"

"Gracious—where?" cried the other girl, giving her head a twist which swept her Gainsborough plumes across Mrs. Fetherel's face.

The first speaker's words had carried beyond her companion's ear, and a lemon-coloured woman in spectacles, who clutched a copy of the "Journal of Psychology" in one drab-cotton-gloved hand, stretched her disengaged hand across the intervening barrier of humanity.

"Have I the privilege of addressing the distinguished author of 'Fast and Loose'? If so, let me thank you in the name of the Woman's Psychological League of Peoria for your magnificent courage in raising the standard of revolt against—"

"You can tell us the rest in the car," said a fat man, pressing his good-humoured bulk against the speaker's arm.

Mrs. Fetherel, blushing, embarrassed and happy, slipped into the space produced by this displacement, and a few moments later had taken her seat in the train.

She was a little late, and the other chairs were already filled by a company of elderly ladies and clergymen who seemed to belong to the same party, and were still busy exchanging greetings and settling themselves in their places.

One of the ladies, at Mrs. Fetherel's approach, uttered an exclamation of pleasure and advanced with outstretched hand. "My dear Mrs. Fetherel! I am so delighted to see you here. May I hope you are going to the unveiling of the chantry window? The dear Bishop so hoped that you would do so! But perhaps I ought to introduce myself. I am Mrs. Gollinger"—she lowered her voice expressively—"one of your uncle's oldest friends, one who has stood close to him through all this sad business, and who knows what he suffered when he felt obliged to sacrifice family affection to the call of duty."

Mrs. Fetherel, who had smiled and coloured slightly at the beginning of this speech, received its close with a deprecating gesture.

"Oh, pray don't mention it," she murmured. "I quite understood how my uncle was placed—I bore him no ill will for feeling obliged to preach against my book."

"He understood that, and was so touched by it! He has often told me that it was the hardest task he was ever called upon to perform—and, do you know, he quite feels that this unexpected gift of the chantry window is in some way a return for his courage in preaching that sermon."

Mrs. Fetherel smiled faintly. "Does he feel that?"

"Yes; he really does. When the funds for the window were so mysteriously placed at his disposal, just as he had begun to despair of raising them, he assured me that he could not help connecting the fact with his denunciation of your book."

"Dear uncle!" sighed Mrs. Fetherel. "Did he say that?"

"And now," continued Mrs. Gollinger, with cumulative rapture—"now that you are about to show, by appearing at the ceremony to-day, that there has been no break in your friendly relations, the dear Bishop's happiness will be complete. He was so longing to have you come to the unveiling!"

"He might have counted on me," said Mrs. Fetherel, still smiling.

"Ah, that is so beautifully forgiving of you!" cried Mrs. Gollinger enthusiastically. "But then, the Bishop has always assured me that your real nature was very different from that which—if you will pardon my saying so—seems to be revealed by your brilliant but—er—rather subversive book. 'If you only knew my niece, dear Mrs. Gollinger,' he always said, 'you would see that her novel was written in all innocence of heart'; and to tell you the truth, when I first read the book I didn't think it so very, *very* shocking. It wasn't till the dear Bishop had explained to me—but, dear me, I mustn't take up your time in this way when so many others are anxious to have a word with you."

Mrs. Fetherel glanced at her in surprise, and Mrs. Gollinger continued with a playful smile: "You forget that your face is familiar to thousands whom you have never seen. We all recognised you the moment you entered the train, and my friends here are so eager to make your acquaintance—even those"—her smile deepened—"who thought the dear Bishop not *quite unjustified* in his attack on your remarkable novel."

V

A RELIGIOUS light filled the chantry of Ossining Cathedral, filtering through the linen curtain which veiled the central window and mingling with the blaze of tapers on the richly adorned altar.

In this devout atmosphere, agreeably laden with the incense-like aroma of Easter lilies and forced lilacs, Mrs. Fetherel knelt with a sense of luxurious satisfaction. Beside her sat Archer Hynes, who had remembered that there was to be a church scene in his next novel and that his impressions of the devotional environment needed refreshing. Mrs. Fetherel was very happy. She was conscious that her entrance had sent a thrill through the female devotees who packed the chantry, and she had humour enough to enjoy the thought that, but for the good Bishop's denunciation of her book, the heads of his flock would not have been turned so eagerly in her direction.

Moreover, as she entered she had caught sight of a society reporter, and she knew that her presence, and the fact that she was accompanied by Hynes, would be conspicuously proclaimed in the morning papers. All these evidences of the success of her handiwork might have turned a calmer head than Mrs. Fetherel's; and though she had now learned to dissemble her gratification, it still filled her inwardly with a delightful glow.

The Bishop was somewhat late in appearing, and she employed the interval in meditating on the plot of her next novel, which was already partly sketched out, but for which she had been unable to find a satisfactory dénouement. By a not uncommon process of ratiocination, Mrs. Fetherel's success had convinced her of her vocation. She was sure now that it was her duty to lay bare the secret plague-spots of society, and she was resolved that there should be no doubt as to the purpose of her new book. Experience had shown her that where she had fancied she was calling a spade a spade she had in fact been alluding in guarded terms to the drawing-room shovel. She was determined not to repeat the same mistake, and she flattered herself that her coming novel would not need an episcopal denunciation to insure its sale, however likely it was to receive this crowning evidence of success.

She had reached this point in her meditations when the choir burst into song and the ceremony of the unveiling began. The Bishop, almost always felicitous in his addresses to the fair sex, was never more so than when he was celebrating the triumph of one of his cherished purposes. There was a peculiar mixture of Christian humility and episcopal exultation in the manner with which he called attention to the Creator's promptness in responding to his demand for funds, and he had never been more happily inspired than in eulogising the mysterious gift of the chantry window.

Though no hint of the donor's identity had been allowed to escape him, it was generally understood that the Bishop knew who had given the window, and the congregation awaited in a flutter of suspense the possible announcement of a name. None came, however, though the Bishop deliciously titillated the curiosity of his flock by circling ever closer about the interesting secret. He would not disguise from them, he said, that the heart which had divined his inmost wish had been a woman's— is it not to woman's intuitions that more than half the happiness of earth is owing? What man is obliged to learn by the laborious process of experience, woman's wondrous instinct tells her at a glance; and so it had been with this cherished scheme, this unhoped-for completion of their beautiful chantry. So much, at least, he was allowed to reveal; and indeed, had he not done so, the window itself would have spoken for him, since the first glance at its touching subject and exquisite design would show it to have originated in a woman's heart. This tribute to the sex was received with an audible sigh of contentment, and the Bishop, always stimulated by such evidence of his sway over his hearers, took up his theme with gathering eloquence.

Yes—a woman's heart had planned the gift, a woman's hand had executed it, and, might he add, without too far withdrawing the veil in which Christian beneficence ever loved to drape its acts—might he add that, under Providence, a book, a simple book, a mere tale, in fact, had had its share in the good work for which they were assembled to give thanks?

At this unexpected announcement, a ripple of excitement ran through the assemblage, and more than one head was abruptly turned in the direction of Mrs. Fetherel, who sat listening in an agony of wonder and confusion. It did not escape the observant novelist at her side that she drew down her veil to conceal an uncontrollable blush, and this evidence of dismay caused him to fix an attentive gaze on her, while from her seat across the aisle Mrs. Gollinger sent a smile of unctuous approval.

"A book—a simple book—" The Bishop's voice went on above this flutter of mingled emotions. "What is a book? Only a few pages and a little ink—and yet one of the mightiest instruments which Providence has devised for shaping the destinies of man . . . one of the most powerful influences for good or evil which the Creator has placed in the hands of his creatures. . . ."

The air seemed intolerably close to Mrs. Fetherel, and she drew out her scent-bottle, and then thrust it hurriedly away, conscious that she was still the centre of an unenviable attention. And all the while the Bishop's voice droned on . . .

"And of all forms of literature, fiction is doubtless that which has exercised the greatest sway, for good or ill, over the passions and imagination of the masses. Yes, my friends, I am the first to acknowledge it—no sermon, however eloquent, no theological treatise, however learned and convincing, has ever inflamed the heart and imagination like a novel—a simple novel. Incalculable is the power exercised over humanity by the great magicians of the pen—a power ever enlarging its boundaries and increasing its responsibilities as popular education multiplies the number of readers . . . Yes, it is the novelist's hand which can pour balm on countless human sufferings, or inoculate mankind with the festering poison of a corrupt imagination. . . ."

Mrs. Fetherel had turned white, and her eyes were fixed with a blind stare of anger on the large-sleeved figure in the centre of the chancel.

"And too often, alas, it is the poison and not the balm which the unscrupulous hand of genius proffers to its unsuspecting readers. But, my friends, why should I continue? None know better than an assemblage of Christian women, such as I am now addressing, the beneficent or baleful influences of modern fiction; and so, when I say that this beautiful chantry window of ours owes its existence in part to the romancer's pen"—the Bishop paused, and bending forward, seemed to seek a certain face among the countenances eagerly addressed to his—"when I say that this pen, which for personal reasons it does not become me to celebrate unduly—"

Mrs. Fetherel at this point half rose, pushing back her chair, which scraped loudly over the marble floor; but Hynes involuntarily laid a warning hand on her arm, and she sank down with a confused murmur about the heat.

"When I confess that this pen, which for once at least has proved itself so much mightier than the sword, is that which was inspired to trace the simple narrative of 'Through a Glass Brightly'— Mrs. Fetherel looked up with a gasp of mingled relief and anger—"when I tell you, my dear friends, that it was your Bishop's own work which first roused the mind of one of his flock to the crying need of a chantry window, I think you will admit that I am justified in celebrating the triumphs of the pen, even though it be the modest instrument which your own Bishop wields."

The Bishop paused impressively, and a faint gasp of surprise and disappointment was audible throughout the chantry. Something very different from this conclusion had been expected, and even Mrs. Gollinger's lips curled with a slightly ironic smile. But Archer Hynes's attention was chiefly reserved for Mrs. Fetherel, whose face had changed with astonishing rapidity from surprise to annoyance, from annoyance to relief, and then back again to something very like indignation.

The address concluded, the actual ceremony of the unveiling was about to take place, and the attention of the congregation soon reverted to the chancel, where the choir had grouped themselves beneath the veiled window, prepared to burst into a chant of praise as the Bishop drew back the hanging. The moment was an impressive one, and every eye was fixed on the curtain. Even Hynes's gaze strayed to it for a moment, but soon returned to his neighbour's face; and then he perceived that Mrs. Fetherel, alone of all the persons present, was not looking at the window. Her eyes were fixed in an indignant stare on the Bishop; a flush of anger burned becomingly under her veil, and her hands nervously crumpled the beautifully printed programme of the ceremony.

Hynes broke into a smile of comprehension. He glanced at the Bishop, and back at the Bishop's niece; then, as the episcopal hand was solemnly raised to draw back the curtain, he bent and whispered in Mrs. Fetherel's ear:

"Why, you gave it yourself! You wonderful woman, of course you gave it yourself!"

Mrs. Fetherel raised her eyes to his with a start. Her blush deepened and her lips shaped a hasty "No"; but the denial was deflected into the indignant murmur—"It wasn't *his* silly book that did it, anyhow!"

Osbert Lancaster

❧

"TAKE ME BACK TO DEAR OLD SHEPHERD'S BUSH"

from *All Done From Memory*

$\mathcal{I}$ was born in the eighth year of the reign of King Edward the Seventh in the parish of St. John's, Notting Hill. At that time Elgin Crescent, the actual scene of this event, was situated on the Marches of respectability. Up the hill to the south, tree-shaded and freshly stuccoed, stretched the squares and terraces of the last great stronghold of Victorian propriety: below to the north lay the courts and alleys of Notting Dale, through which, so my nurse terrifyingly assured me, policemen could only proceed in pairs.

The Crescent, like all border districts, was distinguished by a certain colourful mixture in its inhabitants, lacking in the more securely sheltered central area, grouped in this case round the church. While residence there was socially approved and no traces of "slumminess" were as yet apparent, there did cling to it a slight whiff of Bohemianism from which Kensington Park Road, for instance, was quite free. Of the residents several were connected with the Stage, and some were foreign, but neither group carried these eccentricities to excessive lengths. Among the former were numbered a Mr. Maskelyne (or was it a Mr. Devant?) who lived on the corner, and, right next door to us, the talented authoress of *Where the Rainbow Ends*, whose daughter, a dashing hobble-skirted croquet player, remains a vivid memory. The foreigners included some Japanese diplomats and a German family connected with the Embassy, whose son, a fair, chinless youth, was always at great pains to model his appearance on that of the Crown Prince Wilhelm, much to the delight of my father whom a long residence in Berlin had rendered expert in detecting the subtlest nuances of this elaborate masquerade. Fortunately my parents' arrival at Number 79 had done much to erase the principal blot on the fair name of the street, as our house had previously been the home of no less equivocal a figure than Madame Blavatsky.

Number 79 was a semi-detached stucco residence on three floors and a basement with a pillared porch, not differing stylistically in any way from the prevailing classicism of the neighbourhood. At the back was a small private garden opening into the large garden common to all the occupants of the south side of Elgin Crescent and the north side of Lansdowne Road. Such communal gardens, which are among the most attractive features of Victorian town-planning, are not uncommon in the residential districts of West London, but are carried to the highest point of their development in the Ladbroke estate. This area, which was laid out after the closure of the race course that for a brief period encircled the summit of the hill, represents the last rational, unselfconscious piece of urban development in London. It was unfortunately dogged by misfortune, and the socially ambitious intention of Allom, the architect, and the promoters' was largely defeated by the proximity of an existing pottery slum in Notting Dale, which received, just at the time the scheme was being launched, an enormous and deplorable influx of Irish labourers working on the Great Western Railway.

How different it all was in the years before 1914! Then the stucco, creamy and bright, gleamed softly beneath what seems in reminiscence to have been a perpetually cloudless sky. Geraniums in urns flanked each brass-enriched front door, while over the area railings moustachioed policemen made love to buxom cooks. And in every street there hung, all summer long, the heavy scent of limes.

The angel who drove the original inhabitants out of this gilt-edged Eden, not with a flaming sword but by a simple vanishing trick, was the domestic servant. The houses, even the small ones like ours, were planned on generous lines and labour-saving was still not only an unrealised but unthought-of ideal. Fortunately my parents whose joint income at the time of my birth amounted to all of £600 a year were able to maintain a cook, a housemaid, a nurse and a boot boy; my mother, moreover, had been through the hard school of a Victorian grandmother's household, and herself undertook such specialised, and now obsolete, labours as cleaning the chandeliers, washing the rubber plant and superintending the linen.

The ideal of the servantless civilisation, already fully realised in the United States, is doubtless a noble one, and those who so bravely, and possibly sincerely, maintain that they feel degraded by being waited on by their fellow human beings compel our admiration, although personally they invariably provoke me to confess that I can tolerate without discomfort being waited on hand and foot. But it is an ideal attended by one grave disadvantage—whom is there left for the children to talk to? A mother's love is all very well, but it is only a poor substitute for good relations with the cook.

In my own case, the centre of the below-stairs world was Kate the housemaid. This remarkable woman, gaunt, near-sighted and invariably prepared for the worst, not only endeared herself to me by acts of kindness to which I could always be certain no strings were attached, but also provided my only contact with the real world which lay beyond the confines of my isolated nursery. Quick-witted and an omnivorous reader of the popular press, it was her habit to converse largely in political slogans and popular catch-phrases. Thus when I was detected sliding unobtrusively into the larder she would call out "Hands off the people's food," and if when driven out she suspected that I still retained some loot she would advance with simulated menace, jabbing the upturned palm of her left hand with the index finger of her right, in a gesture which a dozen cartoons of the then Chancellor of the Exchequer, Mr. Lloyd George, had rendered universally familiar, exclaiming "Put it there!" And always when I asked what was for dinner she would remind me of Mr. Asquith and bid me "Wait and see." But by no means all of her sources of verbal inspiration were political; better even than the Harmsworth Press she loved the music hall, and her evenings off were regularly spent at one or other of the many suburban houses then still happily flourishing on the sites of future Odeons. Her favourite performers were Wilkie Bard, George Mozart and Alfred Lester, and while engaged on her endless scrubbing and dusting she could usually be heard informing the household that she had got a motto, or wanted to sing in opera, or desired to be taken back to dear old Shepherd's Bush.

The popular music of the Edwardian era played an important role in the national life: these music-hall songs and ballads have today been so weakened and degraded by intensive plugging and self-conscious revival over the air that they are now as far removed from their former spontaneous popularity as are the careful prancings of latter-day Morris dancers from the village revels of the Elizabethans. In the strictly stratified social world of my childhood they seemed to me in my bourgeois pram to be the one thing enjoyed in common by the world represented by the whistling errand-boy and the ladies I oc-

casionally observed, humming gaily, if a little off key, as
they emerged from the glittering paradise of *The Devonshire Arms* (in passing which my nurse always developed
an additional turn of speed and on which she would never
comment), and the world of which the pillars were Kate
and my father. I specify my father rather than my parents
as his taste was almost identical with Kate's (he perhaps
rated Harry Lauder a little higher than she did), whereas
my mother's was more accurately represented by "Traü-
meri" and "Songe d'automne," beautiful works, doubtless, but hardly with so universal an appeal.

A few additional figures there were who stood in a
rather closer relation to the small world of Number 79
than the anonymous ranks of passers-by I observed from
my pram: they, while obviously debarred from the full
club privileges of Kate, the cook, my parents and the boot
boy, yet enjoyed, as it were, the facilities of country membership. The Italian organ grinder, a martyr to gastric
troubles, who regularly appeared every Thursday afternoon; the crossing sweeper in Ladbroke Grove whose
function the internal combustion engine was even then
rapidly rendering as decorative as that of the King's Champion; the muffin man, the lamplighter and the old gentleman, who came out on winter evenings to play the harp
by the foggy radiance of the street lamp—Dickensian
figures who have obviously no role to play in the Welfare
State and have left no successors. Doubtless their disappearance should be welcomed, and yet they did not appear
to be either downtrodden or exploited: indeed, the impression they gave was chiefly of a proper consciousness
of the important role in the social fabric played by muffin
men, lamplighters and organ grinders. Certainly their
spirits seemed higher and their manners were undoubtedly better than those of the majority of the present-day
beneficiaries of enlightened social legislation. Even the

crossing sweeper, despite his ostentatious rags and traditional whine, displayed a certain individuality and professional pride which one seldom observes in the hygienically
uniformed Municipal Refuse Disposal Officer.

Apart from such figures, my relations and, later, fellow-
pupils at my kindergarten, the most vivid and indirectly
influential personality of my early childhood was our next-
door neighbour to the west, old Mrs. Ullathorne. This
imposing and always slightly mysterious *grande dame* with
whom I was bidden to tea at regular intervals, represented
an era which, even at that date, seemed almost incredibly
remote. She had enjoyed, so it was said, a considerable
success at the court of Napoleon the Third, and there
were prominently displayed amongst the palms and bibe-
lots of her crowded drawing room innumerable *carte de
visite* size photographs of dashing cuirassiers in peg-top
trousers sporting waxed moustaches and elegant lip
beards, and of crinolined beauties who had somewhat
surprisingly elected to put on full ball dress and all their
diamonds for a good long read, of what appeared from
the binding to be books of devotion, seated on rustic
benches in a vaguely Alpine landscape. Certainly Mrs. Ullathorne herself gave a very definite impression of belonging to another, and far more sophisticated, world than that
of Edwardian Notting Hill. Alone among all our female
acquaintances she was heavily and unashamedly made-up
(even the dashing daughter of our playwright neighbour,
who was thought to be a Suffragette and known to smoke,
never, I fancy, went further than a discreet use of *papiers
poudrés*). But the style in which her maquillage was conceived proclaimed her way behind, rather than daringly
ahead, of the times. The whole surface of her face was
delicately pale and matt, and only by imperceptible degrees did the pearly white take on a faint rosy flush above
the cheekbones; the eyebrows, which although carefully

shaped were not plucked thin, were a deep uncompromising auburn, contrasting very strikingly with the faded parma violet of the lids. Her toupet, a rich mahogany in colour, was dressed in tight curls and fringes in the manner of the reigning queen. The whole effect was one of extreme fragility which, one felt, the slightest contact or even a sneeze would irretrievably wreck, and was as far removed from that achieved by modern methods as is a Nattier from a Modigliani.

Whether due to Mrs. Ullathorne's long residence in foreign parts or to her extreme age, she displayed another peculiarity which set her still further apart from the rest of my world—she invariably insisted that in place of the customary handshake I should bow smartly from the waist and kiss her hand. This was for me always rather an alarming ordeal, and I can still see that long white hand delicately extended, crisscrossed with the purple hawsers of her veins standing out in as high relief as the yellowish diamonds in her many rings, and experience once more the ghastly apprehension that one day, overcome by unbearable curiosity, I should take a sharp nip at the most prominent of those vital pipelines.

The influence which the old lady exercised on my early development was not, however, direct, but the result of a gift. One day she presented me with a large quarto volume bound in dark green leather into which, with incredible neatness, she had in childhood pasted scraps.

Although I can still vividly remember the enchantment which was renewed every time I opened that magic volume, it is only quite fortuitously that its peculiar flavour, recognisable if faint, now and then returns to me. No effort of conscious memory will work the miracle, but just occasionally the sight of swans upon a castle-lake, or some peculiar combination of Prussian blue and carmine, or the feel beneath the fingers of the embossed paper lace

on an old-fashioned Christmas card, will play the part of
Proust's Madeleine and fire the train. Many must have
received such volumes in childhood, but not many I fancy
so perfect an example of the genre as this; for the artists
of no age have ever surpassed those of the romantic period
in the production of keepsakes and *culs de lampes,* and
this volume had been compiled at exactly the right moment. The shakoed, hand-coloured infantrymen, who so
gallantly assaulted that vaguely Oriental stronghold, were
the soldiers of Louis Philippe subduing the fierce Goums
of Abd-el-Kader; this mysterious steel-engraved lake shad-
owed by twilit mountains was Lamartine; and the rather
overplumed knights, their armour gleaming with ap-
plied tinsel, were undoubtedly setting out for the Eglin-
ton Tournament.

The charm and excitement of those vividly coloured
vignettes must have made a powerful appeal to the imagination of any child but in my case it was reinforced by
the contrast they provided to the illustrations in my
other books. My mother suffered from that perpetual
illusion common to all parents that the books which had
meant the most to her in her own childhood (or possibly
those which, later in life, she had persuaded herself had
then been her favourites) would awaken a similar delighted response in her offspring. My nursery library was
therefore well stocked with the illustrated fairytales of
the late seventies and early eighties. It cannot be denied
that the skill of the great nineteenth-century school of
English wood engraving was then at its height and that
many of these volumes were, in their way, masterpieces.
Nevertheless, not only did I dislike them all with the solitary exception of Tenniel's *Alice,* but certain of them
awoke in me feelings of fear and revulsion.

I do not think, looking back, that my reaction was
purely personal nor wholly abnormal. Children are all

firmly in favour of representational art up to a certain point (my lack of enthusiasm for Walter Crane, for instance, was caused by his tendency to subordinate accurate representation to decorative embroidery and was of a wholly different kind to my dislike of Linley Sambourne), but that point is reached when realism is carried over into the third dimension. They will welcome, and indeed demand, the maximum amount of realistic detail provided it is flat, but once an artist starts to give his illustrations depth and to visualise his figures in the round, his pre-adolescent public will begin to lose interest. Thanks to the incredibly responsive instrument which such figures as the Dalziels had made of the wood engraver, the book illustrators of the eighties were able to exploit the third dimension, which still possessed in this medium the charm of comparative novelty, to their hearts' content, and they certainly made the most of the opportunity. The buxom flanks of the Water Babies sprang from the flat page with a startling illusion of rotundity; the more unpleasant creations of Hans Andersen's imagination displayed a devastating solidity; indeed, certain artists went rather too far in their three-dimensional enthusiasm and overstepping the bounds of realism achieved an effect which can only be described, in the strictest sense of the word, as surrealist. In our own day this irrational element in the wood-engraved illustrations of the late nineteenth century, against which I as a child had unconsciously reacted (in exactly the same way, incidentally, as did my own children some twenty-five years later), has been recognised and skillfully utilised for his own terrifying purposes by Max Ernst in such works as "Le Lion de Belfort" and "La Femme à Cent Têtes."

Thus the world of Mrs. Ullathorne's scrapbook, with its brilliant green lawns and flat improbable trees peopled by kindly gendarmes in enormous tricornes and little

girls in pork-pie hats and striped stockings practising arch-
ery in château parks, took on in addition to its own proper
attraction the welcome character of a safe retreat from
that other, boring yet terrifying, world of all too completely realised fantasy.

The work from which, next to the scrap book, I derived
the greatest enjoyment was also uncontemporary, being
two bound volumes of the *Picture Magazine,* to which my
father had regularly subscribed during his school days at
the very end of the Victorian age. This admirable period-
ical nicely combined instruction with amusement, and
among the regular features were a series of simple pseudo-
scientific experiments (a cock mesmerised into following a chalked line with its beak and a daring criminal
escaping from Vincennes by means of a home-made para-
chute), accounts of travel and exploration (whiskered
tourists being hauled up to the monasteries of the Mete-
ora in nets), and, best of all, strip cartoons by Caran
d'Ache. In addition were included from time to time four-
page supplements of photographs of the most distinguished figures in one particular walk of contemporary
life—soldiers, scientists, painters. . . . Of these my
favourite was that devoted to the rulers of sovereign states
who, thank Heaven, were at that date far more numerous
than they are today.

Those long rows of royal torsos adorned with every
variety of epaulette, plastron, and aiguillette, the necks
compressed into collars of unbelievable height and tight-
ness, the manly, if padded chests, hung with row upon
row of improbable crosses and stars and criss crossed by
watered silk ribbons and tangles of gold cords, sur-
mounted by so many extraordinary countenances adorned
with immense moustaches, upstanding in the style of
Potsdam or downsweeping in the style of Vienna, some
fish-eyed, some monocled, some vacant, some indignant

but all self-conscious, had for me a fascination which never failed. And nor, when I had learnt to read, did the captions prove a disappointment; such names as Meck-lenberg-Schwerin, Bourbon-Parme, Saxe-Coburg-Gotha held for me a flavour of high romance to which the very difficulty of pronouncing added rather than detracted. How drab by contrast did the still small handful of republican presidents appear, and how deep was my contempt for those pince-nezed, bourgeois figures to whom a gaudy silken diagonal across their stiff-shirted bosoms could not lend an air of even spurious distinction!

Incredible as it may seem, many of these paladins who now appear far more remote from our modern experience than Attila or Ivan the Terrible were actually still more or less firmly on their thrones at the time when I first grew familiar with their appearance. The whiskered porcine features of Franz Josef were still regularly revealed to his loyal Viennese as he drove every morning through the Hofburg; hardly a day passed without his German colleague, dressed as an Admiral, a Hussar, a Uhlan, a Cuirassier, or a Highland sportsman, making an appearance in the illustrated papers; and somewhere hidden away in the heart of the plaster mazes of Dolmabagh-chesh, that last bastard offspring of a frenzied rococo which had reared itself so surprisingly on the shores of the Bosphorus, apprehensive, invisible but undoubtedly there, was Abdul the Damned.

Of all this I was at that time naturally unaware. All these characters were no more and no less real to me than Jack the Giant Killer and the Infant Samuel of whom my mother was acustomed to read aloud, or Hacken-schmidt and the Terrible Turk, in whose exploits the boot-boy took so keen an interest. Only Kaiser Wilhelm was for me in any way, and that very remotely, connected with real life; for I had once been sent a box of toy soldiers by an old friend of my mother, who was one of that monarch's A.D.C.s, and whose photograph in the full-dress uniform of the Prussian guard stood on the piano.

Less colourful but more familiar were the pages devoted to the more prominent contemporary divines. No flourishing moustachios nor jewelled orders here, but every variety of whisker from the restrained mutton-chop to the full Newgate fringe, and billowing acres of episcopal lawn. At the time these portraits were taken the social prestige of the Establishment, and even, on a different level, of Nonconformity, was at its height, and although it had become a little dimmed in the intervening years it was still comparatively great. How complete has been the subsequent eclipse, a brief study of the representative novels of high life during the last half century will amply demonstrate; although the regiments of handsome curates, worldly Archdeacons and courtly Bishops who thronged the pages of late Victorian fiction thinned out a lot in Edwardian times, a sharp-tongued Mayfair incumbent or two, ex-curates doubtless of Canon Chasuble, still make a regular appearance in the tales of Saki; but in all the works of Michael Arlen I cannot recall a single dog collar and the solitary cleric to appear in the novels of Mr. Waugh is Fr. Rothschild, S.J.

In real life, anyhow in the society in which my parents moved, the clergy still played a prominent and honoured role. Their merits as preachers were eagerly discussed and the exact degree of their "Highness" or "Lowness" keenly debated. Many of the originals of those portraits were, therefore, quite familiar to me by name as being preachers under whom members of my family had at one time or another sat, while on the knees of one of them, Prebendary Webb-Peploe, a celebrated Evangelical preacher from whose well-attended Watch Night sermons the more impressionable members of the congregation were regularly carried out on stretchers, I myself had once had the honour of being perched.

It may seem strange that my infant literature should have been so exclusively out of date, but at that time the modern renaissance of the children's book was in its infancy, and the prevailing standard of contemporary productions was unbelievably low. Exceptions there were, however, and I can vividly remember the pleasure I derived from the *Nursery History of England*, illustrated by that happily still flourishing artist, George Morrow, and, a little later, from the works of Edmund Dulac.

To the enjoyment of the pictures, appreciation of the text was soon added, as thanks to the brilliant educational methods of my mother I learned to read at a very tender age. Her system, simple as it was effective, was based on a chocolate alphabet. This was spread out twice a week on the dining-room table and such letters as I recognised I was allowed to eat; later, when my knowledge of the alphabet was faultless, I was entitled to such letters as I could form into a new word. Although never strong in arithmetic I soon grasped the simple fact that the longer the word the more the chocolate, and by the time I could spell "suffragette" without an error this branch of my education was deemed complete and a tendency to biliousness had become increasingly apparent.

Once my ability was firmly established I read everything on which I could lay my hands, from *The Times* leaders to the preface to the Book of Common Prayer. The impressive zeal was not, I fancy, the result of any exceptional thirst for knowledge, but rather of boredom, and was far commoner among children at that time than it is today. Such cinemas as then existed were regarded by my parents as undesirably sensational and notoriously unhygienic, and there was no compulsion on grown ups to make any pretence of enjoying the company of the young who were, quite rightly, expected to amuse themselves. The only addition which modern science had made to the sources of infant pleasure available to my parents, or even my grandparents, was the gramophone. On this archaic machine I was permitted, as a great treat, to listen to the exaggeratedly Scots voice of Harry Lauder, just audible through a barrage of scratching and whining, singing "Stop your tickling Jock," or to the waltzes of Archibald Joyce rendered, rather surprisingly, by the Earl of Lonsdale's private band and recorded on discs half an inch thick by Messrs. William Whitely.

My appearances in the drawing room, where the gramophone was kept, were determined in accordance with fixed rules, as indeed were those of almost all the children of my generation—on weekdays half an hour before going to bed and half an hour in the morning to practise my scales, the latter period being prolonged to an hour on Tuesdays when Miss Pearce, poor long-suffering woman, came to wrestle with my highly personal rendering of "The Merry Peasant." Apart from these daily occasions, the only times when the room knew me were when there were visitors.

The pattern of social life in archaic Bayswater, and all points west, differed almost as much from that prevailing today as it did from that of mediaeval times. Fixed rules prevailed governing the exact hours and days on which visits took place, the number and size of the cards left and when and how they should be "cornered," the clothes to be worn, and the length of time which one was expected to stay; even such trivial gestures as those with which the ladies, once perched on the Edwardian Hepplewhite chairs, were accustomed to throw back their veils and roll down their gloves at the wrists, were formal and standardised. There was no casual dropping in for drinks, as drinking between meals was confined exclusively to

the restorative masculine whiskey and soda (or among
the older generation ("a little b. and s.")—almost exclusively, for curiously enough I do recollect among certain
of my older female relatives the ritual partaking of a glass
of port wine and a slice of plum cake at eleven o'clock in
the morning, although this was generally regarded as an
old-fashioned survival only to be justified on grounds of
old age or a delicate constitution. There was no ringing
up and asking people round for a little cocktail party
as we had no telephone and cocktails were still unknown,
save perhaps to certain rather "fast" Americans—the sort
of people who patronised those "tango teas" of which the
papers spoke.

Where no casual appearance could possibly take place,
and all was fixed and preordained, I knew exactly
when the summons to present myself below would come.
My mother, like all the ladies of her acquaintance, had
her Thursdays, when the silver teapot and the best
china would be shiningly conspicuous and her friends and
relations would dutifully appear to be entertained with
cucumber sandwiches, *petit fours*, slices of chocolate
cake and, in winter, toasted buns. Those who could
not come, either because the number of their friends who
had also chosen Thursday as their "At Home" day pre-
cluded a personal appearance at each or for some other
valid reason, sent round their cards.

My own entry was always carefully timed by Nurse to
coincide with the moment when the teacups, with which
I was hardly to be trusted, were already distributed and
the sandwiches and cakes were waiting to be handed
round. My performance on these occasions was invariably
masterly. Clad in a *soigné* little blue silk number, with
Brussels lace collar and cut steel buckles on my shoes,
in which I had recently made my first public appearance

as a page at a wedding in All Saints, Margaret Street, I
passed round the solids in a manner which combined
efficiency with diffidence in exactly the right proportions.
Moreover, although conspicuously well behaved, I could
always be relied on to go into the *enfant terrible* act at
exactly the right moment, and produce embarrassing questions or comments of a laughable kind that yet just
stopped short of being offensively personal or too out-
spokenly apt. The freely expressed admiration which my
performance always produced was almost as gratifying to
me as it was to my mother, particularly in such cases
where I considered it was likely to pay a handsome divi-
dend next Christmas. Only among my Lancaster relations
was the rapture apt to be a little modified; my Aunt Hetty,
for instance, was more than once heard to remark that if
Mamie were not careful dear little Osbert would soon
be developing a deplorable tendency to "play to the gallery."

The only other times (apart from the many-coursed
dinner parties of the period, a fixed number of which my
parents were accustomed to give during the year, which
naturally affected my life not at all) on which visitors
appeared was when country relatives were in London and
were of sufficient age or importance to be asked to tea or
luncheon for themselves alone. The most memorable of
these was my Great-Aunt Martha, not only for her own
personality and appearance which were remarkable
enough, but also for the manner of her arrival. Having
been born early in the reign of George IV she was relatively fixed in her ways, and when she came to stay with
her younger brother, my grandfather, the victoria and
the greys were put at her disposal: their use in London
had otherwise come to be increasingly abandoned in favour of the Renault, and they were only still maintained,

I fancy, out of respect for Mundy, the elderly coachman, and a deep-rooted enthusiasm for harness horses which was general in my father's family.

I can still recall the stately dignified clop-clop, quite different in rhythm from that of the brisk single-horsed baker's van or the heavy proletarian tattoo of the pantechnicon, which announced that Aunt Martha was rounding the corner, and which I had been eagerly awaiting at the nursery window for half an hour or more. Quickly snatching up some lumps of sugar from Nurse, I was down the stairs and at the horses' heads almost before the footman was off the box. Looking back, I confess myself lost in admiration at my youthful temerity, as nowadays my reluctance to go fumbling round the muzzles of relatively unfamiliar quadrupeds would hardly be so easily overcome.

Great-Aunt Martha, although even older than Mrs. Ullathorne, gave no such impression of fragility; on the contrary she appeared, and indeed she was, exceedingly robust and just about as fragile as well-seasoned teak. Her eyebrows which were thick as doormats were jet-black and her hair, which she wore severely parted in the middle and swept smoothly down over each cheek, was only streaked with grey. She never appeared abroad save in the prescribed Victorian uniform for old ladies—black bonnet enriched with violets, a black jet-trimmed shoulder cape and very tight black kid gloves—which was becoming increasingly rare even at that date and now only survives among pantomime dames. Her features were strong and masculine and bore a close resemblance to those of Sir Robert Walpole as revealed in Van Loos' portrait, and she retained a marked Norfolk accent. Tolerant and composed, she radiated an air of genial and robust common sense, which none of the rest of the family displayed, anyhow in so marked a degree; and alone of all the Lancasters she professed a keen interest in food and was reputed to be the finest hand with a dumpling between Kings Lynn and Norwich. In addition she was never at any pains to conceal an earthy relish for scandal which, linked to a prodigious memory, made her a far more entertaining, and quite possibly a more accurate, authority on the genealogies of most Norfolk families than Burke.

Despite her outward Victorianism, Great-Aunt Martha nevertheless always gave a strong but indefinable impression of belonging to a still earlier era. This must, I think, have arisen largely from her gestures, for gestures remain the surest and least easily eradicable of all period hallmarks. Tricks and turns of speech are good guides but are generally indetectable when combined with a strong regional accent; clothes and hair styles may be deliberately and consciously adopted for their period value; but gestures are easy neither unconsciously to lose nor deliberately to acquire. One has only to compare the most accurate reconstruction of a twenties scene in a modern revue with a thirty-year-old film to appreciate this truth; no matter how skillfully the accents and fashions of the epoch may have been recaptured on the stage the film will always reveal a dozen little gestures—a peculiar fluttering of the hand or some trick of standing—which at the time were so natural as to be completely unnoticeable, and of which even the most knowledgeable spectator with an adult memory of the period and the keenest eye for detail will have remained completely unaware and may even, on seeing them again after a lapse of thirty years, fail to realise are the very hallmarks of that genuineness of which he is nevertheless completely convinced.

The particular gesture of Aunt Martha's which I found so revealing and which, had I not seen her so frequently employ it, I should have come to consider a stereotyped illustrator's convention, no more having an origin in nature than the Fascist salute or the sudden heart-clutching of an Italian tenor, was that with which she invariably registered surprise. This was an emotion constantly evoked in her by the unexpected brilliance (as she thought it) of her great-nephews and nieces or the extraordinary things of which the newspapers were nowadays so full. Maintaining her usual upright but placid attitude when seated, she would suddenly elevate her eyebrows to a remarkable height and in perfect unison raise her hands, which had been lying quietly in her lap, smartly at right angles to her wrists with palms outward, at the same time, but more slowly, lifting her forearms until the tips of her outspread fingers were level with her shoulders, in a manner that was perfectly familiar to me from the illustrations of Cruikshank.

Such visits as those of Aunt Martha were, however, few and far between, and the rhythm of our daily life, monotonous as it would seem to a modern child, was but seldom interrupted by these intrusions from the outside world. Thus the drawing room saw me chiefly in its familiar everyday dress, very different from the unnatural spruceness and formality it assumed on social occasions, and so it remains in my memory. Summoned down for my daily visit I would take my accustomed place beside my mother for the evening reading. My enjoyment at this performance depended in a very large measure on the choice of the book, which was governed partly by the day and partly by my mother's mood.

On Sundays and holy days, or on occasions when some recent display of temper or disobedience on my part was thought to have merited implied reproof, the volume chosen was a ghastly selection of fables, illustrated in that wood-engraved style I so much abominated. What particularly infuriated me about the author, and still infuriates me, was not so much his unctuous style, nor even the pious nature of the themes, but his abominable deceit. The hero, some gallant knight, would don his armour, leap on his trusty steed and go galloping off in pursuit of dragons in the most approved style, and then, just as my interest was getting aroused, it was revealed that the armour, on the exact style and manufacture of which I had been excitedly speculating, was the armour of Righteousness, the steed one learnt answered to the name of Perseverance, and the dragons against which the hero was off to do battle were called Self-Love, Indolence and Bad Temper. Thus one cold puff of piety instantly and irrevocably shattered the warm colourful world of romance and fantasy which had been building up in my imagination, and my rage, though concealed, was boundless. But it was years before the sight of that thick little royal blue volume, so guileless and optimistic is the infant mind, warned me to expect the worst.

But in the course of time my so evident lack of response led to the gradual abandonment of this depressing volume, and the occasions on which I was firmly removed from the study of some illustrated volume of my own choice to listen to the far from hair-raising adventures of some smug paladin of evangelical piety became fewer and fewer. And in the picture which I chiefly retain of these early evenings of my childhood it plays no part.

The firelight is gleaming and flashing from the polished brass of the heavily defended hearth; on one side sits my father, freshly returned from the city, reading one of the pastel-coloured evening papers of the time; on the other my mother, studying with well-founded distrust the double-page spread of the interior of the newly launched *Titanic* in the *Illustrated London News*. The pleasantly depressing strains of "The Count of Luxembourg," rendered of course by the Earl of Lonsdale's private band, faintly echo amidst the shiny chintz and gold-mounted watercolours, speaking of a far distant world of dashing

Hussars and tight-waisted beauties in long white gloves with aigrettes in their golden hair, forever dancing up and down some baroque staircase of exceptional length. While in the middle, flat on his stomach, lies a small boy of engaging appearance poring over an enormous green volume, the faintly dusty smell of the fur hearthrug heavy in his nostrils, perfectly happy counting the medals stretched across the manly chest of the Hereditary Prince of Hohenzollern Sigmaringen.

Clare Leighton

"THE ANNUAL EXODUS"
from *Tempestuous Petticoat*

"The Annual Exodus," which describes an Edwardian family's yearly journey to a summer home, is a chapter from Clare Leighton's book, TEMPESTUOUS PETTICOAT, an account of her childhood in the St. John's Wood section of London. Miss Leighton's mother, Marie Connor Leighton, wrote rather melodramatic serials for the London *Daily Mail*. Mr. Leighton wrote adventure stories for boys. Clare Leighton, who has lived in this country for several years now, is a distinguished wood engraver and writer.

$\mathcal{W}$inter passed, with its fog and rain, Across the road, now, in the garden of the house opposite, the almond was in sudden bloom. The thrushes and black-birds sang in the trees of St. John's Wood. Little rivers of gold ran down our garden path, on each side of the paved walk, as the crocuses opened to the sun.

Our mother was feeling sad at the coming of spring.

"It brings so many promises it never keeps," she sighed to our father as she looked out of the study window. "And it makes me feel ill and unhappy. I always need a little time in which to be physically fit to claim relationship with the spring. Besides, it's all nonsense to say the spring is meant for the young. It isn't. It's only bearable when you're really old. But then, it actually manages to make you feel old. That blackbird's song takes away all your contentment, and first thing you know you are wanting something without being able to find out what it is you want. Oh, dear me, how I wish it were still the autumn. That is the season for youth and work. The poets knew this. You remember the poem that begins: 'God in His heart made autumn for the young'?"

And she burst out weeping, even while she was quoting this verse. We grew shy, and turned away in confusion as we saw tears drop from her eyes onto the bundle she carried in her arms, till the ink of her outlines was blotted and smudged.

But we did not feel sad about the coming of spring.

We knew that in a few more weeks the trunks would be hauled upstairs for the annual migration to Lowestoft.

Each spring the family moved to a house in East Anglia. This annual migration had an Old Testament flavor to it, as though we moved out of Ur of the Chaldees into Canaan. It ought never to have been negotiated in a modern conveyance like a railway train. There should have been camels as beasts of burden, and rivers and deserts to cross.

The first few years of my life we had rented a furnished house for two or three months each summer on the South Coast. It had been exciting to go to a different resort every season, and later on, when we went always to the same place, we often hankered after this change of scene, as over the years of our childhood we grew to know each bush and stone near Lowestoft. For the time came when the Leighton family decided it should have a permanent seaside home, and we bought a half-built house in East Anglia, on a cliff overlooking the North Sea.

"Of course," my mother said, "if we could have found a suitable house for sale that had been lived in and mellowed, it might have been better—though then we'd have had to spend quite a time getting rid of the mental atmosphere left behind by the people who'd lived there before. But as things are, the fact that The Red Croft was only half-built when we bought it ought to make everything pretty safe."

My mother had a deep superstition against building a house. Nothing on earth could have persuaded her to do so.

"But it isn't merely a whim of my own," she protested. "It's a superstition that goes right back to the days of the Bible. Don't you remember the proverb that comes somewhere: 'Fools build houses and wise men live in them'? They knew perfectly well that the surest way to achieve a premature death is to build a house for yourself. It is flagrantly tempting Providence. If you look around you'll see I am right when I say that no one ever lives to enjoy a house he has built."

The migration started a week or two before we actually took the journey by train, for there was so much to be packed. Countless linen chests and trunks appeared on the landings, and in odd corners of all the rooms. I never knew where these were kept over the rest of the year, because there were depths in that St. John's Wood house which we were not allowed to penetrate. Two staircases in Vallombrosa were forbidden to us: the pitch black stairs to the basement, and the equally dark stairway, shut off by a door, that led to the servants' bedrooms in the attic. Between these two floors lay our world; but the outer darknesses were the unknown. Sounds came to us from these regions. The ring of the alarm clock that wakened the servants before sunrise on winter mornings broke into our sleep in the night nursery. As we walked through the hall on our way out, we could hear Dolly stoking the kitchen range, and could imagine the glow of the great banked fire that cooked our dinner. But it never worried us to realize that the servants lived in perpetual gaslight and saw no sun. Only once in all my childhood did I visit our kitchen. That was when our mother and father were away and tremblingly I crept down the basement stairs, challenged by Roland, but terrified of rats and mice.

Though the trunks stood waiting, there was one unpleasant ritual to perform before the packing could take place. My mother's furs must be put away for the summer. Her ermine stole and muff, her sable stole and her skunk-trimmed velvet coat must be protected in pepper from the ravages of moths.

My mother had a great love for furs, and considered that she looked her best in the winter, when she was justified in wearing them. In fact, one of the main reasons for her dislike of the summer months was that she could not be seen in these furs.

"That," she said, "is essentially a sign of breeding. All the common people of the world, you will notice, look their best in flimsy, cheap, gay-colored little cottons and prints. They are the people who are happiest when they are shouting to each other across a tennis court. But the really worth-while women are those who feel most at home in rich furs. And they are in their element when they are quietly indoors. You will see, my child, if you keep your eyes open, that there is a strong line of demarcation between the people who can't seem to wait for the summer, and those who understand the quality of chrysanthemums, and an early dusk, and the magic of lamplight. And nearly always, as I say, it's a case of breeding."

Furs were not only a romantic delight to my mother. They were a symbol.

It was always an especial sorrow to her that she should think it unhealthy to wear a fur coat. I remember her weeping one day because a rich friend, knowing herself to be dying, had asked if she might present my mother with her chinchilla coat.

"I simply had to tell her No," sobbed my mother. "I treasure my health more than a chinchilla coat, and it wouldn't be worth it if I were to die of pneumonia. You notice that no opera singer ever wears a fur coat. She daren't risk catching pneumonia or bronchitis. And neither can I."

And now the romantic half of the year had ended. Her furs must be packed away. Tears fell upon sable and ermine. They were not only caused by pepper.

My mother had no faith in such moth preventatives as camphor. Nothing advertised on the market was to be trusted. She must use household pepper. This pepper arrived in great five pound paper bags, and my mother sprinkled it among her furs with the same lavish abandon with which she pasted her papers together with Stickphast or sealed her envelopes with scarlet wax.

"I dare not let anyone else do this," she said. "My aim is to keep my furs from the moths, and not merely to be able to say that they have been put away. Nobody but myself would think it worth while to rub the pepper thoroughly into the entire surface of the skins."

And so, over several days, my mother dictated her stories to Walmy while she peppered her furs. My mother sneezed. Walmy sneezed. My father bound his nose with a hankerchief as he wrote his stories, and yet he sneezed. Even the dogs seemed affected. But still my mother went on dictating, while she scattered the pepper around her as though it were a libation to some god.

These peppered furs were wrapped securely in old newspapers, and tied with an elaborate network of string. They were put for safety in the top part of the wardrobe in the night nursery, which was the only place in the house with a key. But the pepper seemed to ooze through the packages, and we always sneezed when we opened the wardrobe door.

This sneezing in the spring, though, was as nothing compared with early autumn, when my mother considered it safe to bring out her furs. Walmy was deputed to shake them free of pepper in the back garden, but in spite of this there was an epidemic of sneezing in the Leighton household for many days.

"Is it absolutely necessary, Chummie, to use quite so much pepper?" my red-eyed father dared timidly one day to ask.

But my mother was scornful.

"If Robert thinks I'm going to slave away all my life writing like this in order to get myself a completely new set of ermine and sable each winter, he's wrong," she declared. "Good furs are like family jewels. They come into the category of heirlooms, and are not to be tossed around as though they do not matter."

Once the furs were safely protected against moths, my mother was free to put her mind to the packing for the annual exodus. Not that she did much, for it was Walmy's business to attend to it. Downstairs in the study Walmy was busy amassing my mother's bundles. Into numberless trunks they went: rubbish and unpaid bills, newspapers and dress designs, old love letters and aired under-garments. Everything that lay about in that study was tossed into these trunks, and nothing was sorted. It is not surprising that our luggage was enormous. Even my father's easel and painting materials had to be strapped together and packed.

The only thing of importance we did not take was the gramophone.

"It makes me quite a little sad to leave it behind," my mother said, "for often, over the summer months at Lowestoft, I find myself needing the emotional stimulation of a love song. But it is unwise to risk breaking such a precious thing by taking it on a train."

And so she removed and hid the sound box of the gramophone, in order that the policeman and his wife, whom we always engaged as caretakers at Vallombrosa while we were away—supposing this to be the safest insurance against burglars—might not use it.

"If it were only the police sergeant himself," my mother added, "I would not even remove the soundbox. You can trust a London policeman with anything on this earth—besides, he is generally asleep all the day, when he might want to play the gramophone, and on his beat at night. But unfortunately he is married—though considering he's out always at night it is beyond my understanding what use he can make of marriage—and you can't really trust a woman even when she is a policeman's wife."

But though the entire household was topsy-turvy, my

mother went on dictating her serials in the rapidly emptying study. Nothing might interfere with this, and Walmy would try somehow to get everything ready even while she still sat before the typewriter. Up to the very last moment the sound of my mother's voice could be heard, in passionate love scenes.

" 'Oh, my heart's darling, my own, my joy,' " our mother called across the table to Walmy as she gathered together some of her manuscripts. " 'Give me one chance to prove my love. Give me time to earn your kisses. Let me woo you and you shall know'—Miss Walmisley, did you remember to pack the outline of that next serial we have to do for the *Weekly Dispatch?* Where was I? Yes: 'and you shall know the happiness of living in the shelter of a good man's love.' "

The dictating continued even through the last midday meal, with the typewriter placed on the dust sheet that cloaked the dining room table, as my mother decided the destiny of a heroine between mouthfuls of mutton chop.

One year a terrible thing happened. The last meal was finished. The last cord was tied around the last trunk. The enameled hip bath, filled with nursery belongings, was ready to be placed on the roof of the omnibus. Dust sheets covered the beds, and blankets and towels were packed away. The entire Leighton tribe, with all the dogs, stood in the hall, ready for departure. We waited like this for over half an hour, and the dogs grew restless and began to whine.

"Dear me," worried our mother. "Whatever can have happened? All these years I've never known the Great Eastern Railway omnibus to be late like this. And stranger still, the carriage from Trinder's Livery Stable is late also. If they don't come soon now we shall miss our train."

The grandfather clock in the hall ticked loudly as we waited. It struck the hour. By this time everyone was agitated.

"I don't see the ghost of a chance now of catching the train," my mother complained. "What on earth can have happened?"

A sniffling sound came from the far end of the hall, where Walmy was hiding.

"Are you perfectly sure you ordered the conveyances for today, Miss Walmisley?" our mother asked. "You'd better look at the carbon copies of the letters you sent."

The sniffle became a sob as Walmy with difficulty undid the enormous corded chest that held my mother's papers. She searched through this confusion, with all eyes upon her. On to the floor of the hall tumbled the old bills and the unanswered letters, the torn newspapers and the dress designs. When finally she found the carbon copies, her sobbing grew louder.

In the agitation of packing she had ordered both the omnibus and the carriage for the following day. It was no wonder they had not arrived.

Walmy ran to the lavatory to finish her sobbing. My mother kept an angry silence.

It was a good-sized gathering when it assembled for the migration. First there were the heads of the tribe, my father and mother. My mother wore her best, biggest, newest hat in order that it might not get crushed in the packing. My father's coat was covered with dog hairs, because there were so many dogs to assemble. There seemed always to be a new litter of Skye terrier puppies. These were placed in a big hamper, and I remember that they had to come into the railway carriage with us instead of being put in the guard's van with most of the dogs, in order that we could feed them during the journey with Brand's Beef Essence on a half crown, slipped into the interstices of the wicker hamper. Evelyn and I were encouraged to do this, to occupy our minds, and so keep us from being sick.

Then, of course, there were we three children. Although

Roland was only five years older than I, he always associated himself with our parents and referred to us two younger ones as "the children," ignoring the three years' difference between me and my little brother. We never resented this, because we loved him. Everything he chose to do must be right. On the occasion of the migration he went to Liverpool Street Station with our mother and father in the separate hired carriage.

Walmy, too, came to Lowestoft with us, and lived in the house over the summer months. This meant that she had to bring her own Skye terrier along, to swell the canine crowd. Our dogs disapproved of this stranger and always started a fight, which added a last minute complication.

And then came the "staff." The old nurse was tired and irritable, wondering at what exact point I would disgrace myself, as invariably I did, by being sick.

"It seems to me, m'say, there's no way as I can stop that there Miss Clare from vomiting," she grumbled. "Even if I lets 'er go without 'er dinner she'd manage it somehow just the same."

Her pockets were stuffed with two or three table napkins, as a precautionary measure.

The undernurse was strapping the last bundles, and the cook, the parlormaid and the housemaid, dressed in their best clothes, waited discreetly downstairs, in a dark corner of the hall, for the omnibus to arrive.

It was an enormous omnibus, as it needed to be, for there were always about eight dogs, as well as the humans. I find myself remembering every bit of that long drive. Past the walled gardens of St. John's Wood, into the grime of King's Cross, and the awful depression of City Road; this was a world we were shielded from. We were not accustomed to such ugliness. The horses that drew the omnibus trotted in a way that made the whole vehicle vibrate. Outside was a grey collection of sordid public houses and chimney pots, beneath a smoke-dimmed sky. Everything smelt of grime and airlessness, frightened dogs and sweaty horses. The ride took so long that it seemed as though we would never reach the station. Suddenly it was all too much for me. True to ritual, I rushed to the hastily opened back window and made my offering to the City of London, while the driver went his way, unaware of the pollution of his omnibus. Out from one of Nurse's pockets came a table napkin, but, as always, it was too late. I had to cross the frightening expanse of Liverpool Street Station with a disfigured coat.

My mother was not exposed to this shame. She and my father and Roland had already arrived at the station, in the carriage hired from Trinder's Livery Stable. They were joined there by a sad little Mr. Bowles and one or two equally sad lesser adorers. Bound together by a common grief, these men forgot their rivalry. We could see them a long way off, at the far end of the platform. My mother's hat looked strangely gay against the grime of Liverpool Street Station, as though an exotic bird had escaped and landed on her head, and the sweep of her fawn-colored shantung dust coat seemed out of place in this smoky setting. She wore this dust coat open, so that the grandeur of her clothes might not be hidden from sight. It was essential that she should be looking her best.

"Don't ever forget, my child," she said to me from time to time over the years, "don't ever forget that the last impression you give a man is important. Never let a man who loves you remember you as anything but your most seductive. If he has seen you for even one careless moment in curling pins, or with a smut on your nose, it is this that he will remember, rather than the times when you were all prepared for him."

And so, now, as she was leaving London for several months, it was especially necessary that Mr. Bowles and the lesser adorers should think of her as they had seen her last on the platform at Liverpool Street Station. She must remain in their memory as a vivid picture of beauty.

But my father had watched for the omnibus to arrive, and hastened to help us as we struggled with the frightened dogs. It was his job to steer all these dogs safely into the guard's van, while Walmy and the two nurses coped with us. As the moment for our departure grew nearer, we saw him taking the dogs, one after the other, for a last short walk up and down the platform, to do their "business," so that they might behave themselves in the van—for quite a few of them lived in the kennels in the back garden, and were not housebroken. Leaning from the window of our reserved compartment, we grew more and more frightened lest the train should start before our father had been able to get himself and the dogs safely inside.

When the train moved out from the smoky station, we saw a group of gloomy men walk slowly down the platform, their heads sunk low. As usual each summer, our mother had left behind her some broken hearts.

I do not know how sad she herself was feeling in the privacy of the separate reserved compartment where she sat with our father and Roland. Evelyn and I were far too much worried with our own terrors just then to be aware of anything. Wedged into corner seats with our backs to the engine, where we had been placed to prevent further train sickness, we did not even hear the ceaseless chatter of the servants.

"How far are we now from Colchester?" we kept on asking in a frightened voice. "Walmy, Walmy, how far?"

We had once been told that the particular part of the earth's surface near Colchester, through which we had to pass, was susceptible to earthquakes. We expected at any moment to be swallowed up in a great opening of the globe, and never felt at ease until we were well past the region.

As we slowed down in the station at Ipswich, a pile of brown wicker tea baskets awaited us. Three of these were delivered into the compartment where our father and mother and Roland sat in state. Four were handed in to us, and Walmy and the old nurse, Evelyn and I started in on our refreshment of strong tea and bread and butter and stale fruit cake. The three servants and the under-nurse, though, were not supposed to have baskets; they rated only separate cups of tea, poured from an enameled urn that was wheeled along the platform.

The journey seemed endless. It was only one hundred and eighteen miles from London to Lowestoft, but jour-neys in those days were weighty things. With the strange way in which memory retains insignificant details over the years, I remember that we took the three-eighteen train in the afternoon. Three-eighteen down, and two fifty-seven back to London in the autumn; train journeys will always be associated for me with the face of a clock marking one or other of these times. I shall see the enor-mous clock in Liverpool Street Station, dim through the veil of fog and smoke, with the hands moving slowly to-wards the moment of departure. Tree o'clock—for we were installed in the compartment a good half hour before the train left—and then the moment when the hands came together, at three-fifteen, and the exciting moment when the minute hand overtook the hour hand, and there were only one or two minutes still to wait.

But the hours passed. Suddenly we could smell the sea. This happened when we stopped at a little place called Beccles. A very old man hobbled alongside the train, shouting the name of the station, and ritual demanded that we should lean out of the window to sniff the air. I am certain the grownups in their separate compartment didn't do this; it would have been too underbred to show such exuberance.

But even though she was a lady by birth, Walmy was

not so well brought up. She could not resist our excitement.

"Marvelous. Marvelous," she always said, drawing a deep breath. "Perfectly marvelous. All the ozone of the whole of the North Sea is in this air. Lo-ar, it's good for us. And after a winter in Bayswater, too." For Walmy lived in a stuffy semi-basement flat in Bayswater, all the time she wasn't with us in East Anglia.

It seemed as if new life had suddenly come to us. The servants began to straighten from their wilted exhaustion and even the puppies within the hamper squealed with unusual vigor.

Those were the days when people had a great belief in "sea air." Our family didn't go to Lowestoft to take a holiday. We never took holidays. We went there so that we children should benefit in our health, and in order that our mother and father might go on working with additional vitality. Nobody in our household ever stopped working. Precisely the same pattern of life was led at the seaside as in St. John's Wood, except for seasonal variations such as tea out of doors on fine days in the summer and slightly different hours of working because Walmy now lived in the house with us. But nobody ever dreamed of taking days off to laze or go gadding. Even Evelyn and I worked hard at our studies during the school holidays, in a desperate effort to improve ourselves.

My mother had profound contempt for people who took holidays. She dismissed them as "having something common in their make-up."

"The only real row I ever have with George," she said, "takes place once a year when I discover that he has sneaked off for a holiday. The poor little man is so timid that he is afraid to tell me; but as he is in the habit of writing me a letter practically each day of the week, it isn't easy for him to hide his movements."

And so my mother's face hardened as, suddenly, after a

week without a letter, a picture postcard came from Mr. Bowles from "some lower middle class place like Switzerland."

"I have always been afraid that there was something just a little suburban and ill-bred about poor George," she would tell my father with a sneer.

And then, for a day or two, she showed a sudden tenderness towards Judge Talbot or Alexander; for neither of them was off on such a plebeian thing as a holiday. My brothers and I felt sorry for Mr. Bowles when next he came to visit us. We knew how coldly aloof our mother could be when she wished.

For several weeks before he took the rash step, Mr. Bowles would work up to it by saying that of course he wouldn't be able, this year, to afford a holiday. My mother would console him, and say that it didn't really matter, did it? He would then hint that his work was growing somewhat stale, because he needed some new setting for his next story. At this point my mother grew suspicious, and that evening she might be heard talking to my father about it.

"George will be off somewhere or other soon, on one of these travel bureau tours," she would say. "You see if I am not right. And if he does have to do it—and, of course, it's partly that common wife of his who forces him to, to save the housekeeping money while he's away—why can't he choose somewhere interesting and original? Why does he have to go off in such an organised manner? It'll be Switzerland again, I expect. That's such a safe place. His wife knows he won't possibly meet anyone dangerous there. You couldn't. It's filled with schoolteachers. Now look at me. I never take a holiday. And what's wrong with me? Why, nothing."

She showed the same contempt for my uncle. My father's brother was an artist. He was a very bad artist, but as he had married a woman with some money this didn't

really matter, because, when she died and left him fairly
well provided for, he could go around with all the outward
and visible signs of bohemianism without the anguish of
having to justify himself by producing any paintings. This
uncle was dearly loved by art societies, as he had all the
time of the world upon his hands and adored being
needed and considered important. And so he was always
organizing artists' trips to picturesque countries. Back
to us, on the East Coast, came romantic postcards from
Palermo, from Spain, from Florence or from Algiers. My
mother tossed them over to my father, with contempt.

"There's Jack at it again," she said. "And can't you see
him, with all those third-rate artists, thinking himself God
Almighty. Little shabby spinsters, who've never in their
lives been further than Hammersmith or West Kensington, supposing themselves suddenly the center of romance, and Jack doxing around with them as though he
were a legitimate sort of Don Juan. And all the silly little
water colors that will come out of it, to be placed on the
walls of suburban villas, and to be shown to visitors with
a 'and that was the year I was in Italy' sort of sigh. And
even Jack himself will be thinking he's truly living at last.
He'll be unbearable when he returns—perfectly unbearable. As if travel ever improved anybody. You've got to
have it in you yourself, and if you have, you don't need
to travel."

But Uncle Jack was wise enough not to come down and
visit us for quite a long time after his return from one of
these "lower class" trips.

And so this move to the seaside was merely a change
of locale, in order that we might benefit by the strong
air of Lowestoft. My mother had tremendous faith in this
North Sea air. Nothing would take her to any "soft, back-
boneless place" like Devonshire. She needed the hard
bracing quality of East Anglia, and never tired of telling

us what happened when she went once to the Lake District.

"That air is no good," she would say. "It just lets you down. Of course those poets wrote. There wasn't any possibility of any vitality to make them do anything else. All your ambition leaves you, and you want to do nothing but live with someone you love in a little rose-covered cottage, on fifty pounds a year, and write sonnets. Now here, on the East Coast . . ."

And she would turn to Walmy and go on dictating the romantic adventures of her latest heroine.

The old judge was always at Lowestoft station to meet us. As the train slowed down, the lumbering figure could be seen vigorously waving a thick stick in the air, to greet my mother. His enormous voice boomed out:

"As I was saying—" But the noise of the porters drowned the rest of the sentence.

My mother and father and Roland, joined now by Judge Talbot, went their way in an open victoria. The rest of us were bundled into the pale yellow omnibus that had been ordered from the Crown Hotel. It was a tight squeeze, for this was a much smaller omnibus than the Great Eastern Railway one in London.

Somewhere, in the luggage van of that train, were the nursery hip bath, my father's easel and the trunks and chests of the Leighton family. But they would appear next morning, by special truck.

The air was filled with the sharp, tangy smell of fish, for Lowestoft was dedicated to the herring. There seemed to be magic in this air. As the yellow omnibus rumbled through the town, burdened with children and servants and dogs, it passed little streets leading to the fish market and the harbor. In the pale light of a spring sunset the world seemed bewitched. It was the dry, clear light of the North. Here we saw none of the violet mist of St. John's

Wood dusks, or the dirty sky of Bethnal Green. Everything was sharp-edged, and pure of color. Excitedly we pressed our noses to the windows of the omnibus as we watched each shop, each street, each loitering fisherman. At this moment we were completely happy.

The yellow omnibus left behind it the town of Lowe-stoft. It reached Gunton Cliff, and stopped at last in front of The Red Croft. The grownups' hired carriage had already arrived, and waited to take the old judge back to his home. But he was not yet ready. He had not seen his "Beloved Beauty" for many long months. As we and the servants, Walmy and the dogs swarmed into the house, his fat body blocked the way.

"The sun has come into my life again," he shouted, just as the undernurse was carrying a heavy case around his enormous bulk. He brandished his stick in the air and almost hit the poor girl in the face. But he did not notice this. He did not see that he was preventing us from entering the house. Neither did he hear our nurse grumbling.

"If that old man doesn't get out of my way," she muttered below her breath, as she tried to force herself past him, "if 'e doesn't let me get through with these children they'll be dropping to sleep all over 'im."

But the fat old judge was in such a delirium of joy that he saw and heard nothing except his own "Beloved Beauty."

"As I was saying . . ." his voice boomed loud above the barking dogs, the moving of luggage and the whimpers of tired children.

My mother stood in the front hall, in her best, biggest, newest hat, unable to get rid of him. Life in the Leighton family over the summer months of the year had started its traditional pattern.

Arnold Bennett

"MRS. ELINOR GLYN"

from *Books and Persons*

Between 1908 and 1911 Arnold Bennett, using the pseudonym Jacob Tonson, wrote a series of weekly articles for the British publication, *New Age*. "Mrs. Elinor Glyn" was one of these. It appeared in the issue of November 10, 1910, and concerned a new novel by the popular author of THREE WEEKS and many other books.

$\mathcal{A}$fter all, the world does move. I never thought to be able to congratulate the Circulating Libraries on their attitude towards a work of art; and here in common fairness I, who have so often animadverted upon their cowardice, am obliged to laud their courage. The instant cause of this is Mrs. Elinor Glyn's new novel, "His Hour" (Duckworths, 6s.). Everybody who cares for literature knows, or should know, Mrs. Glyn's fine carelessness of popular opinion (either here or in the States), and the singleness of her regard for the art which she practises and which she honours. Troubling herself about naught but splendour of subject and elevation of style, she goes on her career indifferent alike to the praise and to the blame of the mob. (I use the word "mob" in Fielding's sense—as meaning persons, in no matter what rank of life, capable of "low" feelings.) Perhaps Mrs. Glyn's latest book is the supreme example of her genius and of her conscientiousness. In essence it is a short story, handled with a fullness and a completeness which justify her in calling it a novel. There are two principal characters, a young half-Cossack Russian prince and an English widow of good family. The pet name of the former is "Gritzko." The latter is generally called Tamara. Gritzko is one of those heroic heroes who can spend their nights in the company of prostitutes, and their days in the solution of deep military problems. He is very wealthy; he has

348

every attribute of a hero, including audacity. During
their very first dance together Gritzko kissed Tamara.
"They were up in a corner; eveyone's back was turned
to them happily, for in one second he had bent and kissed
her neck. It was done with such incredible swiftness.
. . ." etc. "But the kiss burnt into Tamara's flesh." . . .
" 'How dare you? How dare you?' she hissed."

Later " . . . 'I hate you!' almost hissed poor Tamara."
(Note the realistic exactitude of that "almost.") "Then
his eyes blazed. . . . He moved nearer to her, and spoke
in a low concentrated voice: 'It is a challenge; good. Now
listen to what I say: In a little short time you shall love
me. That haughty little head shall be here on my breast
without a struggle, and I shall kiss your lips until you cannot breathe.' For the second time in her life Tamara went
dead white. . . ." Then follow scenes of revelry, in which
Mrs. Glyn, with a courage as astonishing as her power,
exposes all that is fatuous and vicious in the loftiest regions of Russian fashionable society. Later, Gritzko did
kiss Tamara on the lips, but she objected. Still later he
got the English widow in a lonely hut in a snowstorm,
and this was "his hour." But she had a revolver. " 'Touch
me and I will shoot,' she gasped. . . . He made a step
forward, but she lifted the pistol again to her head . . .
and thus they glared at one another, the hunter and the
hunted. . . . He flung himself on the couch and lit a
cigarette, and all that was savage and cruel in him flamed
from his eyes. 'My God! . . . and still I loved you—
madly loved you . . . and last night when you defied me,
then I determined you should belong to me by force. No
power in heaven or earth can save you! Ah! If you had
been different, how happy we might have been! But it is
too late; the devil has won, and soon I will do what I
please.' . . . For a long time there was silence . . . Then
the daylight faded quite, and the Prince got up and lit a

small oil lamp. There was a deadly silence . . . Ah! She must fight against this horrible lethargy . . . Her arm had grown numb. . . . Strange lights seemed to flash before her eyes—yes—surely—that was Gritzko coming toward her! She gave a gasping cry and tried to pull the trigger, but it was stiff. . . . The pistol dropped from her nerveless grasp. . . . She gave one moan. . . . With a bound Gritzko leaped up. . . ."

"The light was gray when Tamara awoke. Where was she? What had happened? Something ghastly, but where? Then she perceived her torn blouse, and with a terrible pang remembrance came back to her. She started up, and as she did so realized that she was in her stockinged feet. The awful certainty. . . . Gritzko had won—she was utterly disgraced. . . . She hurriedly drew off the blouse, then she saw her torn underthings. . . . She knew that however she might make even the blouse look to the casual eyes of her godmother, she could never deceive her maid." . . . "She was an outcast. She was no better than Mary Gibson, whom Aunt Clara had with harshness turned out of the house. She—a lady!—a grand English lady! . . . She crouched down in a corner like a cowed dog. . . ." Then he wrote to her formally demanding her hand. And she replied: "To Prince Milaslavski. Monsieur, —I have no choice; I consent.—Yours truly, Tamara Loraine." Thus they were married. Her mood changed. "Oh! What did anything else matter in the world since after all he loved her! This beautiful fierce lover! Visions of enchantment presented themselves. . . . She buried her face in his scarlet coat. . . ." I must add that Gritzko had not really violated Tamara. He had only ripped open her corsage to facilitate respiration, and kissed her "little feet." She honestly thought herself the victim of a satyr; but, though she was a widow, with several years of mar-

riage behind her, she had been quite mistaken on this
point. You see, she was English.

"His Hour" is a sexual novel. It is magnificently sexual.
My quotations, of course, do less than justice to it, but I
think I have made clear the simple and highly courageous
plot. Gritzko desired Tamara with the extreme of amorous passion, and in order to win her entirely he allowed
her to believe that he had raped her. She, being an English
widow, moving in the most refined circles, naturally regarded the outrage as an imperious reason for accepting
his hand. That is a summary of Mrs. Glyn's novel, of
which, by the way, I must quote the dedication: "With
grateful homage and devotion I dedicate this book to Her
Imperial Highness The Grand Duchess Vladimir of
Russia. In memory of the happy evenings spent in her
gracious presence when reading to her these pages, which
her sympathetic aid in facilitating my opportunities for
studying the Russian character enabled me to write. Her
kind appreciation of the finished work is a source of the
deepest gratification to me."

The source of the deepest gratification to me is the
fact that the Censorship Committee of the United Circulating Libraries should have allowed this noble, daring,
and masterly work to pass freely over their counters. What
a change from January of this year, when Mary Gaunt's
"The Uncounted Cost," which didn't show the ghost of a
rape, could not even be advertised in the organ of the
Times Book Club! After this, who can complain against
a Library Censorship? It is true that while passing "His
Hour," the same censorship puts its ban absolute upon
Mr. John Trevena's new novel "Bracken." It is true that
quite a number of people had considered Mr. Trevena
to be a serious and dignified artist of rather considerable
talent. It is true that "Bracken" probably contains noth-

ing that for sheer brave sexuality can be compared with a score of passages in "His Hour." What then? The Censorship Committee must justify its existence somehow. Mr. Trevena ought to have dedicated his wretched provincial novel to the Queen of Montenegro. He painfully lacks "savoir-vivre." In the early part of this year certain mysterious meetings took place apropos of the Censorship, between a sub-committee of the Society of Authors and a sub-committee of the Publishers' Association. But nothing was done. I am told that the Authors' Society is now about to take the matter up again. But why?

Ellen Glasgow

"A SECOND START IN LIFE"

from *Life and Gabriella*

Ellen Glasgow's LIFE AND GABRIELLA covers the period from the middle nineties to 1914, and the writing of the novel occupied the author between the years 1899 and 1916. The book tells the story of a Richmond, Virginia, girl who has grown up in genteel poverty and married a wealthy but worthless young New Yorker, George Fowler. Deserted by her husband, Gabriella is determined to earn a living for herself and her two children. Since she is too much a "lady" to have any kind of professional training, she decides to try her hand at retail selling, the only kind of work in which she has had any experience. She approaches the proprietress of the fashionable house of Dinard. The plight of the well-bred woman forced by circumstances to earn her living and keep up appearances was a popular theme in Edwardian fiction. It occurs, for example, in such well-known novels as Edith Wharton's THE HOUSE OF MIRTH, published in New York in 1905, and in Arnold Bennett's THE OLD WIVES TALE, which first appeared in England in 1908.

In her book, A CERTAIN MEASURE, Ellen Glasgow wrote that "Madame Dinard, the modiste, was an actual person, and the fashionable house of Dinard was an actual establishment."

7he Irish woman, voluble, painted, powdered, bewigged, and with the remains of her handsome figure laced into a black satin gown, nodded her false golden locks and smiled an ambiguous smile when she heard the explanation of young Mrs. Fowler's afternoon call.

"But, no, it ees impossible," she protested, forgetting her foreign shrug and preserving with difficulty the trace of an accent. Then, becoming suddenly natural as she realized that no immediate profit was to be derived from affectation, she added decisively, "you have no training, and I have quite as many salesladies as I need at this season. Not that you are not chic," she hastened to conclude, "not that you would not in appearance be an adornment to any establishment."

"I am willing to do anything," said Gabriella, pressing her point with characteristic tenacity. "I want to learn, you know, I want to learn everything I possibly can. You yourself told me that I had a natural gift for designing, and I am anxious to turn it to some account. I believe I can make a very good milliner, and I want to try."

"But what would Madame Fowler, your mother-in-law, say to this? Surely no one would want to earn her living unless she was obliged to."

For Madame had known life, as she often remarked, and the knowledge so patiently acquired had gone far to confirm her natural suspicion of human nature. She had got on, as she observed in confidential moments, by believing in nobody; and this skepticism, which was fundamental and rooted in principle, had inspired her behaviour not only to her patrons, but to her husband, her children, her domestic servants, her tradespeople, and the policeman at the corner. Thirty years ago she had suspected the entire masculine world of amorous designs upon her person; to-day, secretly numbering her years at sixty-two, and publicly acknowledging forty-five of them, she suspected the same world of equally active, if less romantic, intentions regarding her purse. And if she distrusted men, she both distrusted and despised women. She distrusted and despised them because they were poor workers, because they were idlers by nature, because they allowed themselves to be cheated, slighted, underpaid, underfed, and oppressed, and, most of all, she despised them because they were the victims of their own emotions. Love was all very well, she was accustomed to observe, as a pleasurable pursuit, but, as with any other pursuit, when it began to impair the appetite and to affect the quality and the quantity of one's work, then a serious person would at once contrive to get rid of the passion. And Madame prided herself with reason upon being a strictly serious person. She had been through the experience of love innumerable times; she had lost four husbands, and, as she pointed out with complacency, she was still living.

In the dubious splendour of her showrooms, which were curtained and carpeted in velvet, and decorated with artificial rose-bushes flowering magnificently from white and gold jardinières, six arrogant young women, in marvellously fitting gowns of black satin, strolled back and forth all day long, or stood gracefully, with the exaggerated curve of the period, awaiting possible customers. Though they were as human within as Madame Dinard—and beneath her make-up she was very human indeed—nothing so variable as an expression ever crossed the waxlike immobility of their faces; and while they trailed their black satin trains over the rich carpets, amid the lustrous piles of silks and velvets which covered the white and gold tables, they appeared to float through an atmosphere of eternal enchantment. Watching them, Gabriella wondered idly if they could ever unbend at the waist, if they could ever let down those elaborate and intricate piles of hair. Then she overheard the tallest and most arrogant of them remark, "I'm just crazy about him, but he's dead broke," and she realized they also belonged to the unsatisfied world of humanity.

Madame, who had slipped away to answer the telephone, came rustling back, and sank, wheezing, into a white and gilt chair, which was too small to contain the whole of her ample person. Though she had spoken quite sharply at the telephone, her voice was mellifluous when she attuned it to Gabriella.

"That gown is perfect on you," she remarked in honied accents. "It was one of my best models last season, and as I said before, Madame, you are so fortunate as to wear your clothes with a grace." She was urbane, but she was anxious to be rid of her, this young Mrs. Fowler could see at a glance. "Your head is well set on your shoulders, and that is rare—very rare! It would surprise you to know how few women have heads that are well set on their shoulders. Yes, I understand. You wish to learn, but not to make a living. That is very good, for the only comfortable way for a woman to make her living is to marry one—a man is the only perfectly satisfactory means of livelihood. I tell this to my daughter, who wishes to go on the stage. If you are looking for pleasure, that is different, but when you talk of a living—well, there is but one way to insure it, and that is to marry a man who is able to provide it—

either as allowance or as alimony. The best that a woman can do gives her only bread and meat—an existence, not a living. Only a man can provide one with the essential things—with clothes and jewels and carriages and trips to Europe. These are the important things in life, and what woman was ever able to procure these except from a man?"

Her face, so thickly covered with rouge and liquid powder that it was as expressionless as a mask, turned its hollow eyes on a funeral which was slowly passing in the street; and though her creed was hardly the kind to fortify one's spiritual part against the contemplation of death, she surveyed the solemn procession as tranquilly as any devoted adherent of either religion or philosophy could have done. Not a shadow passed over her fantastic mockery of youth as she glanced back at her visitor.

"But you have worked—you have supported yourself," insisted Gabriella with firmness.

"Myself and six children, to say nothing of three husbands. Yes, I supported three of my four husbands, but what did I get out of it?" replied Madame, shrugging her ample shoulders. "What was there in it for me? Since we are talking freely, I may say that I have worked hard all my life, and I got nothing out of it that I couldn't have got with much less trouble by a suitable marriage. Of course this is not for my girls to hear. I don't tell them this, but it is true nevertheless. Men should do the work of the world, and they should support women; that is how God intended it, that is according to both nature and religion; any priest will say as much to you." And she, who had defied both God and Nature, wagged her false golden head toward the funeral procession.

"Yet you have been successful. You have built up a good business. The work has repaid you."

"A woman's work!" She snapped her gouty fingers with

a playful gesture. "Does a woman's work ever repay her? Think of the pleasures I have missed in my life—the excursions, the theatres, the shows. All these I might have had if I hadn't shut myself up every day until dark. And now you wish to do this! You with your youth, with your style, with your husband!"

She protested, she pleaded, she reasoned, but in the end Gabriella won her point by the stubborn force of her will. Madame would take her for a few weeks, a few months, a few years, as long as she cared to stay and gave satisfaction. Madame would have her taught what she could learn, would discover by degrees the natural gifts and the amount of training already possessed by young Mrs. Fowler. Young Mrs. Fowler, on the other hand, must "stand around" when required in the showrooms (it was just here that Gabriella won her victory); she must assist at the ordering of gowns, at the selections, and while Madame's patrons were fitted, young Mrs. Fowler must be prepared to assume graceful attitudes in the background and to offer her suggestions with a persuasive air. Suggestions, even futile ones, offered in a charming voice from a distinguished figure in black satin had borne wonderful results in Madame's experience.

"I began that way myself, Mrs. Fowler. You may not believe it, but I was once slenderer than you are—my waist measured only nineteen inches and my bust thirty-six—just the figure a man most admires. The result was, you see, that I have had four husbands, though it is true that I supported three of them, and it is always easy to marry if one provides the support. Men are like that. It is their nature. Yes, I began that way with little training, but much natural talent, and a head full of ideas. If one has ideas it is always possible to become a success, but they are rarer even than waists measuring nineteen inches. And I had charm, though you might not believe it now,

for charm does not wear. But I made my way up from the
bottom, first as errand girl, at the age of ten, and I made
it, not by work, for I could never handle a needle, but by
ideas. They were once plentiful, and now they are so
scarce," she broke off with a sigh of resignation which
seemed to accept every fact of experience except the fact
of age. "It was a hard life, but it was life, after all. One is
not put here to be contented, or one would dread death
too much for the purpose of God." In spite of her uncompromising materialism, she was not without an ineradi-
cable streak of superstition which she would probably
have called piety.

"I am ready to begin at once—to-morrow," said Gabriella, and she added without explanation, obeying, perhaps, an intuitive feeling that to explain a statement is to
weaken it, "and I should like to be called by my maiden
name while I am here—just Mrs. Carr, if you don't mind."

To this request Madame agreed with effusion, if not
with sincerity. For her own part she would have preferred
to speak of her saleswoman as young Mrs. Fowler; but
she reflected comfortably that many of her patrons would
know young Mrs. Fowler by sight at least, and to the others she might conveniently drop a word or two in due season. To drop a word or two would provide entertainment
throughout the length of a fitting; and, for the rest, the
mystery of the situation had its charm for the romantic
Irish strain in her blood. The prospect of securing both
entertainment and mystery at the modest expenditure of
fifteen dollars a week impressed her as very good business,
for she combined in the superlative degree the opposite
qualities of romance and economy. To be sure, except for
the advertisement she afforded and the gossip she provided, young Mrs. Fowler might not prove to be worth
even her modest salary; but there was, on the other hand,
the remote possibility that she might turn out to be

gifted, and Madame would then be able to use her inventiveness to some purpose before the gifted one discovered her value. In any case, Madame was at liberty to discharge her with a day's notice, and her salary would hardly be increased for three months even should she persist in her eccentricity and develop a positive talent for dressmaking. And if young Mrs. Fowler could do nothing else, Madame reflected as they parted, she could at least receive customers and display models with an imposing, even an aristocratic, demeanour.

To receive Madame's customers and display Madame's models were the last occupations Gabriella would have chosen had she been able to penetrate Madame's frivolous wig to her busy brain and detect her prudent schemes for the future; but the girl was sick of her dependence on George's father, and, in the revolt of her pride, she would have accepted any honest work which would have enabled her to escape from the insecurity of her position. Of her competence to earn a living, of her ability to excel in any work that she undertook, of the sufficiency and soundness of her resources, she was as absolutely assured as she had been when she entered the millinery department of Brandywine & Plummer. If Madame, starting penniless, had nevertheless contrived, through her native abilities, to support three husbands and six children, surely the capable and industrious Gabriella might assume smaller burdens with the certainty of moderate success. It was not, when one considered it, the life which one would have chosen, but who, since the world began, had ever lived exactly the life of his choice? Many women, she reflected stoically, were far worse off than she, since she started not only with a modicum of business experience (for surely the three months with Brandywine & Plummer might weigh as that) but with a knowledge of the world and a social position which she had found to be fairly market-

able. That Madame Dinard would have accepted an unknown and undistinguished applicant for work at a salary
of fifteen dollars a week she did not for an instant imagine. This inadequate sum, she concluded with a touch of
ironic humour, represented the exact value in open market
of her marriage to George.

In the front room, where a sparse mid-winter collection
of hats ornamented the scattered stands, she stopped for
a few minutes to inspect, with a critical eye, the dingy
array. "I wonder what makes them buy so many they
can't sell?" she said half aloud to the model at which she
was gazing. "Nobody would wear these hats—certainly
nobody who could afford to buy Parisian models. I could
design far better hats than these, I myself, and if I were
the head of the house I should never have accepted any of
them. I suppose, after all, it's the fault of the buyer, but
it's a waste—it's not economy."

Lifting a green velvet toque trimmed with a skinny
white ostrich feather from the peg before which she was
standing, she surveyed the august French name emblazoned in gold on the lining. "Everything isn't good that
comes from Paris." She thought, with a shrug which was
worthy of Madame at her best. "Why, I wonder, can't
Americans produce ideas themselves? Why do we always
have to depend on the things the French send over to us?
Half the hats and gowns Madame has aren't really good,
and yet she makes people pay tremendous prices for
things she knows are bad and undistinguished. All that
ought to be changed, and if I ever succeed, if I ever catch
on, I am going to change it." An idea, a whole flock of
ideas, came to her while she stood there with her rapt gaze
on the green velvet toque, which nobody had bought, and
which she knew would shortly be "marked down," august
French name included, from forty to fifteen and from fifteen to five dollars. Her constructive imagination was at

work recreating the business, and she saw it in fancy made over and made right from the bottom—she saw Madame's duplicity succeeded by something of Brandywine & Plummer's inflexible honesty, and the flimsy base of the structure supplanted by a solid foundation of credit. For she had come often enough to Dinard's to discern the slipshod and unsystematic methods beneath the ornate and extravagant surface. Her naturally quick powers of observation had detected at a glance conditions of which the elder Mrs. Fowler was never aware. To sell gowns and hats at treble their actual value, to cajole her customers into buying what they did not want and what did not suit them, to give inferior goods, inferior workmanship, inferior style wherever they would be accepted, and to get always the most money for the least possible expenditure of ability, industry, and honesty—these were the fundamental principles, Gabriella had already discovered, beneath Madame's flourishing, but shallow-rooted, prosperity. Brandywine & Plummer did not carry Parisian models; their shop was not fashionable in the way that the establishment of a New York dressmaker and milliner must be fashionable; but the standard of excellence in all things excepting style was far higher in the old Broad Street house in the middle 'nineties than it was at Madame Dinard's during the early years of the new century. Quality had been essential in every hat that went from Brandywine & Plummer's millinery department; and Gabriella, deriving from a mother who worked only in fine linen, rejected instantly the cheap, the tawdry, and the inferior. She had heard a customer complain one day of the quality of the velvet on a hat Madame had made to order; and pausing to look at the material as she went out, she had decided that the most prosperous house in New York could not survive many incidents of that deplorable sort. To be sure, such material would not have been supplied to Mrs. Pletheridge, or even to the elder Mrs. Fowler, who, though Southern, was always particular and often very severe; but here again, since this cheap hat had been sold at a high price, was a vital weakness in Madame's business philosophy.

On the whole, there were many of Madame's methods which might be improved; and when Gabriella passed through the ivory and gold doorway into the street, she had convinced herself that she was preëminently designed by Nature to undertake the necessary work of improvement.

Edgar Saltus

❮❮◆❯❯

"THE MODES OF TO-MORROW"
from *The Pomps of Satan*

$\mathcal{S}$omebody or other, an archbishop, perhaps, declared with obvious regret that a woman gowned in the height of fashion possesses a serenity of mind joined to an elevation of spirit which the consolations of religion are incompetent to provide.

We have not a doubt of it. But in what does fashion consist? Women have been known to state that they would rather be dead than out of it, yet when a definition was sought no adequate description could be obtained. For it is one of the charms of women that in explaining everything they explain nothing. That is quite as it should be. It is for them to exhilarate and for us to expound. Yet of their clothes we know little. A little is a great deal. But in a matter such as this no mere man may know much. It is even discomforting to reflect that when the hour comes in which all secrets are revealed Fashion may resolve into Isis still unveiled.

Meanwhile, to the masculine eye at least, the vagaries of it are as recondite as the forecasts of the weather. The mysteries of time and space—mysteries so mysterious that science has reduced them to figments of fancy—are not more enigmatic.

Perhaps, then, it will be safe to say that fashion is an active abstraction—a phrase which does not mean anything, but which sounds very well. In any event, it is a form of debauchery of which the door is closed to man.

There are exceptions, however. The deponent has seen six-footers loll about and admire their hunting togs. And there are other instances. There is, for example, a certain marquis and there is also a certain clergyman. The former one day was standing bareheaded in Lincoln & Bennett's, waiting to be waited on. A prelate entered, marched up to him, took his hat off, and asked him if he had one like it. The marquis examined it, handed it back, and with a sweetness which was silken, replied: "No; and if I had I'll be shot if I'd wear it." The clergyman wanted to assist at a table-d'hôte and could not. Through a tailor's defection he had no trousers to wear. He said he was not a bit more particular than other people, but he had noticed that a clergyman going in to dinner without trousers was almost sure to excite remark. Fashion is not, therefore, a purely feminine vice. There you have at least two men who were slaves to it.

At the risk of writing ourselves down as something else, we should like to call ourselves a third. For, though our ignorance of fashion is abysmal, our admiration is without bounds. Apart from the pleasures of pure mathematics, we know of nothing more intoxicating. Behind its history is the history of love. Whoever invented the one invented the other. In days when tattooing was apparel it has been authoritatively surmised that woman's attractiveness was so meagre that she was as incapable of detaining men as animals are of detaining each other. There were herds, not homes. The development of the wardrobe was the development of the affections. The heart of man began to beat when woman ceased to resemble him. But it was not until meditation had made her modest and fashion fastidious that his enthralment was complete. Then at once where the boor had been the knight appeared. In place of the female came the woman. Hitherto she had served. Thereafter she began to reign. In the States to-day she rules the roost. Fashion has done it. Hence our admiration for that active abstraction. Hence, too, the serenity of spirit which a well-dressed woman displays.

That serenity is quite natural. Barring such abominations as golf skirts and blouses, smart women have never got themselves up more fascinatingly than they do to-day. In the old prints of earlier days they are astounding to behold. Frocks were masonry and chignons architecture. Caricaturists represent *les très grandes dames* followed by carpenters widening and heightening the doors through which they pass. In one sketch a hairdresser is shown on a ladder arranging topmost curls. On the head of the Duchesse de Chartres a *coiffeur* succeeded in exhibiting her entire biography. The hair of the Princess de Machin was manipulated into a cage, in which were loosed three thousand butterflies.

After the amputations of the Revolution fashion must have become simpler, but through epochs which we lack the art to describe it remained unalluring until Worth took a hand. The women he turned out looked like angels, only, of course, much better dressed. To-day the girls to whom Doucet has ministered are a caress to the eye. Personally, if we may refer to ourselves, there are frocks of Félix that have seemed to us more satisfactory than old masters, and there are also confections of Paquin that we have found as exhilarating as cups of champagne.

In what manner they are evolved and through what process, after their evolution, these ruedelapaixian seductions, primarily and, it may be, uniquely designed to pleasure some Princesse Lointaine, repeat themselves indefinitely, and variously vulgarised, reappear on the banks of the Neva, at the Golden Gate, in Bloomsbury and Bucharest, in Kandahar and Chicago, the Lord in his wisdom and mercy only knows, and in so saying it may be that we exaggerate, for, sure of nothing, we cannot be sure of that, although, indeed, there has just occurred to us an incident highly enlightening.

Some years ago the Queen of the Wends, Queen of the Goths, the Queen Matchmaker, who was the late Queen of Denmark, was also Queen of the Bicycle. In her obituaries the fact was not noted. Compared with her other titles it may have seemed unimportant. But it is only unimportant things that are really momentous. Louise of Hesse-Cassel became the progenitrix of sovereigns, and left the course of events unaltered. She got on a wheel one day and changed the face of the earth.

The event occurred before the flood, a full decennium ago, at a time when no decent person would have been found dead on a bicycle. It was at her summer court on the Baltic, through the wide leisures of which the selectest princesses and the least exclusive princes lounged, that the deed was done. What the mother of an empress *in esse* and of another *in posse* does, smaller fry copy. The young royals, her grandchildren, followed suit. Photographed, bike in hand, their pictures emerged in shop windows. At sight of them Paris went mad. Then New York caught a fever, which afterward spread to London, and ultimately was reported to have assumed epidemic proportions in Melbourne. So runs the world away. Meanwhile, the queen had put her wheel aside. Imitation is flattery's most odious form. None the less, a fashion had been set, industries founded, manufactories multiplied, and all through a monarch's whim, because of a summer day an entirely amiable lady had seen fit to mount a wheel.

That wheel has since been relegated to the provinces. In its place is the auto. Presently that will pass. Fancies vary, follies ditto. The one thing constant is change. Yet, as with the bike, so with bonnets. What great ladies do lesser ladies copy. Therein is the mode's *modus operandi*. These premises admitted, there arises the interesting problem, What shall the woman of the future wear? But, before deciding, it will be useful to determine what sort of a person that woman will be.

Could the subject be considered from the standpoint of Dr Schenck's promise that sex may be determined by maternal nutrition, it is obvious that woman would be scarce as Madeira and just as heady. But though Dr Schenck promised he did not fulfil. As a consequence, the subject becomes more complex. At the same time, women being all alike in this that they are every one of them different, it follows that what is true of them today was true in the past and will be in the future. Individually diverse, collectively they are undistinguishable. To the naked eye at least. And it was certainly to remedy this defect that Fashion was invented. For however fancies may vary and follies change, however distressing last year's hat may look, woman herself does not alter. It is the mode that passes, not the model. The eternal feminine is everlastingly the same. To tell, then, what sort of a person the coming woman will be, take a receipt from astrology and first hatch her milliner.

Even so and even otherwise, though it is the mode that passes and not the model, though through the change of years and the convolution of things the heart of archaic Eve beats throughout femininity to-day, the beauty of the lady has developed. Yet, as nothing is constant but change, that beauty is doomed to diminish. In the part of the world from which we write it cannot help itself. Beauty's patent of nobility is to be useless. Therein is the sorcery of the rose. It charms and does nothing. Commerce, combinations, concentration, and all that in them is, whether utilitarian, progressive, or both, are beauty's antitheses. The trend of the age is, as we have elsewhere noted, to things very large and very ugly. In their construction, development, and expansion we all either actively or passively collaborate. We cannot do otherwise. The Zeitgeist will not let us. It has us fast in its maw. For the bewilderments of feminine witcheries it cares not a rap. That for which it does care is progress. In moulding us to its will it moulds our senses and muddles our souls. The instincts it instils we will transmit. As a consequence the babies to come may develop both brains and brawn, yet never beauty. Now add the column up. The result is plain women.

And so much the better. Plain women are currently considered neglectable quantities. Such consideration comports an error that is profound. Memoirs and missions have acquainted us with many who dressed, undressed, and disgressed divinely. The picture gallery of heroines is crammed with others who understood very well that, while beauty may allure, graciousness enchains. A service of Sèvres with nothing on it is less appetising than a *petite marmite.* Unaccompanied by other attributes, beauty alarms when it does not weary. Moreover, it is only the solely beautiful who are really plain. A really plain woman is one who, however beautiful, neglects to charm. By the same token a beautiful woman who contents herself with being merely beautiful is far plainer than a plain woman who does nothing but beautiful things. It is for this reason that the most beautiful woman in the world is always the woman whom we have yet to meet. It is for this reason, too, that in the Evangel of Woman it is written, or rather will be when the Evangel appears: Blessed are the plain who succeed in charming, for theirs and theirs only is the Kingdom of Love.

But let us consider the subject less seriously. Beauty is relative. Perfect beauty is a phrase and nothing else. Once upon a time a philosopher produced a large volume, in the course of which he proved that God is perfection. Then he produced a second volume, equally large, in which he proved that perfection does not exist. It were impossible to be more exhaustively witty. Subsequently another philosopher produced a supplementary work, in which he proved that in the absence of perfect beauty a lady who is equally ugly all over is more satisfactory than one unequally fair. It were impossible to be more profound. These views, however, public opinion has failed to endorse. But that is natural. Moreover, there is a disease of the eye that is catalogued as hemiopia. Of any given object the patient sees but half. It is one of Satan's greatest *tours de force* to have afflicted us all with that malady and rendered us blind to feminine defects. It must amuse him not a little to see how we are all taken in. Were it otherwise men would devote themselves to pious works. For that matter, it is only those who have penetrated the guile of the Very Low that do. As a consequence, when, in the future, women are plain, men will occupy themselves only with virtuous deeds. And is not that a consummation devoutly to be wished?

Yet because the coming Eve is to be plain it by no means follows that she will be painful. On the contrary. In the good old days of the glory that was Greece, a woman whose peplon did not hang right in the back, whose general appearance was not modish, there and then, as we have somewhere remarked, became a disturber of the peace, and as such liable to a fine that varied with degrees of slatternliness from ten to a thousand drachmæ. Penalties not similar but cognate will, we assume with entire readiness, be visited by the legislators of the future on the woman who shall in her attire presume to neglect to charm. But we assume with equal readiness that such neglect will be rare. For while by that time hemiopia may have become curable and feminine defects be recognised and endured, it follows for that reason that women— *celles de la haute, bien entendu*—will be tricked out, adorned, and embellished, as were never even the goddesses of old.

How the ladies of the middle classes shall then appear interests us no more than how they appear to-day. We take it, however, that among them there will be some quite vulgar enough to be pretty. But about the plain yet peerless peris of the peerage of this and other lands there will be garments immaterial as moonbeams, gorgeous as quetzals, at once shadowy and stunning, luminous as the zaïmph of Tanit, coruscating as the shower of Danæ, the triumph of art, poetry, and the Rue de la Paix. For in default of feminine perfections such things as these must be, if only to perpetuate the species, and with it the jubilance and the guile of Satan and his pomps.